IN PRAISE
OF
SOCIOLOGY

1917.

THE AUTHOR

Born in Falkirk in 1952, Gordon Marshall was educated at Falkirk High School and at the Universities of Stirling and Oxford, before taking up a post as Lecturer in Sociology at the University of Essex. He has since lectured widely in North America, Scandinavia and East Asia, and has been a Morris Ginsberg Fellow at the London School of Economics and Political Science, and Visiting Professor at the University of Uppsala. His previous publications include *Presbyteries and Profits* (Oxford University Press, 1980), *In Search of the Spirit of Capitalism* (Hutchinson, 1982), and many articles on sociological theory and social stratification. Most recently he has co-authored *Social Class in Modern Britain* (Hutchinson, 1988). He now lives in Wivenhoe and is presently Senior Lecturer in Sociology at the University of Essex.

IN PRAISE
OF
SOCIOLOGY

Gordon Marshall

London
UNWIN HYMAN
Boston   Sydney   Wellington

Published by the Academic Division of
Unwin Hyman Ltd
15/17 Broadwick Street, London W1V 1FP, UK

Unwin Hyman Inc.,
8 Winchester Place, Winchester, Mass. 01890, USA

Allen & Unwin (Australia) Ltd,
8 Napier Street, North Sydney, NSW 2060, Australia

Allen & Unwin (New Zealand) Ltd in association with the
Port Nicholson Press Ltd,
Compusales Building, 75 Ghuznee Street, Wellington 1, New Zealand

First published in 1990

British Library Cataloguing in Publication Data

Marshall, Gordon
  In praise of sociology.
  1. Sociology
  I. Title
  301

  ISBN 0-04-445687-5
  ISBN 0-04-445688-3 Pbk

Library of Congress Cataloging in Publication Data

Data applied for

Typeset in 10 on 11 point Bembo by
Nene Phototypesetters Ltd, Northampton
and printed in Great Britain by
Billing and Sons, London and Worcester.

For Bob and Ina

Contents

Tables and figures

Acknowledgements

In writing this book I have accumulated the usual debts against the goodwill of friends and colleagues. My thanks, therefore, to Joan Busfield, George Kolankiewicz, David Lee and Ken Plummer for invaluable advice on the contents of the hesitant first draft. I wrote it during the course of a busy academic year – for others as much as myself – and I appreciate the efforts that were made to find time for reading and discussing my manuscript. Gordon Smith, at Unwin Hyman, exercised his usual sound editorial judgement and made numerous worthwhile suggestions. Fortunately, he is an amicable as well as a thorough professional, so I was allowed to indulge my writer's obstinacy and ignore a fair proportion of them. If I have exploited his tolerant nature then I hereby apologise. A particular debt is also owed to the two people to whom the book is dedicated. But for their parental encouragement I would probably still be serving drinks in a certain pub somewhere in central Scotland – and so forced to listen all day to never-ending tapes of Andy Stewart and the Tartan Lads. The thought still makes me break out in a cold sweat. Finally, for reasons that are altogether too complex to explain here, I would also like to express my gratitude to the manufacturers of the Decca Yacht Navigator IV, and the man or woman who invented the autohelm.

Gordon Marshall,
Yacht *Alana*,
April 1989.

1 The theme

On the morning of 16 February 1988 the *Guardian* newspaper carried a full-page article on the decline of British sociology. Published under the headline 'Who needs sociologists?' it made grim reading over breakfast. Apparently there had been a 'terrible eclipse' of the discipline during the 1980s: governments and university authorities had become hostile, departments were closed, and as a result many sociologists were disheartened, anxious about their public image and uncertain as to the merits of the subject itself.

The author of the report, journalist Alan Rusbridger, expressed a measure of sympathy for his sociological interviewees. Their studies did seem to have been singled out for particularly close scrutiny by an unsympathetic government. However, Rusbridger also implies that a good deal of the criticism was justified, since (as is commonly believed) sociologists are often politically biased and methodologically inept. He underlines this conclusion by a frankly mischievous resort to stereotypes throughout the article. Thus, Rusbridger metaphorically steps back in amazement when his investigations lead him to an interview with a most exotic creature, a *right-wing* professor of sociology. He expresses even greater incredulity at the claim made by another professor that British sociological research is generally rather rigorous and therefore highly *respected* in the world at large. Surely not, replies the sceptical journalist, since sociologists have been the standard Westminster music-hall joke for so long that they are themselves now hopelessly confused about where the subject should go. He, by contrast, can offer an immediate and comprehensive diagnosis of the sociological disease. In future, sociological studies must be empirical, statistically sophisticated, policy-oriented and completely free of jargon. Less 'political posturing' and more 'relevant research' is Rusbridger's prescription for the recovery of the patient.

As a professional sociologist, I was not unduly surprised by the tone of this article, or the unsubstantiated nature of the claims it makes about the anti-capitalist and anti-empirical bias of British sociology. The popular image of sociology in this country combines hysterical newspaper accounts of Militant infiltration in trade unions with farcical campus novels about the swinging 1960s – a sort of *Red Robo meets the History Man*. However, I was angered by the fact that supposedly responsible journalism continued to depict sociology as left-wing rhetoric masquerading as scholarship; the *Guardian* ought to know better.

In all probability nothing more would have come of my irritation had I not been scheduled that afternoon to teach a class on *The Authoritarian Personality*, a well-known study of prejudice in modern societies, conducted in the aftermath of the Jewish Holocaust of the Hitler years. Searching for secondary materials on this subject, I turned to John Madge's book on *The Origins of Scientific Sociology*. This is based on a course of lectures given to graduate students at Brooklyn College in the late 1950s. Madge, a visitor from England, had the idea of teaching research methods by giving an historical account of the development of empirical sociology. To that end he selected twelve classic studies of American sociology (one of which was the research on authoritarianism) and devoted a separate chapter of his book to each. His choice was governed by three criteria: each text had to make a significant contribution to investigative technique, to the development of sociological ideas, and to the understanding of social problems. The dozen finalists were all highly innovative in one or all of these respects. They embraced a wide range of topics including suicide, race hatred, productivity in industry and sexual behaviour. In justifying his particular selection, Madge argues that he would have liked to include a work of British sociology as the main subject of one of his chapters, but 'did not feel able to do so'. This is understandable enough. He was writing in the late 1950s, at a time when there were still only half a dozen or so departments of sociology in this country, all but one (at the London School of Economics) having been newly set up after the Second World War. As a modern science of society the subject was still in its infancy in Britain when Madge was selecting the studies to be included in his text. By comparison, sociology had long been established in the United States, where it was taught in most major universities. Not surprisingly, therefore, American sociology offered much more to choose from by way of technical innovation and empirically tested propositions.

Madge's book has many virtues. It makes sociological theories relevant by showing how empirical research inspired by such ideas greatly enhances our understanding of social processes and problems. It also makes sociology accessible by discussing the various studies in more or less everyday language. His text can readily be understood by those without a professional training in the subject. In this way the non-specialist might reach an informed assessment of the merits of the sociological approach – and so go beyond the merely impression-istic accounts that appear in the media. The selected case-studies are themselves a testimony to the scholarly achievements of American sociology. Indeed, it struck me almost immediately that here was the perfect rejoinder to Rusbridger's scepticism about the possibilities for a scientific sociology. If the proof of the pudding is in the eating then

Madge's volume offers an immensely satisfying meal. Unfortunately, of course, his recipe contained no British ingredients. But would it be possible, after three decades of empirical research by sociologists in this country, to concoct an equally appetizing dish from entirely home-grown produce?

Convinced that this question could be answered in the affirmative, I quickly set about choosing my favourite sociological studies of postwar Britain, arriving that same evening at the selection included in this book. At the request of my publisher, I have restricted the discussion to ten texts. But, like Madge himself, I could easily have included another two – or, for that matter, a further twenty. These ten will suffice to make my point. Note that the texts themselves are discussed in no particular sequence – and certainly not according to any supposed order of merit.

In compiling my list of British sociological classics I applied the same criteria as Madge himself. Candidates were required to show theoretical sophistication, methodological innovation and practical application. One additional – and rather crucial – qualification was that texts had to be readily available on my office bookshelves during that particular day. Given these requirements it is quite clear that this volume does *not* represent 'the very best of' British sociology. Strictly theoretical contributions have been excluded, as have largely descriptive ethnographies, although in both cases this means that acknowledged masterpieces must be omitted. The subject matter has been restricted to modern British society – the principal concern of most empirical researchers – which precludes several excellent studies of other societies, produced by British sociologists, but who were writing as outsiders. Historical subjects have been similarly excluded. This is perhaps the most serious omission, since many fine sociological projects have in fact examined the emergence of the modern world, and so been concerned with the societies of the nineteenth century or even earlier. Finally, of course, an indeterminate number of worthy investigations have been overlooked because of my own inadequacies. I have a broad but not exhaustive knowledge of the now extensive literature available within British sociology. Some areas – the sociology of science, for example, which looks at (among other things) the social implications of natural scientific discoveries and origins of new technologies – I simply do not feel qualified to discuss at any length.

Clearly, therefore, this book is not a comprehensive survey of the terrain covered by sociologists. There are many introductory textbooks already available which perform this particular task admirably. Nor does my selection amount to a systematic history of modern British sociology. This, too, is readily available from other sources. Furthermore, the texts I have chosen are not simply the ten most influential or widely known sociological publications, indeed several

sold in rather small numbers even for academic texts. They are (with
due apologies to their authors) certainly not the most accessible pieces
of sociology to have appeared over the years. They are, instead,
simply a small sample taken from the prodigious amount of good
sociology produced in this country during the past quarter of a
century or so. The final selection reflects the many idiosyncrasies of
my own knowledge and preferences. The only common denominator
to the studies is that they are all, unquestionably, *good* sociology.

II

The texts cover a broad range of topics that are of general as well as
narrowly political or policy interest. John Goldthorpe's study of *Social
Mobility and Class Structure in Modern Britain*, the first work discussed,
addresses itself squarely to a subject that has often been described as
'the great British obsession', namely, social class. It is based on a
survey of the social mobility experiences of some 10,000 adult men
living in England and Wales during the early 1970s. Goldthorpe
calculates the chances of men from working-class origins arriving at
middle-class employment, as compared with those of men who
started from middle-class backgrounds retaining these, and examines
the extent to which these relative chances for upward social mobility
may have altered during the twentieth century. His findings lead him
to the rather controversial conclusion that significant changes in the
shape of the class structure during recent years (due, for example, to
the expansion of the professions and decline of manfucturing) have
not actually made that structure more open. The reasonably affluent
Britain of today is no more a classless or fluid society than it was
during the interwar years of economic depression. All that has
happened is that as the proportion of middle-class jobs in the
occupational structure has grown, so middle-class parents have become proportionately more successful at securing these new positions
for their own children. The liberal strategy of piecemeal egalitarian
reform, via the expansion of education and welfare, has clearly failed.
On the other hand, there has been a substantial shrinkage in the
relative size of the manual workforce during recent years, so Goldthorpe also dismisses as no less unconvincing the Marxist scenario of
radical political upheaval by a unified proletarian mass. Here, then, is a
critical appraisal of the achievements of modern consensus politics –
but it is patently not anti-capitalist. Nor, obviously, is it anti-
empirical. The conclusions are based on extensive research employing
modern and highly sophisticated techniques of quantitative analysis.
Nevertheless, as I hope to show, the argument itself is relatively
straightforward.

  The next chapter continues with the themes of meritocracy and class by looking at the experiences of eighty-eight working-class children who were educated in Huddersfield grammar schools during the late 1940s and early 1950s. These form the basis of a study by Brian Jackson and Dennis Marsden, *Education and the Working Class*, first published in 1962. At that time there was great public concern about the 'wastage of talent' and in particular the problem of early leaving among able working-class children who entered selective schools but failed to stay on until the sixth form. Jackson and Marsden offer a highly original explanation for this phenomenon, centring on the 'culture clash' between the mores and values of the working-class neighbourhood and those of the grammar school. From detailed and probing interviews, they tease out the often painful ways in which the sons and daughters of manual workers were required to estrange themselves from family and neighbourhood in order to be educationally successful. Many, of course, refused to pay this price for intellectual enlightenment. However, this is not really the principal theme of the Huddersfield study. Jackson and Marsden are particularly concerned with the 'cultural costs' of social mobility, both for the individual working-class child winning through to a middle-class life and for the moral order of the society itself. As I make clear in the text, I am frankly unconvinced by the authors' rather romantic view of the communal and solidaristic aspects of working-class life although my own views on this subject are certainly no less controversial. Nevertheless, I know of no better sociological account of the personal costs of class mobility, and one has to turn to literature to find a more moving description of the trauma induced among working-class children by their first sustained encounter with a middle-class institution.

The third of my classic texts is Peter Townsend's massive and controversial survey of *Poverty in the United Kingdom*. This is certainly the most complete account of household resources and social deprivation ever to have been produced in this country. I argue that two rather bold theses hold the many and complex arguments of the book together. The first is Townsend's insistence that poverty should be conceptualized in relative rather than absolute terms. The notion of 'relative deprivation' is thus pivotal to his study. The second thesis is that poverty can nevertheless be measured objectively. This leads Townsend to arguments about a national 'style of life' that is customary among a majority of the population and which can be operationalized in terms of a 'deprivation index'. Denial of access to the items in this index, through lack of individual or household resources, is in Townsend's view the defining characteristic of poverty. According to this criterion, approximately one-quarter of all households in Britain were either in poverty or on its margins, when the survey was fielded in the late 1960s. Needless to say, this finding attracted considerable criticism – especially from those with a political axe to grind on the subject of deprivation. However, Townsend's results have actually stood up to critical scrutiny surprisingly well, in view of their inevitably controversial nature. My own, admittedly idiosyncratic view is that they are probably more significant than is conventionally assumed in the mainstream literature on social policy. In fact, they can easily be seen as unambiguous proof of the fundamental conflict between social justice and market value in British society. The 'essentially contested' definition of poverty brings the universal principles of citizenship to bear on the unprincipled or free market. Successive British governments have failed to resolve the conflict between these contradictory axial principles of social order – and the continuing debate about adequate definitions of material poverty, and appropriate public policies towards it, merely underlines this fact.

Chapter 5 looks at the impact of technological and commercial change on companies involved in the electronics industry. In *The Management of Innovation*, Tom Burns and G. M. Stalker argue that different forms of business organization are appropriate for different economic environments, and that rapidly changing technical or market conditions require firms to adopt 'organic' systems of management. Some companies were quicker than others at adapting in this way to the postwar restructuring of the electronics market, and as a result became commercially more successful than their rivals. In the course of the research, Burns and Stalker also explored the 'informal organization' of the twenty companies involved, and this led them to conclude that the political system and status structure within each concern exerted a major influence on its economic efficiency. These findings were crucial to the development of the so-called rational systems perspective, a major advance in organization theory during the early 1960s, and one which I discuss at some length in the chapter. I also propose the perhaps rather contentious thesis that most of the insights into behaviour in organizations that are suggested in recent influential management texts were already available in Burns and Stalker's analysis of almost thirty years ago. If this sounds like an argument for managers to read more sociology, that is precisely what is intended.

The sixth chapter describes probably the best-known piece of empirical research in British sociology, namely, the *Affluent Worker Study*, conducted in Luton in the mid 1960s by John Goldthorpe, David Lockwood, Frank Bechhofer and Jennifer Platt. Rather ironically, since my own expertise lies in the field of social stratification broadly defined, I found this chapter particularly difficult to write. So much has already been said about the Luton project that it is extremely difficult to be original in reviewing it. Its principal claim – that there has been a convergence in the normative orientations of some sections of the working class and certain lower white-collar groups – has been subjected to almost continuous empirical investigation, more or less since it was first proposed, as indeed have the allied themes of working-class 'privatism' and 'instrumental collectivism'. If readers of my own text have previously been introduced to sociology, even cursorily, then they will almost certainly already have encountered some of this literature. In the end, therefore, I opted for an unorthodox approach. Rather than rehearse familiar arguments for and against the project, I chose instead to devote at least part of my discussion to a publication which is not strictly part of the *Affluent Worker* research itself, but is nevertheless so obviously a development of it that one can legitimately consider it in this context. The article in question, which was written by Goldthorpe and offers a sociological explanation for the high rates of inflation in Britain during the 1970s, not only sheds light on the earlier project, but also provides a pertinent reminder of the relevance of sociological research to the formation of economic policy. The punchline here is rather obvious – economics is simply too important to be left to the economists.

I also offer a rather bad-tempered conclusion to Chapter 7. In the early 1960s John Rex and Robert Moore studied the Sparkbrook area of Birmingham as part of the Survey of Race Relations in Britain. At the heart of their research was an investigation of the multi-occupied lodging-houses in this inner-city 'zone of transition'. They explain how, in the 'great urban game of leapfrog', the various 'housing classes' in the city come to be resident in specific territories and types of accommodation. For reasons that were not difficult to discern, coloured immigrants to Birmingham during the postwar years lacked both of the primary resources necessary for securing access to good quality housing, namely, either a substantial income or suitable length of prior residence in the locality. They were, therefore, forced into multi-occupation of large houses in the inner city. These properties were soon subject to rapid physical deterioration for reasons beyond the control of the inhabitants themselves. The problem of the 'twilight zones', where large, old houses, too good to be classified as slums, had become multi-occupied lodging-houses, rapidly became a 'race problem' about which, as the researchers found, the city had got itself into a state of near-hysteria. Rex and Moore conclude their report, which was published under the title *Race, Community, and Conflict*, with a series of policy recommendations designed to eliminate the discriminatory elements in the city's housing allocation. They also warn that, if the desire of immigrants to improve their situation continues to be frustrated by racialist practices and policies, the long-term prospect must be 'for some sort of urban riot'. Predictably enough, this warning went unheeded by those in authority. And yet, twenty years and a long series of precisely such riots later, I find myself having to defend my profession against critics and policy-makers who complain that sociological research should be 'more relevant' to this country's social and economic problems; were this accusation not so tragically ill-informed, I might find it laughable.

Stanley Cohen's *Folk Devils and Moral Panics* is the subject of Chapter 8. This is an investigation of subcultural deviance, especially the societal reaction to it, based on a case-study of the Mods and Rockers of the mid 1960s. Cohen advances the rather controversial thesis that, by a process of 'labelling' and 'deviance amplification', the various social control agencies attempting to undermine these subcultures actually accomplished quite the opposite. By instigating what Cohen calls a 'moral panic', the media, police, courts and other 'moral entrepreneurs' helped to create, rather than eliminate, the collective disturbances which took place at English seaside resorts between 1964 and 1966. Cohen's compelling, convincing and often amusing account of these highly ritualized Bank Holiday gatherings shows that the majority of teenage participants were quite unlike the press stereotypes of the Mod or Rocker. Most identified with neither group and had, in fact, travelled to the seaside specifically as spectators. However, the combination of press misreports, provocation by the police and over-reaction by the courts so dramatized a number of quite unexceptional and relatively infrequent events of minor hooliganism that the crowds of youthful holiday-makers became part of a generalized vision of mass civil disobedience and profound social malaise. Rather interestingly, Cohen's arguments could easily be extended to contemporary examples of subcultural deviance, such as football hooliganism and mugging. They therefore raise the thorny problem of the 'policy relevance' of sociological analyses of such phenomena. Both Cohen's own conclusions about policy and my observations on these will, I hope, come as a pleasant surprise to the many critics who complain that sociology lacks policy application. By defending the independence of sociology from political considerations, I trust also that they will thoroughly annoy ideologues, both of the Right and Left alike.

Chapter 9 deals with cultic religious beliefs. In *The Road to Total Freedom* Roy Wallis traces the history of Scientology, from its origins in the rather diffuse Dianetics movement of the early 1950s, through to the established but controversial sectarianism of the mid 1970s. He argues that, as it emerged, Scientology developed many of the ideological and structural characteristics of a totalitarian organization. Needless to say, representatives of the movement challenged Wallis's findings, principally on the grounds that an outsider such as he could not possibly comprehend their faith: understanding was the prerogative of the believer. In this way, Wallis's research raises a general question which invariably surfaces whenever scepticism is expressed about the scientific standing of sociological studies, namely, why should one privilege the sociologist's version of events if contradictory stories are told by others? Fortunately, Wallis himself has rather a lot to say about the relationship between competing sociological and 'commonsensical' accounts of social action, and even more fortuitously I find myself in almost complete agreement with his principal conclusions. We both insist, to put it bluntly, that sociology is simply more scientific than commonsense.

The penultimate chapter examines research into the social origins of mental illness. For almost two decades, George Brown and his co-workers at the University of London have been investigating the relationship between stressful life-events and psychiatric disorder, particularly schizophrenia and clinical depression. For the sake of brevity I concentrate almost exclusively on the most popular of the group's many publications, *Social Origins of Depression*, co-authored by Tirril Harris and Brown himself. In many ways this is a particularly difficult text for non-sociologists to comprehend. For one thing, the first third of the book (fully one hundred pages) is devoted exclusively to the discussion of research methodology, including the complex technical issues surrounding the construction of measurement scales, coding of empirical materials and logic of causal analysis using crosstabulated survey data. Some understanding of psychiatry is also required in order to follow the authors' occasional excursions into the realms of clinical casework. I hope I have managed to clarify both matters to the satisfaction of the non-specialist reader. My chapter argues that Brown and Harris provide convincing evidence linking various stressful life-events to the onset of severe depression. This requires them to overcome the possible contamination of causal analyses that can arise from the tendency among psychiatric patients to search retrospectively for potential provoking agents which might help explain mental illness. That is, depressed respondents make an *ex post facto* 'effort after meaning' which leads them to reinterpret their biography, assigning significance after the onset of disorder to an event that happened beforehand which they would not necessarily have considered noteworthy prior to the illness. (This provides an 'explanation' for the patient by making sense of his or her otherwise mysterious disorder.) In order to eliminate this and other similar confounding influences, Brown and his colleagues were required to perform a number of sophisticated statistical analyses, considering the relative merits of different mathematical techniques for identifying and disaggregating causal effects. These proved to be highly controversial and provoked a lengthy debate in the academic journals. I have derived a certain amount of malicious satisfaction from reporting some of the more obscure technical aspects of this exchange, precisely because the fact that it took place at all gives the lie to the myth that British sociologists are wholly innumerate and entirely lacking in respect for social statistics.

Finally, in Chapter 11, I describe a study that has always seemed to me to represent British sociology at its penetrating best. Elizabeth

Bott's *Family and Social Network* was first published in 1957, but more than three decades later her arguments still seem breathtakingly original, and remain central to our understanding of the lives of ordinary families in late twentieth-century Britain. Her book had an enormous influence on subsequent sociological studies, both in this country and abroad, although that is not why I have included it among my selected texts. Rather, I have always been impressed by the way in which she links different aspects of social life, which on the face of it would seem to be quite unrelated, by identifying the social processes which connect an individual's personal relationships to his or her general views of society. Only a sociologist could see the possible implications of a family's social network for the type of conjugal roles adopted by husband and wife. No one but a sociologist could then go on to link both of these to the norms and ideologies subscribed to by the marital partners. Without sociological under-standing of precisely this kind, welfare workers or clinicians attempting to help families through their troubles may inadvertently increase the strain on spouses, by thrusting on them an ideal which they neither understand nor endorse. Only a sociologist could have undertaken this research and only a sociologist could have obtained these insights. For this reason I have chosen to let discussion of Bott's text serve also as a general conclusion to my argument as a whole. If critics cannot see the merits and relevance of her project, then I despair of ever converting them to the cause of good sociological scholarship.

III

These ten studies are by no means the most accessible products of modern British sociology. Some employ advanced statistical tech-niques to analyze their data. Others assume a good deal of background or even specialist sociological knowledge on the part of the reader. Most draw extensively on complex concepts and theories in order to explore their various subject matters. All were written so as to be read by other professional sociologists.

My own concerns are somewhat different. This book is aimed at the student rather than the academic specialist. It assumes no prior acquaintance with the subject and so devotes a substantial part of each chapter to expounding the principal arguments of the study in question. Of course, sociology students are in some respects well catered for, there being a large number of comprehensive introduc-tory texts already available in the libraries. But these are often rather formal – offering exhaustive and even-handed accounts of competing theories and explanations. My treatment is more specialized and partisan. It deals with only a small selection of the empirical materials available and does not attempt to offer a complete coverage of any issue. This is not a comprehensive textbook. On the other hand, it has been designed to be read as a whole, rather than merely dipped into. These particular studies have been chosen precisely because they illustrate what I take to be good sociological practice. The underlying argument about the value and values of sociology runs through all ten chapters. In that limited sense, at least, my choice of materials represents a manifesto for the proper agenda and techniques of sociological scholarship. Finally, of course, I also seek to convince at least some sections of the general public (including, I hope, a few of the many and vociferous critics of contemporary British sociology), that my discipline is at least as rigorous and relevant as any other social science, and probably more so than most. One should not need to be a practising sociologist in order to appreciate the merits of a sound sociological analysis.

Some generalization and simplification is therefore unavoidable in my presentation. For example, the social context of the various studies is invariably sketched with a particularly broad brush, as is the relevant intellectual ancestry. I have also dispensed with the usual academic etiquette of footnotes and citations, although I freely confess to having drawn on the works of others for background and appraisal, and some acknowledgement of this is made in the section on Further Reading. I trust my professional colleagues will overlook this apparent lack of concern for details. Of course, they will almost certainly dispute my choice of texts. I fully anticipate their cries of derision because I have omitted classic works by Runciman, Gallie, Bernstein, Wilmott and Young, Pahl, Oakley, Willis – or a host of others far too numerous to mention. In reply I can only plead the defence of pragmatism. In the interests of variety I have tried to cover a range of substantive areas and methodologies. Forced, therefore, to choose between several excellent studies of the same general type, I have made some painful (and inevitably arbitrary) decisions about which texts to exclude. If my final choice of British sociological classics does not correspond to that of my colleagues, then this is only because we have such a wealth of riches from which to choose.

On the other hand, I make no apology for the fact that my selection spans four decades of research, since it is my belief that none of these books is in any sense dated. All have stood up remarkably well to subsequent close inspection, or in some cases sustained critique, and all are relevant to the great public debates of the late 1980s. It is for this last reason that I have written about them in the historical present as much as in the past tense. Governments have yet to learn the lessons that are here on offer.

2 Social class and social mobility

I

The first text I want to consider is John H. Goldthorpe's *Social Mobility and Class Structure in Modern Britain*, published originally in 1980, then in an expanded second edition in 1987. Written in collaboration with Catriona Llewellyn and Clive Payne, this is a report of the principal findings of the Oxford Study of social mobility among men in England and Wales. Although it is the most recent of the ten studies under consideration, there are, nevertheless, several good reasons why it offers a convenient starting-point for our discussion. One is that it deals with the subject of social class – and it is this topic, above all others, that is associated most commonly with sociology in the minds of its critics. Another is that popular perceptions are, in this case, well grounded in the reality of British sociology: a disproportionately large amount of sociological discussion in this country has indeed focused on the issues of class analysis. Finally, and most importantly, Goldthorpe's subject matter is the class structure of contemporary Britain – in other words the stratification system of the society as a whole. The nine remaining texts I have selected concentrate instead on one constituent group within that structure – such as black immigrants, grammar-school children, religious sectarians, or industrial managers. Goldthorpe's general and inclusive concerns mean that he paints an overall picture into which these more specialized investigations can conveniently be set.

What then does this broad canvas look like? The most useful way of introducing Goldthorpe's own, rather complex ideas about class stratification in modern Britain is to consider the more straightforward interpretations which he specifically rejects. Two such interpretations have had wide (including popular) currency in the years since the Second World War: liberal (usually American) theories of industrial society, and Marxist (usually European) theories of capitalist society. These make quite contradictory predictions about likely transformations in the class stratification of Western societies – including Britain – on the basis of secular trends that are allegedly immanent in all technologically advanced nations.

The liberal perspective was most influential during the 1950s and early 1960s, and although it has somewhat declined in popularity since then, there are still many enthusiastic advocates of the 'logic of industrialism' thesis writing today. These would include, among others, Daniel Bell, Clark Kerr, Edward Shils, Seymour Martin Lipset, and Peter Berger. Such writers argue that certain underlying processes of convergence in industrialized countries will, among other things, transform the class structures of Western democracies. Tendencies intrinsic to the production process – in particular, both the sectoral shift from manufacturing to services in advanced economies and the increasing automation of work generally – will generate uniformity in hitherto distinctively class (democratic capitalist) and mass (state socialist) societies by increasing the numbers of occupations that require specialized knowledge and skills and by decreasing those involving only routine tasks and minimal qualifications. This upgrading of the occupational structure will expand the middle class – those commanding high economic rewards and prestige from relatively skilled employment – and create a demand for highly trained professionals, technicians, administrators and managers which cannot be met simply by the 'internal recruitment' of children from existing middle-class homes. Necessarily, therefore, these structural changes alone will be sufficient to generate substantial net upward mobility, as people from working-class origins move in to fill the new middle-class positions that have been created. Additionally, however, so liberals argue, advanced industrialism promotes the use of meritocratic criteria for occupational advancement, and this too will enhance the overall rates of social mobility, making the new post-industrial societies more open and more egalitarian than their early industrial predecessors. These changes, together with the widespread adoption of progressive systems of taxation and improved social welfare, will then lead to a general embourgeoisement of hitherto class-divided societies. Relative homogeneity of living standards will generate cultural homogeneity around middle-class values, norms and lifestyles. Crucially, all of this is to be achieved by evolutionary rather than revolutionary means. An expanded and benign state will regulate competition in the general interest: rigid systems of class stratification will gradually give way to a fluid occupational structure reflecting meritocratic outcomes based on equality of opportunity, and ideological battles will succumb to a new conservatism compatible with the new egalitarianism. Class conflicts will vanish to be replaced by consensus politics.

Marxist writers, by comparison, see changes in the class structure in terms almost completely opposite to those outlined by theorists of post-industrialism. During the 1970s and early 1980s, Harry Braverman, Guglielmo Carchedi, Erik Olin Wright and Rosemary Crompton, among many others, offered the argument that changes in the labour process were evidence of a long-term trend towards proletarianization rather than embourgeoisement of the class structure. In their view, the imperatives of capitalist production (particularly the drive for greater profitability) compel the owners and managers of industry to simplify and fragment work-tasks, in order to increase output and maintain control over labour. A deskilled workforce is relatively powerless to resist demands for greater productivity: in-tractable workers can simply be fired in favour of easily trained replacements. Automation thus serves merely to confine real technical expertise to an ever smaller proportion of the labour force. Similarly, the shift from manufacturing to services creates an expansion of middle-class positions that is more apparent than real, since the low level of skill required in many of the new nonmanual jobs renders them indistinguishable from the routine or 'degraded' work done by most blue-collar employees. For Marxists, then, the reality of all wage labour under capitalism is that it is necessarily exploitative and is organized only in the interests of the capitalist class. Putative rates of upward mobility from manual to nonmanual employment only mystify the class struggle and obscure the essential continuity of class stratification. In due course, it is argued, the historical tendency of workers towards workplace and communal solidarism will re-emerge; the mystifications of bourgeois ideology or hegemony will become transparent; and class-based action by a unified proletariat will overthrow the structures of property and power which underpin late capitalism.

To some extent the disagreement between these frameworks may simply reflect the changed economic circumstances of the long postwar boom as compared with those of the recessionary 1970s and 1980s. As the age of affluence gave way to economic stagnation, so the liberal perspective became less fashionable among social theorists generally. But it is clear to Goldthorpe that, beyond any empirical dispute about the facts of class stratification, these contradictory interpretations also arise as a direct consequence of the contrasting socio-political objec-tives pursued by the two schools of thought. In order to protect their liberal or (conversely) socialist values, both seek to interpret the present characteristics of the occupational structure in the context of some underlying developmental logic of industrial (or capitalist) societies, rather than attempt serious empirical investigation of that structure itself. They offer substantively opposed but equally histori-cist accounts of class processes. That is, present events are invariably seen by liberals as part of a long-term historical trend towards greater social equality, or by Marxists as evidence of a similar tendency towards class polarization. For this reason both groups are inclined to what Goldthorpe calls 'wishful rather than critical thinking' in the interpretation of empirical materials.

Just how plausible, then, are the many liberal and Marxist accounts of social stratification in advanced societies? It is against this back-ground that the arguments of Goldthorpe's *Social Mobility and Class Structure in Modern Britain* can best be understood. His book offers, quite simply, a systematic test of the central propositions about class processes (or their demise) advanced by these popular and politically inspired theories of social change.

II

Obviously, a clear definition of social class is a necessary prerequisite to any description of class processes, so Goldthorpe addresses this issue in some detail. He starts from the observation that all capitalist societies have a broadly similar social division of labour, involving employers, the self-employed, employees and domestic labourers. These categories themselves – in particular that of employee – tend to be internally differentiated by variable conditions of employment. That is, some employees are better off than others, such as would typically be true if one compared managers or supervisors with those actually working on the shop-floor. Classes are then aggregates of individuals, or families, who occupy similar locations in this social division of labour over time. These locations are defined by differences in the 'market situation' and 'work situation' of the various occupations. For Goldthorpe, then, the occupational order forms the backbone of the class structure in advanced societies.

What does he mean by market situation and work situation? Both terms describe the conditions characteristically associated with different occupations. The former refers to the source, level and security of the income associated with any job. That is, whether the returns come from investments, selling one's labour, or from self-employment; how much is earned; and the likely chances of continued economic advancement through promotion or incremental wage increases. Work situation describes the location of particular jobs within structures of authority, and thus the degree of control that is exercised at work, in particular the amount of autonomy typically enjoyed while performing the work-tasks involved in the particular occupation.

By this theoretical reasoning Goldthorpe arrived at the seven-category class scheme shown in Table 2.1, although for the sake of brevity he often uses a collapsed version that distinguishes only between the service, intermediate and working classes. The types of occupational group found within each social class are fairly self-evident from the labels attached to the classes. In practice, when Goldthorpe and the other members of the Oxford Mobility Project conducted their national sample survey in 1972, they allocated respondents to the various class categories by using a threefold procedure. First, individuals were placed in an occupational group (for example, plumber, teacher), according to how they described their work. Occupational title is taken by Goldthorpe to be a good operational measure (or indicator) of market situation. Then, interviewees were given an employment status which reflected their social relationships

Table 2.1   Goldthorpe class categories, and distribution of respondents to Oxford Social Mobility Inquiry, 1972

Class			%
SERVICE	I	Higher-grade professionals, self employed or salaried; higher-grade administrators and officials in central and local government and in public and private enterprises (including company directors); managers in large industrial establishments; and large proprietors.	13.6
	II	Lower-grade professionals and higher-grade technicians; lower-grade administrators and officials; managers in small business and industrial establishments and in services; and supervisors of nonmanual employees.	11.5
INTERMEDIATE	III	Routine nonmanual – largely clerical – employees in administration and commerce; sales personnel; and other rank-and-file employees in services.	9.2
	IV	Small proprietors, including farmers and smallholders; self-employed artisans; and all other 'own account' workers apart from professionals.	9.4
	V	Lower-grade technicians whose work is to some extent of a manual character; and supervisors of manual workers.	11.6
WORKING	VI	Skilled manual workers in all branches of industry, including all who have served apprenticeships and also those who have acquired a relatively high degree of skill through other forms of training.	21.2
	VII	All manual wage-workers in industry in semi- and unskilled grades; and agricultural workers.	23.5
Total			100.0

(N = 9,434)
Source: Social Mobility and Class Structure in Modern Britain, Table 2.1.

at work, such as self-employed without employees, or manager in a large establishment. This offered, for Goldthorpe, a satisfactory measure of work situation. In both cases the categories and definitions adopted were those commonly used by the Office of Population Censuses and Surveys, which lists in its classification of occupations well over 500 occupational titles, together with nine employment statuses. Finally, a social class position was obtained for each individual by cross-classifying his occupation (let us say plumber) and employment status (employee, supervisor, self-employed, and so on), each possible legitimate combination having previously been allocated to one of the seven Goldthorpe class categories. The percentages reported in Table 2.1 were those obtained by the Oxford researchers. Here, then, is their 'class map' of England and Wales in the 1970s. (Scotland and Northern Ireland were studied by separate research teams based at the Universities of Aberdeen and Belfast respectively, but since the major findings of these studies do not differ to any significant degree, the reference to Britain in the title of Goldthorpe's volume is not entirely unjustified, especially since the principal Scottish and Irish results were incorporated into the second edition of the text.)

It would be easy, but nevertheless wrong, to think of these classes as if they were arranged hierarchically in some form of layer–cake model of class privilege. Goldthorpe is insistent that classes exist only in process rather than structure. This is because *individuals* are mobile, in different directions and with variable degrees of permanency, through the various *locations* themselves. In other words, having identified the structure of class positions, the researcher must then examine the degree of *demographic class formation* within that structure: that is, the extent to which classes are identifiable as collectivities whose members are associated with particular sets of positions over time. A more appropriate metaphor here might therefore be that of a river flowing out to the sea. As the water (people) pours downstream, some parts rush on more quickly than others, and so rapidly reach the estuary. But much water is held back, swirling around to form pools, a few of which are so large and deep that they remain relatively undisturbed by the small volume of liquid passing over their surface and on down to the coast. Similarly, as we shall see, some positions in the class structure (that of the routine clerical workers of class III, for example) are like river rapids, in that most of the individuals in them are 'flowing through', rather than being retained; while others, such as the semi–skilled and unskilled manual class VII, are like river pools because the proportion of the membership that is lost, compared to that which is retained, is very much lower.

Moreover, having ascertained the likely demographic identity of the various classes, one must then determine the extent of *socio-political class formation*; that is, the degree to which identifiable classes form distinctive life–styles, patterns of association, socio–political orientations and modes of action. Is it the case, for example, that members of the service class (classes I and II) share a common class identity, vote for the same political party, or have similar sorts of attitudes and values?

We can see, then, that Goldthorpe's programme for class analysis offers a comprehensive means of linking the structure of class positions to an understanding of patterns of collective action. His class scheme attempts to combine occupational categories whose members typically share similar market situations and work situations. But such an exclusively structural approach to class would be inadequate to the explanation of social order and collective action because some individuals – to an extent yet to be determined – proceed through that structure in a series of class trajectories. A satisfactory class analysis must therefore take seriously the issues of class formation, both in the demographic and socio-political senses, and this is why Goldthorpe insists that the question of social mobility should be central to any investigation of social inequality in modern Britain.

III

The empirical results subsequently reported by Goldthorpe are too numerous to document fully in this short chapter. Moreover, his analysis contains a good deal of impressive statistical tabulation, involving specialist indices such as disparity and odds ratios, as well as the fitting of a series of multiplicative or log-linear models. Fortunately, it is not necessary to pursue the details of these here, since the central argument of the book is relatively straightforward and can be illustrated without recourse to the complex accompanying calculations.

In fact it is necessary only to present the two most important tables from his report in order to grasp the significance of Goldthorpe's findings. The first of these is shown here, in somewhat simplied form, as Table 2.2. This records the basic intergenerational mobility experience of the respondents to Goldthorpe's inquiry, contrasting their own present social class ('What is your job now?'), with their class backgrounds ('What was your father's – or other head of household's – job when you were aged 14?'). The top half of Table 2.2 measures class distribution or 'outflow' by showing the amount and pattern of mobility experienced by men of different class origins. Thus, for example, we can see that among those who started from class I (top service-class) origins (7 per cent of the total sample), some 45 per cent are themselves in class I locations, with another 19 per cent in class II positions, 12 per cent in class III, and so on along the row. Only 6 per cent of men from class I origins had been downwardly mobile to class VII (unskilled manual) destinations at the time of Goldthorpe's study. By comparison, only 6 per cent of men from class VII had been upwardly mobile into class I occupations, although another 8 per cent reached class II, and 8 per cent class III. Of men from class VII backgrounds, 35 per cent were themselves in class VII occupations. The bottom half of Table 2.2 then presents the same data but in 'inflow' terms. This gives a picture of class composition by identifying

Table 2.2   Intergenerational class mobility among men in England and Wales

(a)   Class distribution of respondents by class of father at respondent's age 14 (% by row)

		Class of Respondent								
		I	II	III	IV	V	VI	VII	(N)	Total %
	I	45	19	12	8	5	5	6	(688)	7
	II	29	23	12	7	10	11	9	(554)	6
Class of	III	18	16	13	8	13	15	17	(694)	7
Father	IV	13	11	8	24	9	14	21	(1329)	14
	V	14	14	10	8	16	21	18	(1082)	12
	VI	8	9	8	7	12	30	26	(2594)	28
	VII	6	8	8	7	12	24	35	(2493)	25
	(N)	(1285)	(1087)	(870)	(887)	(1091)	(2000)	(2214)	(9434)	
	Total %	14	12	9	9	12	21	23		100

(b)   Class composition by class of father at respondent's age 14 (% by column)

		Class of Respondent								
		I	II	III	IV	V	VI	VII	(N)	Total %
	I	24	12	9	6	3	2	2	(688)	7
	II	13	12	8	4	5	3	2	(554)	6
Class of	III	10	10	10	6	8	5	5	(694)	7
Father	IV	13	14	12	37	11	10	12	(1329)	14
	V	12	13	12	9	15	11	9	(1082)	12
	VI	15	21	25	19	29	39	30	(2594)	28
	VII	13	18	24	19	29	29	39	(2493)	25
	(N)	(1285)	(1087)	(870)	(887)	(1091)	(2000)	(2214)	(9434)	
	Total %	14	12	9	9	12	21	23		100

Note: Percentages may not add up exactly because of rounding.
Source: Social Mobility and Class Structure in Modern Britain, Tables 2.1, 2.2.

the class origins of the respondents within each social class. So, for example, we see that, among those presently to be found in social class I, 24 per cent hail from class I origins, 13 per cent from class II origins, and so forth down the column to the 13 per cent who have been recruited from class VII backgrounds. Correspondingly, of the men currently in class VII locations, only 2 per cent are from class I origins, with another 2 per cent from class II origins, and so on down to the 39 per cent who are themselves from class VII social backgrounds.

Clearly, there are a large number of interesting detailed comparisons that could be made by using the information contained in Table 2.2, but the full and rather far-reaching implications of the data can best be seen in the more general conclusions drawn by Goldthorpe himself. Three of these would seem to be particularly important. First, there has been a clear shift away from manual labour towards both routine and skilled white-collar work, with the proportions in classes I, II and III increasing while those in V, VI and VII have decreased. This is obvious from a comparison of the marginal percentages in Table 2.2. Of the fathers, 7 per cent were in class I as compared with 14 per cent of sons. A further 6 per cent of fathers were in class II – as against 12 per cent of sons. Conversely, while 28 per cent and 25 per cent of fathers were in skilled and unskilled manual occupations (classes VI and VII) respectively, these proportions have declined to 21 per cent and 23 per cent among sons. The effect of this is to make the class composition of the service class (classes I and II) rather heterogeneous. Around one-third of this class has been recruited from working-class backgrounds, with slightly more than one-third upwardly mobile from intermediate classes, and slightly less than one-third having come from established service-class origins. The working class, by comparison, is substantially self-recruiting. Almost 70 per cent of those in classes VI and VII are second-generation working class. Relatively few manual workers are recruited by downward mobility from intermediate and service-class origins. In other words, there has been substantial net upward social mobility within the structure, if one compares the class distribution of fathers with that of sons.

Second, by inspecting the pattern of class distributions, we can see that the proportion of sons who are in service-class occupations increases as one moves up the scale of relative privilege in class backgrounds. Thus, rather small proportions of those from class VI and VII backgrounds are distributed to class I and II destinations (the figures are 17 per cent and 14 per cent respectively), as compared with the much larger percentages of those from service-class backgrounds who themselves return to service-class occupations (64 per cent in the case of class I and 52 per cent in that of class II). Comparing the cells in the top left-hand corner of the class distribution table with those in the bottom right, it will be seen that the general tendency is for respondents having service-class backgrounds to retain these by achieving service-class destinations, while those from the working class are returned to manual labour. Another way of expressing this is to say that those from service-class origins have greater *chances* of finding service-class employment than those from working-class backgrounds. Indeed, these relative mobility chances can be calculated from the figures shown, and expressed as a series of precise odds. Table 2.3 summarizes the overall mobility trends evident in Table 2.2 as a series of so-called odds ratios. (In addition, however, respondents have been broken down into four age-groups or birth cohorts, comparing the mobility trajectories of those born between 1908–17, 1918–27, 1928–37 and 1938–47 – the latest year of birth for those old

Table 2.3 Relative mobility chances in terms of odds ratios, by birth cohorts

Pairs of origin classes 'in competition'	Birth cohort	Pairs of destination classes 'competed for'		
		S vs I	S vs W	I vs W
S vs I	1908–17	3.06	4.86	1.59
	1918–27	3.12	4.32	1.39
	1928–37	3.47	4.90	1.41
	1938–47	2.89	5.97	2.06
S vs W	1908–17	4.16	12.85	3.09
	1918–27	4.54	13.83	3.05
	1928–37	5.72	17.37	3.04
	1938–47	4.29	15.56	4.91
I vs W	1908–17	1.36	2.56	1.94
	1918–27	1.45	3.20	2.20
	1928–37	1.65	3.55	2.15
	1938–47	1.10	2.61	2.38

Key: S = Service (classes I and II).
I = Intermediate (classes III, IV, and V).
W = Working (classes VI and VII).
Source: Social Mobility and Class Structure in Modern Britain, Table 3.5.

enough to have been included in Goldthorpe's sample.) The figures in Table 2.3 are thus a measure of the chances of achieving alternative class destinations. It is perhaps easiest to think of these as analogous to the betting odds in a horse race. Where the chances of a horse finishing first in a race are very good, in other words the horse is a 'favourite', then it will be offered to the betting public by the bookmakers at odds of, say, 2 : 1. If one bets £1, and the horse wins, one gets £2 back. On the other hand, if the horse is unlikely to come first and is therefore an 'outsider', it might be offered at odds of, say, 20 : 1. The comparison of these relative odds is then a measure of the (ten times) greater chances of the favourite as against the outsider winning the race.

Similarly, mobility odds ratios show the outcome of the competition between individuals of different class origins to achieve (or avoid) one rather than another destination in the overall structure, and so measure the relative chances of those from the various class backgrounds arriving at more or less privileged class destinations. Where a competition is perfectly equal – in other words the odds for a particular movement are even – then the ratio will be 1 : 1 (or simply 1). In fact, if we examine the competition between men from service-class and working-class backgrounds competing for service-class (and to avoid working-class) destinations (that is, the middle of the nine cells in Table 2.3), we see that the odds ratio here is over 12 : 1 for the oldest cohort, over 13 : 1 for the next oldest, 17 : 1 for the next to youngest, and 15 : 1 for the youngest. These ratios are a measure of the advantage held by service-class men over working-class men in this particular competition. Or, to put the matter another way, the chances of someone starting in the service class being found in the service class, rather than in the working class, are anything between 12 and 17 times greater (depending on age) than the same chances for someone starting in the working class. The individual odds reported elsewhere in Table 2.3 are perhaps less striking, although the overall pattern is consistent with the degree of class inequalities in mobility chances that are so evident in the service-class to working-class transition. Thus, for example, men from service-class origins have on average a four or five times greater chance of arriving at service-class rather than intermediate-class destinations, than have working-class men; men from intermediate-class backgrounds are twice as likely, as compared to men from working-class backgrounds, to arrive at intermediate rather than working-class destinations; and so on.

Finally, by comparing the pattern of odds for each transition across cohorts, we can examine changes in the mobility chances of people from particular class backgrounds over time. In fact, the changes are very slight and Table 2.3 shows no obvious tendency for the inequalities in the odds ratios to decline. The pattern of unequal mobility chances between classes is much the same from one cohort to another. Relative mobility rates – what Goldthorpe calls 'social fluidity' – have remained fairly constant throughout the course of the twentieth century. This is a particularly striking finding when one remembers that the youngest cohort, unlike the others, will have benefited from all the post-1945 reforms associated with the expansion of education and the welfare state. Despite this, the degree of class inequality in mobility opportunities among the youngest men in the study has not been diminished, and is as great as that found among men born before the First World War. Indeed, by incorporating into his analysis results from the mobility data that were gathered as part of the British General Election Study of 1983, Goldthorpe showed in the second edition of his text that the pattern of social fluidity found for the middle decades of the century extended well into the 1980s. The stability of relative rates, which the initial analysis of the 1972 survey suggested went back at least to the 1920s, was unaltered by the inclusion of even the most recent data. In 1983, the model of 'constant' (or unaltered) social fluidity was as acceptable for men aged 20–34 as it was for those in the 35–49 or 50–64 age-groups. In other words, the chances of intergenerational class mobility were the same among men born in the 1950s as among those born in every previous decade since the Great Depression.

IV

These, then, are the principal substantive findings reported in *Social Mobility and Class Structure in Modern Britain*. Before moving on to an appraisal of their significance, both as a general observation about inequality in this country and with particular reference to liberal and Marxist claims about social class, it is worth considering a number of possible objections to Goldthorpe's analysis.

Like other social sciences, sociology proceeds by means of a critical exchange of ideas and information, governed by the established canons of good scholarship. Sociologists scrutinize each other's arguments, looking for such things as logical inconsistencies, empirical inaccuracy, or lack of a satisfactory fit between theory, data and interpretation. All of the texts selected for inclusion in this volume have therefore been subject to close examination from within the discipline. Indeed, most have initiated lengthy debates, not only within the sociological community, but also among an interested audience of policy-makers, political activists and (occasionally) the subjects of the particular studies themselves. Goldthorpe's volume is no exception.

One strand of criticism deals with the definition of social class. This, it will be remembered, is rooted in the notions of market situation and work situation. These concepts have been central to the mainstream of class analysis in Britain and are generally held to provide a perspective on class relationships that can be traced to the classical writings of the German sociologist Max Weber. They offer an alternative to the Marxian proposition that it is relations of production – and in particular the distinction between those who own capital and those who merely sell their labour power – that are the determining elements in class structures. Marxists such as Wright and Crompton have argued that, in studying occupations as the basis for his class analysis, Goldthorpe has substituted categories defined by technical relations of production (the prevailing state of technology) for those which are properly defined by social relations of production (possession of productive resources).

The thrust of this criticism is perhaps best illustrated by reconsidering Goldthorpe's concept of the so-called service class. He sees professional, administrative and managerial employees as sharing a common class position because of the 'code of service' which regulates their employment. Unlike waged manual or routine nonmanual workers, these salaried employees have relative security of employment; enjoy high incomes with good prospects of advancement; and are in large measure free of direct control by others, so that they exercise considerable discretion or autonomy in their jobs. Lawyers, personnel managers, civil servants and the like are not usually subject to the same close supervision of their work as are shop-floor factory employees or ordinary clerical staff. The bureaucratic imperative to delegate authority, together with the growth of occupations requiring specialist knowledge, means that members of the service class must be trusted to fulfil their responsibilities in a manner consistent with organizational goals or professional values. Their conditions of employment therefore embrace a moral element that is not normally found in the case of rank-and-file wage workers. This element is recognized in a modification of the usual market relationship between employer and employee. Unlike wage workers, who exchange discrete amounts of labour for wages on a fairly short-term basis (and are therefore paid by the hour or week), the salaried service class are offered annual and incremental incomes, job security and career opportunities in exchange for the faithful discharge of their specific responsibilities. In other words, professional, managerial and administrative personnel are differentiated from other grades of employee by virtue of their distinctive market situation and work situation.

In this way the service class comes to contain all of the relatively privileged salaried employees among Goldthorpe's respondents. However, this category is the elite grouping in his class schema, and so also includes proprietors of large concerns, company directors and those who have no specific occupation but whose income is derived instead from inherited wealth or from capital investments. Critics have therefore maintained that, although Goldthorpe's approach reserves a distinct class location for the 'own-account' workers of the petit bourgeoisie, it is unwarrantably imprecise in its application to the upper echelons of the class structure, since it places the classic bourgeoisie (or, in Marxist terminology, the owners of the means of production) alongside top managers and rather ordinary professionals, in the same broad class category. How satisfactory is it, for example, to conceive of Robert Maxwell and Gordon Marshall as having the same class standing – of whom the former actually owns Derby County Football Club (among numerous other rather more lucrative investments) while the latter could at present ill-afford the price of a season ticket to go and watch their soccer matches?

However, Goldthorpe rather convincingly defended his practice, both on theoretical and pragmatic grounds. He points out that the distinction between employer, self-employed and employee is, among the relatively privileged, often ambiguous – as in the cases of working proprietors or managers holding sizeable ownership assets. The different labels are sometimes merely a convenient device introduced for purposes associated with national insurance or income tax payments. Moreover, the study of class processes via national sample surveys, as in the case of the Oxford Mobility Project, would select very few large-scale capitalists for interview, were the sample to remain representative of the population as a whole. Indeed, given the acknowledged lack of a suitable sampling frame, studies of specifically elite mobility have necessarily fallen back on more *ad hoc* procedures to generate respondents. In any event, these more specialist investigations have already confirmed what one might have suspected from casual observation, namely, that elite groupings are characterized by a high degree of intergenerational self-recruitment, and so form a cohesive but rather small fraction of the population. Thus, Goldthorpe argues, in the absence of sufficient numbers to permit reliable analysis, it makes little practical or sociological sense to distinguish 'the capitalist class' from employees having a high, secure and steadily rising income, and who exercise discretion or authority at work. His interest is in mass rather than elite mobility. In this regard, the notion of the service class may be a less tidy concept than that of the classical Marxist bourgeoisie, since the former, unlike the latter, embraces both employers and employees alike. But it is certainly a more practical proposition in survey research designed to reveal the overall contours of the class structure; and, in any case, is probably closer to the reality of modern corporate Britain, in which two-thirds of publicly quoted stocks and shares are now held by institutional rather than private investors, and managed by top administrators enjoying precisely those privileged conditions of service-class employment highlighted by Goldthorpe's approach.

A second line of criticism accepts the criteria of market situation and work situation as the defining characteristics of social classes, but questions Goldthorpe's operational procedure for generating classes from occupational data. He claims to have assigned an appropriate class standing to each combination of occupational title and employment status

in the light of the available information from official statistics, monographic sources etc., regarding the typical market and work situations of the individuals comprised: e.g. on levels and sources of income, other monetary and non-monetary benefits, degree of economic security, chances of economic advancement, and location in systems of authority and control.

In fact, we are never shown the 'available information' in question. This omission becomes crucial when it is remembered that the class categories he arrives at were designed explicitly for a study of social mobility among men only: it was male pay and authority (market and work situations) which Goldthorpe had in mind when constructing his schema. Not surprisingly, therefore, a number of critics have suggested that this operational logic makes the resulting class analysis (and the class categories themselves) sex-specific. In particular, feminists such as Stanworth point to the generally accepted wisdom that the occupational division of labour is sex-segregated, since women are concentrated in some occupations rather than others; and, within specific occupational categories, tend to have inferior conditions of pay and service to corresponding males. Similarly, it is often alleged that by making the family rather than the individual the unit of class analysis, Goldthorpe has simply prejudged a number of empirically unresolved issues. He interviews male 'heads of household' and allocates class positions to families according to the occupational standing of putative heads. Critics maintain that this procedure ignores the difficulties raised by growing numbers of single-female or jointly-headed households; fails to address the problem of 'cross-class' families, in which the husband and wife are both in paid employment, but in different class positions; and overlooks the possibility that women's earnings may have affected class formation, class inequalities and collective action in numerous ways, ranging from expanding home-ownership among the working class to reconciling intergenerationally stable proletarian men to their class immobility.

Goldthorpe subsequently defended his 'conventional' approach (of sampling only 'heads of household') against these changes – though perhaps less convincingly than in the case of criticisms directed at the concept of the service class. In a long-running debate in the academic journals, he pointed out that all the available evidence suggested that families rather than individuals were the units not only of demographic class formation, but also of socio-political class formation. For example, as regards the former, the duration and timing of a wife's employment (including her return to work after childbirth) were typically conditioned by the class position and mobility experience of her husband; while, in the case of the latter, the voting intentions and class identities of married women are generally found to be a function of their husbands' jobs rather than their own occupational experiences. Furthermore, most married women in employment had an occupational standing inferior to, or at best equal to that of their spouses. Few cross-class marriages comprised service-class women having working-class husbands. These and similar data suggested that the conjugal family remained the unit of class fate, class formation and class action. Goldthorpe concludes, therefore, that one can legitimately ignore women in a *class analysis* of social stratification because their employment experiences are irrelevant to the processes of class formation. The sex-specific nature of his class categories is, in his eyes, not an issue.

My own view of this matter is that the parties to the debate were in large measure talking at cross purposes. Goldthorpe contends that the position of the family as a whole within the class system derives from the 'family head', or member having the greatest commitment to and continuity in the labour market; and that, empirically, it is usually husbands who are in this position. A good deal of evidence to support this claim has actually been generated by feminists themselves. It shows that women are (still) constrained to take primary responsibility for childrearing and household tasks; are invariably discriminated against in the labour market; and so placed in subordinate and disadvantaged positions relative to men. In challenging Goldthorpe on this point, his critics are caught in the dilemma of seeming to argue both that the nuclear family and capitalist labour market oppress women, yet that their oppression is insufficient to support the logic of conventional class analysis.

On the other hand, Goldthorpe's insistence on the family as the *unit* of class analysis unnecessarily restricts the *scope* of his class analysis, and in a manner that belies the importance of women's participation in paid labour as a key factor shaping men's occupational mobility. His own interest is in the relationship between demographic and socio-political class formation. He concludes that, since women's class identities and votes (class socio-political traits) seem largely to be a function of the occupational standing of the men to whom they are attached (class demographic characteristics), this then justifies an exclusive concern with the mobility experiences of the latter in any class analysis. However, a mass of data accumulated over the past decade or so confirm that the way in which people are allocated to places in the occupational structure over time – the very processes of demographic class formation – are strongly influenced by gender, so that the career trajectories of men, and their associated class experiences, cannot be explained without reference to the very particular ways in which women participate in paid employment. There are relatively few male clerical and secretarial employees because this is commonly seen to be 'women's work'. Conversely, men are more readily promoted to service-class positions because rather few top managerial or administrative posts are held to be 'suitable' for females. Goldthorpe does not deny that this is the case – but he will not accept that these issues form part of the legitimate concerns of class analysis. For him, demographic class formation is interesting only to the extent that it sheds light on socio-political class formation; and, as the data show, certain (rather restricted) socio-political characteristics among women are conditioned primarily by the class standing of their husbands.

Arguably, however, studies of class formation should also investigate those mechanisms which help to generate classes as persistent demographic collectivities. Class structures are obviously 'gendered', since women are systematically discriminated against in the labour market, such that the overall effect of their participation in paid work is to privilege men. The sexual division of labour tends to confine women to part-time employment, less skilled jobs and careers which are interrupted by childrearing responsibilities and by the primary consideration that is given to the worklife requirements of husbands. But women continue (for the most part) to live in families, and this too has consequences for their life-chances and social actions, including, for example, their voting behaviour. This means, of course, that an approach which takes the individual as the unit of class analysis is no less legitimate than one which takes the family as the basic unit. Clearly, both are important, though perhaps for different purposes. In short, social classes comprise neither individuals nor families, but individuals in families.

In the second edition of *Social Mobility and Class Structure in Modern Britain*, Goldthorpe attempted to defend his position by switching attention from the pattern of overall (or so-called absolute) mobility rates among men and women to the matter of relative chances or social fluidity. By using occupational data from the aforementioned British General Election Study of 1983, which sampled both sexes, he was able to demonstrate, rather convincingly, that there was no significant difference between the mobility chances of women in competition with other women, when compared with men in competition with other men. He concludes that, since relative rates within the sexes are the same, one can on these grounds alone ignore women's occupational experiences in any class analysis. But the problem with this argument, to my mind at least, is that the competition for class places is not sex-segregated. Women have to compete for positions in and advancement through the occupational structure, not only with other women but also with men, and in this latter competition their chances are not equal. Women are discriminated against precisely because they are females – as Goldthorpe himself readily concedes elsewhere. It is rather as if one were to look separately at the chances of black and white people in South Africa for achieving service-class positions from working-class origins, discover that these were broadly similar, and then conclude that blacks could be excluded from a class analysis of that country since looking at whites alone would not lead to any false conclusions about class inequalities. Most sociologists would not wish class analysis to be as strictly defined and limited in its aspirations as this. In the real world, class and gender (and race) intersect; and, many would argue, what happens at these intersections is not only inherently sociologically interesting, but also crucial to a full understanding of class processes.

Finally, however, the distinction between absolute and relative mobility rates, the central methodological device in Goldthorpe's analysis of class mobility, was itself the subject of a critical commentary by other mobility researchers. No one has doubted Goldthorpe's principal finding that his results confirm the seeming paradox of having absolute mobility increase but relative mobility stagnate. In other words, his data suggest that there has been a net upgrading of the class structure, with perhaps as many as one-third of those presently in the service class having arrived there from working-class origins. However, they also show clearly that this upward mobility is not the result of changes in relative mobility rates, since these are fairly constant across successive cohorts entering employment. The implication is obvious. Such upward mobility as has occurred is the result of changes in the *shape* rather than the *openness* of the class structure. The growth of the service class and contraction of the working class, at least throughout the course of the present century, have been caused by changes in the occupational structure in Britain: the decline of manufacturing and manual labouring, together with the expansion of the services sector and of professional, administrative and managerial jobs. It does not stem from a reduction of the inequalities in class mobility chances. More 'room at the top' has not brought greater equality of opportunity to get there, because proportionately more of the new middle-class jobs have been captured by the children of those already in privileged class locations, so providing for a remarkable stability in *relative* chances for mobility during the period covered by Goldthorpe's analysis.

This does not mean that British society is entirely closed to social mobility. Goldthorpe is arguing simply that the expansion of the salaried service class, which is evident in the comparison between the proportion of fathers and sons in classes I and II, is almost wholly attributable to structural changes alone. It is not a testament to greater equality of opportunity between the various social classes. Nevertheless, critics such as Peter Saunders have argued that the emphasis placed on unchanging relative mobility chances paints an unduly pessimistic picture of British society, depicting it as more closed and thereby more static than is warranted by the evidence of the total mobility pattern. Goldthorpe's own figures suggest that only about one-third of families will have experienced no intergenerational upward mobility on the part of at least one member – and some of these will already be in the service class and so have nowhere higher to aspire. Most ordinary people will simply have perceived mobility around them – rather than have calculated it as constant relative chances of different origin groups entering various destinations. Goldthorpe's emphasis on the latter measure therefore tends to direct attention away from the considerable level of fluidity which, despite the class structure, clearly does exist.

In Goldthorpe's defence it can be argued that this criticism is largely the result of a rather partial reading of his text. In fact he devotes a good deal of space to describing the fairly high levels of mobility that can be observed in the intermediate-class positions of his schema. He notes, for example, that men who are of class III (routine nonmanual) or class V (lower-grade technical or supervisory) origins are rather widely dispersed across the class positions. This is confirmed by the class distribution figures in Table 2.2, which show what the lowest values on the main diagonal (indicating strict intergenerational stability) are for classes III and V, at 13 per cent and 16 per cent respectively. Moreover, further analysis also confirms that even those men who appear as intergenerationally stable in these classes will have experienced a good deal of worklife or career mobility, and that a rather large proportion of men in other class positions will have held intermediate-class occupations at some stage in their lives. It is true that class IV, the self-employed, show a stronger tendency to intergenerational immobility. One-quarter of men having self-employed fathers are themselves in self-employment; or, looking at this in terms of class composition, well over one-third of those presently in class IV hail from class IV social backgrounds. Here too, analysis of worklife mobility data confirms that there is a high probability of men from petit bourgeois origins themselves moving into self-employment when the opportunity arises, and doing so in spite of previous failures at working on their own account. However, the unquestionably low degree of both intergenerational stability and worklife continuity that is revealed within class III and class V positions suggest that these groups have highly fluctuating memberships, and therefore a weak demographic identity. Not surprisingly, therefore, Goldthorpe suspects that they also lack a coherent or unified socio-political class identity. Since there is a high frequency of intergenerational and career mobility from routine nonmanual to other occupational groupings, the class affiliations of intermediate workers are probably as diverse as their class trajectories, and certainly cannot be read off from the structural location of class III occupations alone. Class, as Goldthorpe rightly insists, is about process as much as position.

V

Notwithstanding the as yet unresolved controversy about the inclusion of women's occupational data in class analysis, what then is the significance of the results obtained from Goldthorpe's study of class inequalities in contemporary Britain?

At first sight the evidence might seem to substantiate liberal theories about long-term transformations in the class stratification of Western societies. Over the past three-quarters of a century or so the proportion of service-class positions in the class structure has doubled: The working class, meanwhile, has shrunk by about one-fifth. The result of these structural shifts is that one-third of those presently in service-class positions have working-class backgrounds. Another third have arrived there from intermediate-class origins. Upward mobility on this scale is clearly at odds with Marxist theories about the rigidity of class structures in advanced capitalism. Nor can these theories be salvaged by recourse to arguments about the proletarianization of the middle layers in the structure. Even if one were to accept that the market situations and work situations of those in intermediate positions had tended as a whole to move closer to those of manual wage-workers – and, as Goldthorpe rightly maintains, the point is debatable – there is a high frequency of mobility (intergenerational and career) from routine nonmanual positions to both manual and skilled nonmanual ones. Consequently, for example, routine clerical and administrative workers are a highly differentiated workforce rather than a somehow uniformly proletarianized mass. Some (mainly older unqualified men) enter clerical work from manual jobs late in life and stay there; others (notably younger men with few qualifications) alternate spells of clerical work with periods of manual labour; while considerable numbers of credentialled men spend only a limited period in clerical jobs early in careers which take them into senior managerial and administrative (service-class) positions. The proletarianization of some, through downward social mobility, is thus more than offset by the upward mobility or embourgeoisement of others.

However, there are also serious flaws in the liberal account, at least where the case of modern Britain is concerned. The notion of relative mobility provides the key to these. Liberals would argue that in the advanced industrial societies of the late-twentieth century, class structures give way to gradational and fluid socioeconomic hierarchies. Goldthorpe's data suggest quite the contrary, and show that class is as important now as it has been in the past, in a demographic sense at least. As a measure of its importance one may cite the odds ratios calculated for the transitions from origins to destinations: for example, that the chances of a man from service-class origins securing service-class rather than working-class employment for himself are more than twelve times greater than those for a man arriving at service-class employment rather than working-class employment from a working-class background, an advantage which has remained unaltered throughout the greater part of this century. Economic development has not reduced class inequalities in terms of the chances of securing advancement to privileged occupational positions.

These and other data relating to the total pattern of social mobility in this country confirm that changes in the British class structure have been considerably more complex than is allowed for within either liberal or Marxist theories. Furthermore, Goldthorpe also claims that these theories are equally suspect in their predictions concerning socio-political class formation, at least in so far as liberals anticipate the end of class conflict and Marxists a revolutionary struggle between proletarians and bourgeoisie.

The liberal perspective is most obviously challenged by the formation of the service class as a coherent demographic entity. The Oxford data show that there is relatively little downward mobility, either of a career or intergenerational kind, from service-class to other occupational levels. Having arrived at service-class destinations, individuals

tend both to retain this class standing and to secure similarly privileged employment for their offspring. The emerging demographic
identity of the service-class, together with a certain amount of
information on life-styles which Goldthorpe reports both in his
mobility text and elsewhere, lead him to speculate that this class is
developing a socio-cultural identity as well. Most service-class members (even those upwardly mobile from working-class origins) have at
least some good friends within the service-class; situational differences
between professional, managerial and administrative positions seem
to have low salience, since there is considerable mobility between
these; service-class men provide 'preferred associates' for each other in
sociable activities; and show a growing awareness of shared class
interests and a common standing. It would therefore be a mistake,
according to Goldthorpe, to assume that the socio-political characteristics of the service class to date offer a sound basis for speculations
about its behaviour in the future. This is still a class in the making. It is
therefore difficult to state conclusively whether past (and present)
socio-political inclinations are a function of the variety in class
background or of the present class circumstances held in common.
However, all the evidence does seem to point to the conclusion that
the service class, as it matures demographically, will form a cohesive
and conservative force within Western societies, and one that seeks to
preserve its relatively favourable market and work situations. As a
collectivity, it has a major interest in and commitment to the status
quo which has so obviously recognized its skills and achievements.
Consequently, service-class organizations may be expected to pursue
exclusionary strategies (such as credentialism) in order to maintain
class differentials in life-chances; and, in Goldthorpe's view at least,
will increasingly protect service-class interests specifically at the
expense of a redistribution in favour of manual workers.

The working class, in its turn, will be in a strong position to assert
its presence in the struggle for distributional advantage. Because of the
contraction in manual occupations, the industrial working class of
twentieth-century Britain has not been required to recruit from
outside its own ranks, for example among the sons of farmers,
agricultural workers, or the self-employed. The data in Table 2.2
show that classes VI and VII are the most homogeneous groupings in
terms of the social origins of their members. In short, the present-day
working class possesses a high degree of demographic maturity, since
it is predominantly second-generation blue-collar. Naturally, this has
favoured socio-cultural cohesion, and therefore enhanced the political
maturity and confidence of the waged workforce. Most manual
workers will have lived a large part of their lives within working-class
families and neighbourhoods. Those who fail to achieve mobility to
nonmanual occupations will not only participate as individuals in any
general economic advance in the country, but also be able to draw on

an established tradition of British labourism in order to secure collective improvements in their working and living standards. Indeed, the primary instrument for the pursuit of group and class interests among waged workers has historically been the organized trade union. However, the apparently undiminished potential of manual workers for communal or solidary action in defence of their own interests does not imply that the working class shares in an intrinsic commitment to communal, rather than merely individual concerns. It is at this point that Goldthorpe parts company with the Marxists. High wage demands may be pursued aggressively, but they testify only to the economic rationality of workers, and imply nothing in the way of discontent that can be channelled in the direction of revolutionary objectives. The history of industrial action by trades unions in this country is testimony to a predisposition towards sectionalism as much as socialism. Nevertheless, the long history of British working–class collectivism does show that manual employees are only very imperfectly accommodated to the capitalist system, and events at the time of Goldthorpe's study (such as the successive waves of strikes during the 1970s) merely underlined his argument that, contrary to liberal expectations, class conflicts showed no signs of withering away in the face of increasing affluence.

In conclusion, therefore, I would argue that Goldthorpe's study is chiefly significant for having shown that the social policies of British welfarism have not minimized class influences on social selection. The persistence of these inequalities in mobility chances is an obvious anomaly in a supposedly meritocratic market society. Such societies are legitimized by the principle of equal opportunities. Consequently, equality of opportunity has been an explicit policy objective of all postwar governments in Britain, Conservative and Labour alike. Relative mobility rates are a measure of equality of opportunity. These rates have not changed significantly in this country since the 1920s. Therefore, the inescapable conclusion must be that the postwar project of creating in Britain a more open society, through economic expansion, educational reform and redistributive social policies, has clearly failed.

However, like all good sociologists, Goldthorpe refused to take the seemingly obvious next step of advising his readers as to how, therefore, they ought to rearrange their lives. By drawing a clear distinction between the analysis of political structures, on the one hand, and the taking of a practical political stand, on the other, he is merely implementing the well-established scientific principle of value-freedom. Again he follows Max Weber in this matter. In a famous essay on 'Science as a Vocation', Weber wrote that all sciences (including sociology) contribute 'methods of thinking, the tools and the training for thought', in the service of 'self-clarification and knowledge of interrelated facts'. Science is not, therefore, 'the gift of grace of seers and prophets dispensing sacred values and revelations, nor does it partake of the contemplation of sages and philosophers about the meaning of the universe.' So, Weber insists, only a prophet or a saviour can give an answer to the question 'What shall we do, and, how shall we arrange our lives?' The problem of class inequalities is a political problem. One's approach to it therefore depends upon the kind of society one wants to have. But, as Goldthorpe rightly insists, he has no more to say about this *as a sociologist* than the man who cleans his street.

Goldthorpe therefore prescribes no particular solution for reducing the marked inequalities of opportunity that are documented in his text. Rather, he merely observes that in so far as governments explicitly set themselves the task of achieving greater social equality by creating a more open society, there are no grounds for supposing that any tendencies in this direction will be generated by economic advances alone. There is no 'logic of development' in modern capitalist societies that automatically translates economic growth into increasing social fluidity. Indeed, in Britain at least, prevailing patterns of class-linked inequalities in mobility chances appear to be of remarkably long standing; and, in the absence of sustained political interventions to the contrary, the inegalitarian tendencies that are inherent in the British class structure must be expected continually to reassert themselves. There are, as Goldthorpe puts it, no easy options for egalitarians. But, if their objectives are to be realized, the sociological analyst can quite legitimately argue that present policies alone will not suffice.

3 Education and culture

I

The evidence from the Oxford Mobility Inquiry shows that some 16 per cent of sons from working-class backgrounds are upwardly mobile and arrive at service-class destinations. The corresponding figure for sons of service-class parents is almost 60 per cent. This is a striking disparity in mobility chances. Relatively few children of manual workers have obtained professional, managerial, or skilled administrative employment, even in postwar Britain. Why is this so? Universal and free secondary education has been available in this country since 1944. Scholarships and then student grants ensured that, in principle, higher education was open to all who were able and might benefit from it. Do the above statistics therefore mean that middle-class children are inherently more talented – proportionately more intelligent – than those from working-class households? Or are there social processes which might explain these differences in recruitment to service-class occupations?

In truth the explanation for class differentials in mobility chances is almost certainly rather complex. But at least part of that explanation would relate to the functioning of the education system. Does it act to inhibit or encourage social change – including changes in access to class privileges and in the composition of elites? Educationalists remain divided on this issue. Two general perspectives can be identified in the literature. The first, which is shared by functionalists, liberals and human capital theorists, is that education is pivotal to modernity and prosperity. It creates knowledge, disseminates skills and matches individuals to jobs in an efficient and equitable manner. It is, therefore, a major stimulus to economic growth and social justice. The second approach, subscribed to by Marxists, interactionists and conflict theorists, suggests that education is principally a means of social control. Schools legitimize structures of inequality by installing acquiescence into the majority in the interests of the powerful. The system is neither efficient nor impartial and is therefore an obstacle in the path of social progress.

Public debate about education in this country has regularly drawn on both theories, in so far as economic efficiency on the one hand, and the creation of a national 'common culture' on the other, have long been established as the twin objectives of government policy towards schools. Social inequality – and in particular social class – has been seen as a major barrier to achieving these goals. Characteristically, therefore, British research in the sociology of education has been concerned with 'political arithmetic', or calculating the chances of children from different social backgrounds reaching successive stages in the educational process. For the same reason, discussion of education in relation to the ideals of social justice or equality of opportunity has centred on the *structure* of the education system and *access* to its various parts by children from different class origins. It is only relatively recently, with the advent of the so-called new sociology of education in the early 1970s, that much attention has been given to the *content* of education. The perceived failure of comprehensive schools to reduce educational inequality led writers such as Basil Bernstein and Michael Young to look at the organization of curricula, at the categories and assessments employed by educators, and at the quality of teacher–pupil interaction. Prior to this period, however, most studies in the old political arithmetic tradition simply documented longstanding class inequalities in access to private as against state education, selective rather than nonselective schools, and to higher education generally, and then attacked these on the grounds that they hindered economic efficiency and perpetuated social divisions. Regarding the first of these objectives, able children from less privileged backgrounds were being denied the chance to develop their talents, so there was an obvious wastage of ability. In respect of the second, these same differences in access to the different types of schooling merely reproduced the social distinctions of class itself, and so retarded the growth of a unified national culture.

Against this background, most educational reformers in Britain have pressed for equality of opportunity, irrespective of social origins. The more radical have sought to erase class differences. The aim of the majority, and ultimately of government policy itself, has been merely to eliminate class differences among children of equal ability. To that end, the Education Act of 1944 raised the school-leaving age to 15, and reorganized the system of state-aided education into primary, secondary and further educational stages. Fees were abolished in the state sector, so that each child could have an education 'appropriate to his age, aptitude and ability'. In practice, this meant that those passing the eleven-plus examination could choose to go to grammar or selective technical schools, rather than the nonselective secondary modern schools. Talented working-class children began to move into the former in large numbers. Strangely, however, relatively few of them successfully completed their course of studies. A series of official reports published in the 1950s and early 1960s drew attention to the different performances of middle-class and working-class children in grammar schools. In particular, they identified problems of early leaving and scholastic underachievement among the latter group. For example, during the 1950s the proportion of grammar-school pupils from skilled manual backgrounds grew to some 45 per cent of the total, while those from unskilled manual origins came to comprise around 15 per cent. However, skilled manual workers' children provided only 35 per cent of sixth formers, while those from unskilled manual backgrounds constituted barely 5 per cent. This, together with similar statistics on A-level examination results, seemed to suggest that the hitherto distinctively middle-class grammar schools had failed to assimilate their new working-class pupils. The selective system of the immediate postwar decade was still working against the interests of working-class boys and girls. Grammar schools remained mechanisms for the transmission of privileges from one generation of middle-class citizens to the next.

Unfortunately, although the arithmetic is telling and certainly impressed many educationalists of the period, none of the reports in question shed much light on *why* it was that the children of manual workers fared relatively badly in their grammar-school careers. What precisely was happening behind the classroom doors so as to perpetuate class differences in achievement among those with equal ability? *Education and the Working Class*, a study by Brian Jackson and Dennis Marsden first published in 1962, provided a particularly convincing answer to this question. By going behind the statistics, to unravel the social processes connecting home and school, this book added a new dimension and depth to the public debates of the early 1960s which preceded the transition to the comprehensive system of education in Britain. It is therefore the second classic text of postwar sociology which I have chosen to discuss.

II

On the face of it the study by Jackson and Marsden has little in common with that of Goldthorpe. Their research strategies, analytical tools and presentation of results are all sharply divergent. Goldthorpe situates his concerns in the context of well-established sociological theories; devises a series of precise hypotheses for testing; applies the most sophisticated statistical techniques to the analysis of data from a representative national sample survey; and presents his most important findings in formal mathematical terms. Jackson and Marsden, on the other hand, admit to not knowing quite why they wrote their book until they had finished it. Their results are presented in the form of quotation, scene and incident. They do not test specific propositions. Rather, to use the subtitle of their book, they simply introduce 'some general themes raised by a study of eighty-eight working-class children in a northern industrial city'. The city is Huddersfield where both authors grew up. Indeed, as they freely admit, their study is based on a sample of ninety working-class children. The fortunes of eighty-eight are reported in some detail. But the experiences of the other two – Jackson and Marsden themselves – are crucial to the interpretation of the findings. If Goldthorpe's text embodies the best of sociology as statistics, then *Education and the Working Class* is the epitome of sociology as autobiography.

Nevertheless, despite these radical differences in approach, there are clear substantive overlaps between the texts. Two issues in particular are common to both analyses. One is the extent to which postwar Britain has achieved the professed goal of social policy by successfully applying meritocratic principles to the allocation of rewards. The other is the individual subjective experience (and possible personal costs) of long-range upward social mobility.

We have already seen that liberal theories of industrialism embrace the ideal of meritocracy. They postulate open, mobile societies in which there is equality of opportunity and distributive justice according to the criterion of 'just desert'. Goldthorpe, of course, challenges these theories by showing that postwar Britain is not a fluid society. Mobility chances are strongly determined by class background: privilege is passed on. Jackson and Marsden complement this critique by examining the 'class wastage' among grammar-school children. They argue that talented working-class pupils who pass the eleven-plus examination nevertheless underachieve – leaving early or securing rather poor A-level passes – because of a culture clash between the codes of judgement and behaviour appropriate to family and neighbourhood, on the one hand, and school on the other. Intellectually able sons and daughters of manual workers were required to reject a whole way of life in order to succeed academically; many could not – or would not – do so.

This, in turn, introduces the second and principal theme of the research in Huddersfield. Mobility from the working to the middle classes carries the possible costs of social isolation and anomie. In his study, Goldthorpe explored this possibility by offering to a small subsample of his respondents the opportunity to write a short life-history describing their mobility experiences. Much of this material is used to demonstrate an affinity between his own class categories and the concepts employed by interviewees in describing their occupational trajectories. That is, most respondents seemed to view their mobility in specifically class terms, and in particular to emphasize the same basic elements of market and work situation that are the focus of Goldthorpe's approach. But consistent with his theme of a 'service class in the making', Goldthorpe also observes in the life-histories of upwardly mobile men a pronounced tendency to judge success in work as beneficial for families and social life generally, since it is seen as having raised material standards and widened the circle of friends and acquaintances. Normatively and relationally these working-class *arrivistes* are coming to resemble the established service-class core. It is this aspect of upward mobility which is central to Jackson's and Marsden's account. Their main concern is with the costs of upward mobility for the working-class child. What is gained and lost in the transition between classes? Is there a price to be paid for access to high culture, intellectual satisfaction and material well-being? Some such children do indeed become fully integrated into middle-class society. But, in the Huddersfield study at least, most of these came from 'submerged' or 'sunken' middle-class backgrounds. Those from unambiguously working-class homes, on the other hand, tended more towards the extremes of non-identification or over-identification with their new class cultures. The former, a minority, were dissatisfied with their work and position in society, doubtful about the worth of their education, and felt keenly certain losses in neighbourhood and family life which it seemed to have compelled. The majority, by contrast, were fully satisfied with their schooling and the social rise it had facilitated. But, as it seemed to Jackson and Marsden at least, these men and women had developed into rigidly orthodox middle-class citizens who now wished to preserve a hierarchical society and all its institutions. They wanted to forget rather than remember their working-class origins. The argument of *Education and the Working Class* thus seems to confirm Goldthorpe's suspicion that the service class in modern Britain may be developing a conservative, self-interested and exclusionary socio-political identity.

In both of these respects, then, the study by Jackson and Marsden serves to corroborate Goldthorpe's conclusions – despite the quite different methodologies and contexts of the two projects. The educational system in Britain neither promotes meritocracy nor encourages a common culture for all citizens. Rather, it functions to maintain both class inequalities in access to middle-class jobs and class cultural conflicts in schools and the wider society generally. Let us look at these arguments in more detail.

III

I have suggested that *Education and the Working Class* focuses on two interlinked themes – those of meritocracy and cultural loss. The key to understanding the connections between them is provided by the sample for the study. Jackson and Marsden selected eighty-eight former working-class children (forty-nine boys and thirty-nine girls), aged between twenty-three and thirty-two, who had successfully completed their studies at one of the four Huddersfield grammar schools during the years 1946–54. The authors then interviewed the parents of these children, most of whom were still resident in Huddersfield, and the children themselves. The majority of the latter had moved away, but were contacted during local visits, or else followed up to their homes elsewhere. Crucially, therefore, the study is based on a sample of former working–class pupils who had, against whatever odds, actually obtained Higher School Certificates and GCE A–levels at the local grammar schools. It is thus perfectly suited to the principal objective of the research, namely, that of examining the costs of upward class mobility and particularly the theme of cultural loss.

So what, in fact, became of those who entered a middle–class world from a working–class background? Of course, almost all were now in professional occupations, in management, industrial research, pharmacy, the civil service, medicine, the clergy and social services. More than half of the sample (forty–six individuals) had taken up teaching. Jackson and Marsden see this outcome as both a function of class background and an indicator of cultural malaise. Most of the pupils had decided on careers very late in their school and college days. To some extent, this is to be explained in terms of lack of knowledge about the professions among their working–class parents, and lack of appropriate advice on the part of the school. But it is also a symptom of the 'drifting, rudderless existence' lived by some of these young men and women. The positive choice of a career assumes that one 'lives to some purpose'. This sense of purpose, according to Jackson and Marsden, is 'nourished from the affective securities of family life and the social strengths of the neighbouring community'. It is precisely these supports that are lost during the process of social mobility. As a result, some working–class pupils simply drifted from certificate to certificate, and let the process of education make the choice of career for them. They added a teaching qualification to their other diplomas and in this way finished up back in the classroom. Not surprisingly, many figured among the one–third or so of the adult men and women whom the authors describe as 'disturbed', although this group also contained other 'unsettled' respondents who had changed jobs frequently and were most uncertain about the overall direction of their careers. Collectively, they tended to complain about the automatism of learning, about the loss of easy and intimate contact with family and neighbourhood, and about the lack of purpose in their lives.

The other two–thirds of the sample are described as a mixture of the 'normal' and the 'orthodox'. Many of the former came from sub-merged middle–class families. Jackson and Marsden describe them as the most positive people who were interviewed: men and women whose bearing was easy and untroubled; who were good at and enjoyed their work; and who expanded their social lives to the full. In short, people who were consciously pursuing a career and ploughing their talents back into society. But this group shaded into those who were excessively orthodox. These were mainly children from aspiring working–class homes who 'impressed by their readiness to accommo-date'. At school, they quickly learned the appropriate tone and accent and thoroughly identified themselves with the aims and practices of selective education. In adult life, though tactful and friendly, they were obsessively keen to engrain themselves in 'established' (that is middle-class) society. They disliked nonconformity and avoided unpleasantness. Theirs was an 'aspirant sociability' that hardened into 'an over-concern with the status quo'.

All three groups showed a strong preference for class homogamy in marriage. Some respondents married the sons or daughters of middle-class families while others were paired with upwardly mobile partners from other working-class homes. Education was the paramount concern. No less than fifty-two individuals had married someone with a grammar-school background. Those with university degrees looked for partners with similar degrees – and so on down the hierarchy of credentials. Perhaps unsurprisingly, the majority were well satisfied with the system of selective education and their own experience of it, with only some of the 'disturbed' minority expressing scepticism about the ability of grammar schools to select and develop all talented children. There was great support for the eleven-plus examination as a device for separating the intelligent from the rest. Comprehensive education was viewed with hostility as a political rather than an educational concept. Most felt that the educational road was wide open for working-class children with ability, so that changes in the selective system were unnecessary, and were the work of 'crackpot psychologists'. Indeed, the principal dissatisfaction expressed in respect of grammar schools was that they were not more like the great fee-paying public schools, especially in their ability to instil leadership into pupils.

Moreover, as these former grammar-school children came to enjoy a middle-class standard of living and style of life, so they also adjusted their political views to chime in with their new class standing. The majority of parents had been Labour supporters whereas most of the children voted Conservative. Many were hostile to the haste, nonconformity and disruption which they associated with Labour Party 'extremism' on issues such as nationalization of industry, support for the welfare state and nuclear disarmament. Labour was, after all, the party of the working class – whereas Conservatism was for 'the country'. The orthodox group in particular were most outspoken in their rejection of labourism in all its forms, including trades unions and the co-operative movement, which were commonly associated with militancy and inefficiency. Of all sons and daughters, 58 per cent located themselves in the middle class, 30 per cent in the working class, and 12 per cent as classless. By contrast, only 30 per cent described their parents as middle-class, while 69 per cent claimed working-class parental identities. Of course, this was only to be expected since almost all these children now held middle-class occupations.

But Jackson and Marsden are particularly interested in the 42 per cent who refused to describe themselves as middle-class, by stretching the working class drastically upwards in order to claim a common class standing with their parents, or indeed the middle class downwards towards the same end. Similarly, 90 per cent of parents described themselves as working class, but more than half claimed that their children were also working class. A quarter of all children voted Labour and even some of the Conservatives had a nagging doubt that they ought to have done so. (This uneasiness was accommodated by relegating voting to the realm of the unimportant.) And almost all were concerned to distinguish that 'respectable' stratum of the working-class from which they had come, and to which their parents belonged, from the 'rough' majority. In all of this Jackson and Marsden detect a latent ambivalence that is a symptom of the cultural loss experienced by most of their sample. The device of stretching one's class, for example, is taken to be a symbolic denial of the material and intellectual gap that had opened up between the generations – a reaffirmation of the solidarity of family life despite the changes wrought by education. It is a recognition that class is

> something in the blood, in the very fibre of a man or woman: a way of growing, feeling, judging, taken out of the resources of generations gone before. Not something to be shuffled off with new possessions, new prospects, new surroundings; to be overlaid perhaps, or felt in new ways.

But, of course, what now overlay the class background of these young men and women was a real change in their social standing: they were materially much better off than their parents, had broader intellectual horizons and access to the dominant high or civilized culture of the society in which they lived. Stretching of class affiliations, the rather apologetic description of oneself as 'left Conservative' and the characterization of social background as specifically 'respectable' working-class are, then, all devices which hark back to lost connections with the working-class home. They are 'addressed to the self', as an 'inner colloquy to soothe the doubts', a 'last protection' against full acceptance of the class barrier between origins and destination.

The most tangible costs of having crossed that barrier are diminished relationships with parents and childhood friends. Jackson and Marsden reserve some of their most painful quotations for the often perplexing familial situations of their former working-class children. Many were now 'strange' with their parents – though the arrival of a new grandchild was often a catalyst for the return to a surer and more affectionate bond between mother and daughter. For the most part, however, relationships between the generations were testimony to a long series of breaks in communication that had started with access to grammar school. Parents were unsure as to what precisely their children did for a living. Pride at seeing one's son or daughter 'getting on' was mixed with a certain resentment at their new 'snobbishness'. For their part, sons and daughters spoke with some embarrassment about the narrowness of their parents' lives and the intellectual poverty of working-class neighbourhoods. Finding themselves much nearer to the 'high places' in our society, few of these former working-class children wanted to remember their origins, so the discharging of duties to kin became simply a painful reminder of the social distance they had travelled since their youth. Consequently, they experienced curiously 'external' feelings about their background and described working-class life as if they were looking in on something almost alien to them. A gap in understanding had been opened up between parent and child during the grammar-school years; by adulthood it had become a class-cultural chasm.

IV

Of course, a sample of successful working-class children is entirely appropriate to the study of upward social mobility, especially if one can also talk to parents, and so grasp, as it were, both ends of the mobility chain. The methodology of *Education and the Working Class* is highly imaginative in this respect. But the authors are also concerned to discover why so many sons and daughters of manual workers fail to do well in grammar school. By means of careful interviewing, and a good measure of sociological insight, they painstakingly construct a plausible explanation for this wastage of talent. Nevertheless, it is surely the major weakness of their study that they seek to draw conclusions about working-class children who fail to stay the educational course from statements made in interview by eighty-eight such sons and daughters who have actually succeeded in doing so.

In fact the first part of Jackson's and Marsden's analysis, based on interviews with parents, tells the story of why proportionately fewer working-class children succeed in passing the eleven-plus and entering grammar schools at all. A number of important factors are identified, but the key element in the equation for success is the drive provided within the family home. In almost one-third of cases this stemmed from the 'sunken middle-class' nature of the household. That is, parents had formerly owned a small business, were themselves from middle-class backgrounds, or had middle-class brothers or sisters. Consequently, they were determined to reclaim the social position of the grandparents by thrusting their own children back into the middle class via the (now free) education offered in the grammar schools. A similar drive towards upward mobility was initiated in authentic (or what Goldthorpe would call 'demographically mature') working-class households, where the father had been promoted to foreman or senior chargehand. These men sought to satisfy their frustrated desire for managerial standing by offering this opportunity to their sons and daughters. Alternatively, there were some families (twenty over the whole sample) in which one of the parents had themselves enjoyed a grammar-school education, usually provided for by a competitive scholarship. Here, the child was born into 'an atmosphere of educational excitement and ambition', made especially intense since the occupational aspirations of the parents had often been thwarted by circumstances beyond their control. Some parents had a lifetime of self-education behind them, either through serious attendance at further education classes, or the dedicated pursuit of a particularly enlightening hobby. Others held responsible offices in a local or working-class organization. In the staunchly Conservative home, grammar school offered a release from the cramped conditions of working-class life, whereas to dedicated Socialist parents it seemed a harbinger of egalitarianism yet to come.

In all of these types of working-class home the pressures on the child to succeed educationally were unusually strong. These were the boys and girls who had a good chance of entering grammar schools alongside talented middle-class youngsters, especially if they came from small families and went to mixed-background primary schools where the influence of a minority of middle-class children and their parents could be directly felt. But this finding only deepens the mystery of working-class wastage at secondary level. How was it that, despite such parental encouragement and support, talented working-class children selected into the grammar schools nevertheless underachieved in relation to their middle-class counterparts? In order to answer this question Jackson and Marsden turned to their interviews with the working-class children who had in fact successfully stayed the A-level course.

These suggested that the first few weeks and months at grammar school were crucial to the child's educational success. It was during this period that new pupils learned either to adapt to, or reject, the culture of the school. This was also the point at which they were allocated to rigid 'A', 'B' and 'C' streams. There was little subsequent movement between these streams. Almost all children placed in B or C classes left before entering the sixth form. Only five of those interviewed by Jackson and Marsden had moved between streams after that first grading. As the authors point out, either this means that the system of assessment was remarkably accurate, or one must wonder 'whether working-class children, lacking a particular kind of parental knowledge and support, and rubbing against the school in all kinds of ways, did not over-accept the gradings given them'.

Such 'rubbing against' the system was the result of a clash between the cultures of school and neighbourhood. This conflict is central to the explanation of working-class underachievement. For most children from blue-collar backgrounds grammar school meant an abrupt ending of all neighbourhood ties outside the school. Pupils were expected to channel their social energies into school activities and clubs. Here, they found themselves surrounded by more middle-class children than they had ever met before: confident, articulate children who seemed familiar with the mores of classroom behaviour, already knew bits of Latin and French, and were sometimes personally acquainted with the teachers as neighbours or family friends. A whole new vocabulary – a largely middle-class discourse of grammatical precision, formal exchanges and distant politeness – had to be learned quickly. New ways of behaving and a new accent had to be developed. Old mannerisms and habits had to be supressed to avoid giving offence to teachers. All of this induced in many working-class pupils a haze which rendered memories of those first few months almost hallucinatory.

Those perplexed by the strangeness of grammar school, and confused by the loss of the neighbourhood that had hitherto loomed large in their social lives, were increasingly unable to turn to parents for explanation and understanding. Jackson and Marsden found that, even among those thrusting parents who wished their children to do well, there was (unless they themselves had attended grammar school) a remarkable ignorance about educational requirements and scholastic practices. Vital decisions, concerning, for example, the choice of subjects to be studied, were taken without knowledge of subsequent entry requirements for universities or particular professions. Parents lacked information about, for instance, the consequences of dropping or keeping Latin or geography and, as a result, many working-class children reached the fifth form only to learn that their career ambitions had been frustrated by erroneous decisions made in ignorance at the age of 12. Moreover, certainly after the first few weeks, most parents were unable to help much with the increasingly complex homework. Providing an appropriate environment for evening study itself introduced another tension into the manual household. Could the family afford to heat a second room exclusively for this purpose? If not, should the wireless in the living room be off or on, and should younger children be banished elsewhere? The necessity – or even the request – for silence offended the life of the family, since it 'was to go against it in its natural moments of coming together, of relaxation'. Similarly, unless the child quickly became bilingual (speaking BBC English in school and the local dialect at home), then he or she was increasingly prone to charges of snobbishness, and again introduced discord into relationships with kin.

These sections of *Education and the Working Class*, in which Jackson and Marsden describe the gradual estrangement of pupil and neighbourhood, are a powerful and moving account of the many, seemingly rather trivial everyday incidents and expectations that create intense social discomfort in the young child. The loss of social life outside school, combined with the demands of ever-expanding amounts of homework, introduced unaccustomed pressures and a new intensity into family relationships. Fathers began to demand clear statements about 'what kind of job' school was leading to. Mothers reacted by protecting the child and pushing him or her on to the next examination hurdle. Children, in their turn, responded by being unusually taciturn at home. This then further bewildered the parents who were already puzzled, sometimes offended, by the social barriers that had grown up between themselves and their son or daughter. Intermittent parental contact with the largely alien culture of the school, and sheer social discomfort during exchanges with middle-class teachers and parents, reinforced the tendency of working-class mothers and fathers to see the relationship between neighbourhood and school as one of 'us versus them'. The working-class child, in order to be educationally successful, had to make the painful transition from one side of this class barrier to the other – largely unsupported by the institutions on either side.

Of course, there were all sorts of minor variations on this central theme, and Jackson and Marsden are careful to document these in full. Some of the pupils studied – fifteen of the eighty-eight – refused to identify with the school and, aware of the conflict between the grammar-school ethos and the norms and values of the neighbourhood, quite deliberately rejected the former in favour of the latter. Basic loyalties, for them, remained local loyalties. All fifteen had nevertheless successfully completed their education: being against the school did not necessarily mean being against schoolwork. Rather, they valued knowledge itself, but rejected the rituals and rites associated with the official side of their education. Indeed, they were found by Jackson and Marsden to have formed themselves into a tight-meshed friendship network or subculture, based on neighbourhood rather than classroom, and incorporating local children who had not passed the selective examination. This subcultural group thus maintained itself within, but against the school throughout all of its six forms. They chose local youth clubs before school teams and recoiled against all images of dominance or leadership: school uniforms, speech days, morning assemblies, prefects, and so on. But the majority of the sample had chosen classroom rather than neighbourhood, and through hard work had become accommodating members of the school community, and ultimately rather successful middle-class citizens.

Given this degree of conflict between the cultures of school and neighbourhood it is not difficult to see why so many working-class children failed to survive beyond the fifth form. Jackson and Marsden suspected that, for some, the initial streaming proved to be a self-fulfilling prophecy: once declared 'C' children they simply began to think, feel, act and learn like 'C' children. In some cases the social unease and bewilderment that working-class parents experienced during encounters with teachers had been sufficient to convince them that the grammar-school education was, after all, of no importance – a conviction which was duly communicated to sons and daughters. Jackson and Marsden say that they are 'unable to estimate' how important this failure of contact between school and parent may be, 'but clearly it could have been decisive in many of those cases where able children have left at fifteen or sixteen'. Other working-class pupils probably found that the expectations of school bit too deeply into the habits of family life and disrupted relationships with relatives and friends to an unacceptable degree. Misunderstandings at home, isolation from kin and resentment among neighbours were simply too great a price to pay for intellectual enlightenment. For any or all of these reasons education might be prematurely terminated. Only a minority survived into the sixth form – though, here again, the authors pay particular attention to the few 'subcultural dissidents' because 'they often represent the very large numbers of gifted working-class children who abandon grammar school at sixteen, and do not progress (as well they might) on to university and the professional life.' 'Certainly', they continue, 'the children we spoke to remembered large numbers of dissident pupils up to the fifth form, but few of these remained at school after this, and only a minority fall on our sample.'

Of course, this whole account of the processes responsible for working-class wastage in grammar schools is simply intelligent speculation, resting on the difficult and painful experiences reported by educationally successful children and their blue-collar parents. However, what makes it convincing as an explanation is Jackson's and Marsden's subsequent study, also reported in their book, of ten Huddersfield early leavers. Discussions with these children, and indeed with their parents, simply confirmed the accuracy of the insights derived from the earlier interviews. All could recall incident after incident which compounded the shock felt at the initial clash of neighbourhood and school cultures. Children were puzzled at their inability to develop an intimate relationship with teachers and grew resentful in continual clashes with the school authorities. Grammar school brought them into an alien world for which the local value-judgements of the largely working-class primary school failed to provide adequate preparation. Bewilderment at 'not belonging' undermined confidence, which resulted in early streaming into the 'B' or 'C' classes, then to a subsequent lack of parental and school encouragement, to minor acts of rebellion against authority and thus further resentment. A vicious circle was set up from which early leaving offered the only escape. As if to place the issue beyond doubt,

Jackson and Marsden also report the details of a parallel study of ten educationally successful grammar-school children from middle-class backgrounds, and these confirm that there is an essential 'continuity of culture' between the established middle-class household and the selective school itself, which makes the transition between the two unproblematic and painless. They share a common vocabulary, range and mode of speech; teachers are often familiar as family friends, neighbours or even kin; and when things go wrong, parents possess the confidence and resources to intervene and protect the child's interests even against the opinions of the school. This is all too obvious even in the supposedly objective assessment of intellect itself. Working-class children who seem unlikely to pass examinations tend to be relegated to the lower streams reserved for the less able. Middle-class children, facing a similar difficulty, are often credited with a 'particular learning difficulty', which is diagnosed in close consultations between parents and teachers and overcome well in advance of any crucial test, if necessary by extensive private tuition.

V

Clearly, the selective school system merely reproduced the social class divisions of the society in which it was situated, rather than (as was its intention) helping to undermine these. Grammar schools did not operate according to meritocratic principles. Working-class pupils were systematically disadvantaged in the classroom. Financial exigency was – perhaps unexpectedly – not a major problem. Jackson and Marsden report the usual difficulties experienced by blue-collar parents in finding the money for such items as school uniforms and travel costs, but these were invariably overcome. The real hurdle was the cultural gap which the working-class boy or girl was obliged to leap in order to belong to the school and be accepted as a praiseworthy individual. Middle-class children entering the system were already familiar with the culture of the grammar school because it was so obviously their own. If working-class children wished to compete on an equal basis they had to scorn the norms and values of their own upbringing; and applaud, instead, not only intellectual enlightenment itself, but also the entire moral order of the 'higher' (middle-class) culture. It is hardly surprising that so many 12 and 13 year-olds were unable or unwilling to play the game.

Naturally, education in the 1960s was (indeed it still is) a contentious political issue, so this assessment was subjected to a good deal of (sometimes deeply emotional) criticism. Much of this originated in the opposition to the comprehensive system mounted by educationalists on the political Right. (It is perhaps worth making the point here, if only parenthetically, that those who accuse sociologists of a collective left-wing prejudice are invariably, and rather peculiarly, blind to academics in other disciplines who make explicit political capital on behalf of the status quo. Why is it, one might well ask, that critical sociological appraisal is regularly dismissed as 'bias', whereas positive endorsement by those grinding a political axe on behalf of the existing order is mysteriously endowed with the quality of value-freedom?)

Defenders of the grammar-school system complained that *Education and the Working Class* gave only a 'surface appearance of fairminded-ness'. In truth, so they claimed, the argument rested on impressionistic evidence and a sociological analysis coloured by personal conviction. The technology of the time scarcely permitted the recording of interviews and many were reconstructed immediately after the event from memory and field-notes. The investigators were intimately involved in their problem and, having preconceived ideas about the centrality of social class to educational achievement, simply found (or reconstructed) what they were looking for. Moreover, the Hudders-field schools were supposedly atypical, having been unusually slow to change their fee-paying ethos during the years covered by the study. Even so, much of what Jackson and Marsden take to be middle-class in the culture of these schools is in fact classless, since the emphasis on correct speaking, requirement to extend one's vocabulary and many other symbols of middle-class strangeness are all universal features of an academic education. There is nothing peculiarly middle-class about them and they are not confined to grammar schools. Indeed, when the Huddersfield researchers encountered working-class parents who positively approved of grammar schools, and pupils who seemed to adapt easily to them, they were forced to invent the category of 'submerged middle class', in order to reconcile these findings with their general thesis that the schools were divisive and a part of the class war. It was claimed, in short, that the analysis was simplistic, and obscured the merits of selective education, since it attempted 'to reduce life to a simple equation: "working-class" is noble, "middle-class" nasty and "upper-class" anathema'.

It is impossible to assess the merits of these detailed criticisms within the confines of this short chapter. In any case, readers must judge for themselves if Jackson and Marsden are guilty of over-interpreting the statements made by interviewees, by considering whether or not the evidence is generally convincing. Needless to say, I myself am persuaded by the analysis. There is, however, a school of thought within sociology which suggests that *all* informal interview-ing techniques employed in this way are inherently problematic. In the first place they yield results for which validity is difficult to assess. Survey data are public property: sceptics may consult the data-tape or even the original questionnaires, via the various data archives, and so judge for themselves the accuracy of fit between theory and evidence.

Historical studies rest on the interpretation of artefacts – letters, diaries, business records, for example – and these too are in the public domain. But outsiders rarely have access to the field-notes or tape-recordings that emerge from the indepth or informal interview. How then are we to know if the published data fairly represent the material collected? Do they actually support the interpretation placed upon them by the field-researcher? The question of reliability raises similar problems. Surveys are (usually) based on representative samples. Historical studies (rarely) generalize beyond the particular instance under investigation. But how representative is the sociological case-study or, in this case, sample of eighty-eight boys and girls who attended four schools in one northern town during a few years in the late 1940s and early 1950s?

The answer, of course, is that we cannot reliably assess the typicality of Jackson's and Marsden's relatively few respondents. But the point of their study is not to paint a picture of the selective system as a whole. Formal surveys had already established that class wastage was a national phenomenon. The authors of *Education and the Working Class* were convinced, with good reason since they themselves had lived through the experience, that the social processes behind the statistics were complex and subtle. Unravelling these would almost certainly require data pertaining to intimate details of family life, embarrassing recollections of offence given and received, and in general an unusual degree of introspection on the part of those participating in the study. Under these circumstances, the methodologies of the case-study and of lengthy, informal interviewing seem highly appropriate. Only by these means might one gain an insight into the changing relationships between parents and children, teachers and pupils, school and neighbourhood that are slowly – and sometimes painfully – built up by the working-class child during the crucial years between taking the eleven-plus and entering paid employment. It may well be the case, as recent research has shown, that a rather larger sample of grammar-school boys drawn from a national data-set will cast doubts on some of the details of the Huddersfield study. For example, there is no reason to suppose (as Jackson and Marsden maintain), that educated working-class mothers are more effective than educated fathers in improving the chances of securing grammar-school places for their children. Fathers seem to be every bit as important as mothers in this matter. But, these and other minor observations apart, I myself see no reason to suppose that the principal arguments of *Education and the Working Class* are not valid for their time and place. Moreover, unless family and education in Huddersfield are peculiar in some respects as yet to be determined, then one can plausibly assume that class processes probably work elsewhere in much the same way.

VI

At a more general level, there are three additional observations that might be made about the Huddersfield study. The first is that personal involvement in a sociological problem, on the part of the researcher himself or herself, is a circumstance that is as likely to operate to the benefit as to the detriment of any particular study. It need not necessarily be a problem. In large part, the promise of sociology consists precisely in its ability to relate biography to history and so lay bare the connections between the personal troubles and public issues in any society. When one talented working-class girl leaves grammar school prematurely then that is her personal problem. The solution will probably be found in her character, lack of skills, or in the private troubles of her immediate milieu. When, as in Huddersfield, a majority of these girls do so, then this is a public issue about the social structure, and the likely causes will be found in the system of education itself, rather than in the diverse personalities of the large numbers of adolescents involved. Indeed, it is a sociological truism that individuals shape their own lives, but only within the confines of social forces and circumstances which are handed down to them by history. Unrestrained free will and comprehensive structural determination are rare conditions of social action. The 'sociological imagination' is quite properly defined, therefore, as 'the capacity to range from the most impersonal and remote transformations to the most intimate features of the human self – and to see the relations between the two'. Seen in this light, the attempt by Jackson and Marsden to measure their own experiences against those whose biography seemed similar is no more and no less than one would expect from the self-conscious and sensitive sociologist.

The second observation is more critical and concerns the wider implications of the argument about cultural loss. Jackson and Marsden argued that material gain was purchased at the cost of cultural deprivation. This was a theme which concerned many intellectuals during the postwar years of rising affluence. The literary critic F. R. Leavis and cultural theorist Richard Hoggart, for example, had argued during the 1950s that the social values and characteristics of advanced industrialism – acquisitiveness, individualism, economic competitiveness, privatism, the growth of suburbia, mass culture, geographical and social mobility – were destroying the 'organic communities' of the pre-industrial era. These earlier towns and villages, based on kinship and neighbourhood, inspired a culture which emphasized rootedness, belonging, co-operation and solidarism. They permitted a more complete expression of individual needs, on the one hand, and close attention to civic responsibilities on the other. The great working-class communities of the 1950s, in the East End of London, in South Wales, Liverpool and elsewhere, were seen to hold the last vestiges of these 'organic values' which might act as a brake on the excessive individualism of the affluent – that is middle-class – life-style. Leavis and Hoggart wished, therefore, to see all that was good in the working-class culture – and particularly the deeply engrained habits of mutuality, solidarism and collective action – added to the common stock of (otherwise middle-class) national values.

Clearly, in taking up the theme of cultural loss, Jackson and Marsden were echoing these sentiments. Not only did working-class children, as individuals, pay a cultural cost for their grammar-school eduation and subsequent class mobility; the country as a whole was also culturally impoverished by material advance. Grammar schools, quite properly, handed down a number of civilizing qualities to their pupils: the capacity for logical analysis, literacy, an appetite for knowledge, and the like. But, quite improperly in Jackson's and Marsden's view, they also insisted that the narrower qualities of style, gentility, individualism, competition and other specifically middle-class characteristics were part of the same civilizing process. Mutualism and collectivism had to be abandoned. To the extent that working-class children succeeded educationally, therefore, the moral order of the country as a whole was impoverished.

With the benefit of hindsight, this argument now seems somewhat romantic and rooted in a rather one-sided reading of English social history. As critics have several times pointed out, if the working-class traditions of collectivism and mutuality stem specifically from the material constraints and deprivations of traditional working-class life, then they represent an instrumental (calculated) response to circumstances rather than a principled commitment to communal values. One might expect, therefore, that the class solidarity of manual workers will persist only in so far as the very conditions which support it remain unchanged. Real material gains – such as might accrue from upward social mobility, progressive social reforms, or the pursuit of sectional gains by some advantageously placed group within the manual workforce – may well then reveal that the culture of the working-class embraces an individualistic as much as a communal frame of reference. The history of trades unionism in Britain, with its many instances of sectional disputes and attempts to preserve craft privileges – running alongside the strenuous attempts to improve conditions of employment and extend political rights throughout the working-class as a whole – suggests that this is quite probably the case. Arguably, therefore, the cultural loss identified by Jackson and Marsden is as much the result of a working-class jump as a middle-class push towards individualism and social exclusivity.

Finally, however, one might note that, irrespective of any theoretical and methodological weaknesses in their study, Jackson and Marsden identified in the schools of Huddersfield a number of substantive issues that were subsequently to be placed high on the agenda of educational reform. In many respects, therefore, their text anticipated the principal concerns of the new sociology of education of the 1970s and beyond. These later debates, conducted in the aftermath of the move to comprehensive education, addressed themselves to the problems raised by the clash between the backgrounds and interests of the majority of children, on the one hand, and the traditional academic values of the former selective schools, now responsible for their education, on the other. The comprehensive reforms made it imperative to look at the content of education: at curricula, the quality of teacher–pupil interactions, the different rewards given for different kinds of skill, the categories and assessments used by educators themselves, the informal cultures of the school, and the educational consequences of all of these. In short, it became necessary to treat what it was to be 'educated' as problematic, to look at the social construction of categories such as 'bright' or 'stupid', and to examine the processes by which some parents, teachers and children were able to impose these constructions or meanings on the activities of others.

In fact most of these themes are introduced in one form or another in the pages of *Education and the Working Class*. For example, Jackson and Marsden attribute the culture clash between school and neighbourhood to a tendency among middle-class teachers to devalue certain working-class skills, values and traditions. Strictly academic qualities – and certain peculiarly middle-class properties – are given pride of place. The dominant values embodied in the school culture are thus treated as absolute, rather than as social constructs pertaining to particular interests, and no less contentious than those of the blue-collar neighbourhood itself. The working-class child who wishes to preserve aspects of his or her class culture is then forced into the role of dissident or rebel. Subcultural resistance to the categories and judgements of the school authorities is created. In sum, as Jackson and Marsden observe, 'every custom, every turn of phrase, every movement of judgement, informs the working-class parent and the working-class child that the grammar schools do not "belong" to them'. It is a measure of the sensitivity of the researchers to the stories told by their respondents that they were able to identify – though, understandably, not pursue in detail – so many of the issues that were to move to centre-stage in later analyses.

Of course, grammar schools are largely a thing of the past. During the fifteen or so years following the Huddersfield study most state secondary schools in Britain were reorganized on a comprehensive basis. By the mid 1970s three-quarters of all secondary school pupils were in these schools. This situation persists today – but perhaps only just. As I write this chapter, a Conservative government is seeking to implement a series of educational reforms which, among other things, will offer popular state schools the opportunity to opt out of local authority control; will define compulsory core curricular subjects in an attempt to concentrate attention on traditional academic skills; reintroduce selectivity based on the testing of measured intelligence; make access to education increasingly dependent on ability to pay; and in numerous other ways channel pupils along rigid 'training' routes leading clearly towards 'suitable employment outcomes'. To the outsider it all looks rather like a concerted attempt to reintroduce the selective school system of the 1950s. Proponents of these reforms might care to read how the original grammar schools were experienced by talented working-class children in Huddersfield before pressing further along this particular route.

4 *Poverty in an affluent society*

I

After completing his research in Huddersfield, Dennis Marsden continued interviewing on behalf of the Institute of Community Studies for another two or three years, before moving to the University of Essex in order to help with the pilot studies for a projected national survey of poverty. That survey was fielded in the late 1960s and, after an extensive period of analysis, the results were eventually published in 1979 as *Poverty in the United Kingdom*. This massive volume of well over a thousand pages was written by Peter Townsend, the principal architect of the poverty project, and is the third distinguished product of postwar British empirical sociology which I have selected for study.

Townsend's poverty project is probably best understood as part of a tradition of research into social problems in Britain that goes back to the nineteenth century. Early and influential studies of poverty, most notably those in London by Henry Mayhew in 1862 and Charles Booth in 1887, and by Seebohm Rowntree in York in 1899 and 1936, helped shape a flow of social legislation which culminated, in the mid 1940s, in the creation of a comprehensive welfare system designed to combat the five 'giant evils' of want, idleness, disease, squalor and ignorance. As we have already seen, the education system was reorganized in 1944, but the immediate postwar years also saw the establishment of the National Health Service (1946); enactment of Family Allowances, National Insurance and National Assistance legislation (1945 to 1948); and the passing of a new Children's Act in 1948. In the wake of these and other reforms, the popular perception among politicians, social commentators and the general public during the 1950s was that material poverty in Britain had finally been overcome. This view was given further credibility by the only major piece of research on poverty to be conducted during the 1940s and 1950s, Seebohm Rowntree's and G. R. Lavers's restudy of York, published in 1951. This showed that only 1·5 per cent of those surveyed lived in poverty in the early 1950s – compared with 18 per cent in the similar survey undertaken by Rowntree himself in 1936. According to Rowntree and Lavers, this remarkable improvement was mainly the result of full employment and rising wage-rates. In the earlier survey, 60 per cent of poverty had been due to low wages or unemployment, but by 1950 this figure had been reduced to a mere

1 per cent. Moreover, the new welfare measures (such as family allowances) had successfully redistributed income and wealth, and so considerably improved working-class living standards. Poverty among the aged remained the only significant blemish on the surface of the new welfare society.

It seemed that poverty had all but been eliminated by a combination of economic expansion and social reform. Indeed, public controversy and political debate shifted instead to the problems of uninterrupted economic growth and the materialism of the new 'affluent society'. Long-established inner-city communities were disrupted as workers moved out to the developing suburbs and fringe council estates. The major difficulty in these new dormitory areas appeared to be social isolation rather than physical deprivation. Full employment encouraged well-placed workers to strike for higher wages in order to furnish their new homes with an ever-expanding range of consumer goods. Labour shortages, rather than unemployment, helped set the political agenda. Successful attempts were made to recruit 'green labour' from the New Commonwealth to fill lower-paid or unskilled jobs that remained unattractive to the indigenous workforce. Harold Macmillan advised the country that 'most of our people have never had it so good' and a leading article in *The Times* rejoiced at 'the virtual abolition of the sheerest want'. Politicians on the Left assumed that fine tuning of welfare payments would solve the few residual problems of economic hardship. Those on the Right expected the wealth-producing mechanisms of the free market to achieve the same end. Either way, the last traces of poverty would soon disappear.

However, throughout the so-called years of affluence a small group of commentators consistently maintained that the problem of material poverty was still widespread. As early as 1952, Townsend himself criticized the narrow definition of 'essentials' used in the third survey of York, and argued for a more generous and realistic definition of 'necessary expenditure'. In subsequent articles in the *British Journal of Sociology*, he suggested that calculations of essential expenditure being used to determine the 'poverty line' should recognize the fact that spending takes place within the context of a social system which encourages people to spend in certain ways, so that 'due regard must be paid to the conventions of sanctioning membership of the community, to the influence of economic and social measures currently adopted by society as a whole... and to the standards encouraged by advertisers, the press, the BBC and the Church'. Townsend identified a number of minority groups, including the old, the widowed, the sick and the disabled, who were unable to participate in the expanding economy and therefore prevented from consuming in ways which had become conventional. Collectively, these groups probably numbered some 7 million people. Other commentators, including Richard Titmuss and Dorothy Wedderburn, challenged the idea that the welfare state had redistributed income substantially in favour of the working class.

Finally, in 1965 Brian Abel-Smith and Peter Townsend working together produced a study of *The Poor and the Poorest*. This book, which is based on data from government income and expenditure surveys, is generally credited with the 'rediscovery of poverty' in the 1960s. The authors argued that, if one adopted the official poverty line (the state minimum standard set by national assistance levels) as a benchmark, then the figures showed only 1·1 per cent of the population in poverty in 1953 and 3·8 per cent in 1960. These were the people entitled to national assistance payments – the forerunner of supplementary benefits – in order to achieve the state's minimum income standard. However, Abel-Smith and Townsend then reasoned that 'the level of living of persons receiving national assistance could be higher than that provided by the basic scale', both because some additional grants were made to beneficiaries, and because most also had access to other resources which were disregarded when the level of benefits was calculated. A more realistic poverty line, therefore, would be set at something like 140 per cent of national assistance rates. Applying this '140 per cent of state minimum' standard to data from the Family Expenditure Surveys for 1953 and 1960, they estimated that 7·8 per cent of the population were in poverty during the earlier period, and 14·2 per cent more recently. Alternatively, these figures could be expressed as 10·1 per cent of all households in poverty in 1953, rising to 17·9 per cent of households in 1960. Contrary to popular opinion, therefore, the numbers in poverty were substantial and had been growing during the 'affluent' 1950s.

As expected, this analysis was considered highly controversial in many quarters, although Abel-Smith and Townsend viewed it merely as a provisional exercise. Their ultimate objective was to conduct a national survey of poverty, of their own design, in order to produce comprehensive and reliable data which overcame the various weaknesses of the available official statistics on income, wealth and expenditure. Funding for such a study was successfully obtained from the Joseph Rowntree Memorial Trust. Abel-Smith withdrew from the project when he took up a political appointment in 1968, leaving Townsend as its sole director and principal author. Fieldwork was completed in 1969. The final report of the survey was published ten years later under the title *Poverty in the United Kingdom*.

II

It is not difficult to see why Townsend took fully a decade to produce his book. By any standards it is a massive volume: almost 1,200 pages of text including some 500 tables and diagrams. The data it reports are in fact taken from a variety of sources. The main national survey, conducted during 1968–9 in each of fifty-one constituencies in the United Kingdom, successfully collected information for 2,052 households (or 6,098 individuals) selected randomly. It therefore contains both 'rich' and 'poor' households in proportion to their distribution throughout the population as a whole. Townsend provides complete details about the selection procedures and there is no reason to suppose that his sample is unrepresentative in any significant respect. At the same time, four parallel local surveys were carried out in Salford, Glasgow, Neath and Belfast, yielding information on a further 1,204 households (3,950 individuals). These additional samples were specifically drawn from poor areas and were designed to yield sufficient numbers of low-income households to allow the researchers to make statistically reliable inferences about the many factors associated with poverty on the basis of the households sampled in their study. In addition, Townsend frequently draws on material from a host of official and other publications, including government reports, ministry memoranda and committee and command papers.

Clearly, therefore, it is impossible to give a comprehensive account of Townsend's numerous findings and recommendations in this short chapter. I propose, instead, to focus on the two interrelated themes which, it seems to me, provide the unifying threads that hold his complex arguments together. These are, first of all, Townsend's insistence that poverty must be defined as a *relative* rather than an *absolute* condition; and, second, his strenuous efforts to distinguish subjective, collective and objective assessments of need in order to measure poverty *objectively*.

The issue of absolute versus relative definitions of poverty is deceptively straightforward. Townsend notes that most previous studies have simply measured household income and compared this with the amount of money required to maintain physical efficiency. In Britain, the pattern was set by Rowntree's first study of York, which defined families 'whose total earnings are insufficient to obtain the minimum necessaries for the maintenance of merely physical efficiency as being in primary poverty'. Basing his calculations on the work of contemporary nutritionists, Rowntree estimated the average calorific needs of adults and children, converted these into appropriate foodstuffs, and then into the cash equivalent necessary for minimum subsistence. Small sums were also added to cover clothing, fuel and other household sundries. A family was judged to be in primary poverty if its total income (minus the cost of weekly rent) fell below this 'poverty line'. Almost all subsequent studies applied a similar concept of subsistence. Indeed, the state minimum income standard is even today derived from these early calculations, since the original 1948 national assistance levels were based on the (slightly expanded) 'human needs scale' used by Rowntree to measure the extent of poverty in his 1936 survey of York. In other words, most definitions of poverty are based on some conception of absolute deprivation, and a level of more or less constant minimum needs. It is assumed that if this is met then the individual can be expected to perform adequately in his or her occupational and other social roles.

Townsend proposes a quite different view of poverty in terms of the concept of relative deprivation. In his view individuals, families and groups in a population are in poverty when 'they lack the resources to obtain the types of diet, participate in the activities and have the living conditions and amenities which are customary, or are at least widely encouraged or approved, in the societies to which they belong'. That is, their resources are so inferior to those of the average individual or family, that they are effectively 'excluded from ordinary living patterns, customs and activities'. Townsend is here building on his much earlier observation that people live in societies which, through their organizations and customs, create similar wants and needs among members. Drinking tea is a good example. Although nutritionally worthless (or even harmful), it is generally accepted as a necessity of life in many societies, and has become both essential for individual well-being and a customary accompaniment of social visiting. Friends and neighbours expect to be offered a cup of tea when they drop in for a chat. Similarly, advertising or imitation by neighbours can establish certain types of clothing or furnishing as essential in a community, so that television or an annual holiday, for example, become part of the style of life to which individuals are expected, or feel prompted, to conform, if they are to be full members of the society. They may therefore be said to be relatively deprived if they lack the resources to purchase particular types or styles of commodities, or to participate in specific social activities.

The concept of resources itself requires clarification. Townsend argues that cash income alone is inadequate as a measure of financial condition, because overall standards of living can be greatly affected by such things as fringe benefits at work, access to free public social services, to income in kind (as might be available to farmers), and possession of capital and other assets. His survey endeavours, therefore, 'to measure all types of resources, public and private, which are distributed unequally in society and which contribute towards actual standards of living'. By measuring the contribution of the various systems of resource distribution in this way Townsend hoped to be able to specify which particular resources could most efficiently be manipulated in order to reduce poverty. The very comprehensive list of items about which information was gathered is shown in Table 4.1.

However, the major operational difficulties of this approach are raised, not by Townsend's pluralistic conception of resources, but by the idea of a style of life which, if it cannot be enjoyed fully, may be said to leave those excluded as 'relatively deprived'. This brings us to

Table 4.1   Types of resource and main systems from which they are derived

Type of resource	Main systems from which derived
1. Cash income:	
(a) Earned.	Wage and salary systems of private industry and the state Self-employment income system Fiscal system
(b) Unearned.	Asset-holdings (rent, dividends and interest from deposits with banks and building societies, insurance policies, land and buildings, government and company securities) Fiscal system
(c) Social security.	Social insurance and assistance Employer sick pay and pensions Family Fiscal system Court maintenance orders
2. Capital assets:	
(a) House/flat occupied by family and possessions.	Family Public authority loans system Building societies and insurance companies Employer subsidy Fiscal system
(b) Assets (other than occupied house).	Employer gift Family Earnings Fiscal system Capital issues system of companies, banks and insurance companies
3. Value of employment benefits:	
(a) Employers' fringe benefits: subsidies and value of occupational insurance.	Industrial welfare system Fiscal system
(b) Occupational facilities.	Industrial planning and management Safety inspectorate Trade union
4. Value of public social services: Chiefly other than cash, including government subsidies and services, e.g. health and education, but excluding social security.	Central and local public education system Central and local public welfare system
5. Private income in kind:	
(a) Home production.	Family Personal leisure Self-employment
(b) Gifts.	Family
(c) Value of personal supporting services.	Family Community

Source: Poverty in the United Kingdom, pp. 88–9.

the second major theme of his study, namely, Townsend's argument that poverty can be measured objectively.

At first sight this seems to be a difficult thesis to sustain. Relative deprivation is normally collectively or subjectively defined. In both cases it is socially constructed; either a population as a whole conventionally acknowledges a particular condition as one of relative deprivation, or, alternatively, the individual so affected feels himself or herself to be deprived relative to others. These usages are rather difficult to employ in a study of poverty. In principle, for example, I might feel myself to be relatively deprived because all of my sailing friends own cruising yachts over 30 feet long whereas my own is a mere 26 feet from stem to stern. Now, I may be deprived relative to them, but surely, as a yacht-owner living in a society containing homeless and undernourished families, I am not in a state of 'material poverty'? Nor, I suspect, would most other people in Britain subscribe to the view that anyone not in possession of a 30-foot yacht was impoverished. Offshore sailing is not an activity which is customary, far less prescribed, within the national style of life. How, then, can one arrive at an objective measurement of poverty – especially when that concept itself is defined in relative rather than absolute terms?

Townsend's solution to this problem is both novel and, as we shall see shortly, highly controversial. While recognizing that styles of living in a society are heterogeneous, and vary according to (among other things) class, race, age and personal taste, he maintains also that there are, in any society, 'types of custom and social activity practised or approved, and home, environmental and work conditions enjoyed or expected by a majority of the national population'. The extent to which groups within a population participate in these can be measured statistically in an operational index of the 'national style of living'. A list of sixty style-of-living indicators was therefore compiled, covering clothing, fuel, lighting, housing facilities, diet, working conditions, recreation, family support, education, health and social relations. Deprivation could then be measured among individuals and families, by determining, in interview, whether or not they lacked these physical amenities, or the ability to participate in the various social activities. Almost all the indicators correlate highly with the measured resources of households: the lower the available resources the higher the level of deprivation.

Townsend then restricted his analysis, 'for illustrative purposes', to a summary 'deprivation index' including only twelve of the original sixty items. These are listed in Table 4.2, which also shows the percentage of the population affected in each case, together with the correlation of the items with household income (as a crude indicator of total household resources). So far, then, he has established that there is a clear relationship between diminishing resources and deprivation. But how can one next draw a poverty line objectively at some point

Table 4.2   The Townsend deprivation index

Characteristic	% of population	Correlation coefficient (Pearson) (net disposable household income last year)	
1. Has not had a week's holiday away from home in last 12 months	53.6	0.1892	S = 0.001
2. *Adults only.* Has not had a relative or friend to the home for a meal or snack in the last 4 weeks	33.4	0.0493	S = 0.001
3. *Adults only.* Has not been out in the last 4 weeks to a relative or friend for a meal or snack	45.1	0.0515	S = 0.001
4. *Children only* (under 15). Has not had a friend to play or to tea in the last 4 weeks	36.3	0.0643	S = 0.020
5. *Children only.* Did not have party on last birthday	56.6	0.0660	S = 0.016
6. Has not had an afternoon or evening out for entertainment in the last two weeks	47.0	0.1088	S = 0.001
7. Does not have fresh meat (including meals out) as many as four days a week	19.3	0.1821	S = 0.001
8. Has gone through one or more days in the past fortnight without a cooked meal	7.0	0.0684	S = 0.001
9. Has not had a cooked breakfast most days of the week	67.3	0.0559	S = 0.001
10. Household does not have a refrigerator	45.1	0.2419	S = 0.001
11. Household does not usually have a Sunday joint (3 in 4 times)	25.9	0.1734	S = 0.001
12. Household does not have sole use of four amenities indoors (flush WC; sink or washbasin and cold-water tap; fixed bath or shower; and gas or electric cooker)	21.4	0.1671	S = 0.001

Source: Poverty in the United Kingdom, Table 6.3.

on the frequency distribution of income and deprivation scores? Surely such a decision is merely arbitrary – or, more accurately, normatively governed. It is presumably the values of the researcher that determine the threshold at which poverty is reached.

In fact this is not the case. Townsend hypothesizes that, as resources for any individual or family are reduced, so there will come a point at which there occurs a *sudden* withdrawal from the various customs which comprise the national style of life. The gradual intensification of deprivation associated with diminishing resources gives way to a dramatic and disproportionate decline in participation in the activities sanctioned by the culture. If this were found to be true, then one could reasonably argue that 'the point at which withdrawal "escalates" disproportionately to falling resources could be defined as the poverty line'. This definition would be objective since it would be defined by observed patterns in the data themselves. But does such a threshold actually exist? The date from the poverty surveys suggest that it may. These show that, if one standardizes for composition of households by expressing income as a proportion of the appropriate supplementary benefit scale rate; groups households by this adjusted income level and estimates the modal (or most common) value of the deprivation index for each group; and plots this modal value against income (expressed logarithmically), then the resulting graph (illustrated in Fig. 4.1) has a kink in its curve. That is, 'as income diminishes from the highest levels, so deprivation steadily increases, but below 150 per cent of

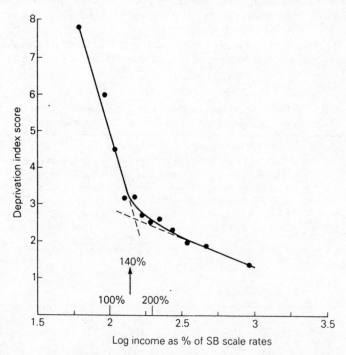

Figure 4.1 Modal deprivation by logarithm of income as a percentage of supplementary benefit scale rates

Source: Poverty in the United Kingdom, Figure 6.4.

supplementary benefit standard, deprivation begins to increase swift-
ly'. Beyond this point people cease, rather abruptly, to participate in
the conventional activities of the society.

The real poverty threshold therefore occurs at about 50 per cent
above supplementary benefit level. This new measure of deprivation
has, as one would expect, a marked effect on the incidence of poverty
in Britain. Applying the state standard (the basic supplementary
benefit levels), Townsend's survey suggests that 7 per cent of
households are in poverty, representing some 3 million individuals.
However, if his new deprivation standard is introduced, these figures
rise to 25 per cent of all households and more than 12 million people.
This total represents between one-quarter and one-fifth of the total
population at the time of the survey – truly a remarkable incidence of
poverty in a supposedly affluent society.

III

Much of the subsequent argument of *Poverty in the United Kingdom* is
a massive elaboration on this key finding. Among other things, for
example, Townsend's data on resources suggest strongly that the
various distribution mechanisms simply reinforce rather than diminish inequalities. As can be seen from Table 4.3, the top 20 per cent of

Table 4.3 Value for previous year, in pounds, of different types of resource to average household in each quintile income group

Quintile	1 Net disposable income	2 Net disposable income less income from property and investments	3 Imputed income from assets	4 Imputed income from employer welfare benefits in kind	5 Imputed income from social service benefits in kind	6 Imputed income from private income in kind	7 Total resources
Top 20%	2,486	2,353	700	330	411	67	3,859
Second 20%	1,420	1,680	333	162	287	66	2,227
Third 20%	1,073	1,052	191	96	225	56	1,620
Fourth 20%	750	725	184	52	156	51	1,168
Bottom 20%	378	359	146	10	105	31	652

Source: Poverty in the United Kingdom, Table 5.29.

households in terms of net disposable income also receive the largest sums from the ownership of assets, from employer welfare payments, social service benefits and private income. Column five of Table 4.3 shows the average estimated value to families of the various health, education, welfare and housing services. The calculations are based on information gathered in interview about the actual use during the previous twelve months of each of these services, including, for example, periods of stay in hospital, visits by district nurses and home helps, dental treatment, receipt of hearing aids and spectacles, attendance at schools and institutions of higher education, and subsidies for accommodation. Perhaps surprisingly, the figures suggest it is the rich rather than the poor who obtain most from the welfare state, with each household in the top quintile benefiting by some £411 as compared with £105 for each household in the lowest rank. This pattern is repeated across the other columns. Although lower-income households are more *dependent* on social services and private income in kind than those with higher incomes (because the value of these services represents a much larger proportion of total income); nevertheless, the 20 per cent of households with the highest net disposable incomes actually received the highest *money value* of each of the additional resources. In other words, adding other resources to cash income, in order to arrive at a more realistic assessment of living standards, simply serves to increase the observable inequalities in the distribution of income itself.

In other chapters Townsend explores in great detail the factors most commonly associated with poverty and hence the identity of those groups in society which run the greatest risks of being exposed to such deprivation. Poverty is found to be associated with a familiar set of circumstances – unskilled manual labour, old age, childhood, disability, unemployment, lack of formal education, membership of a racial or ethnic minority, and single parenthood – although the relative importance of these factors has changed over the years. Individuals with these characteristics have greatly increased chances of finding themselves among the poor. Consequently, for example, of those households containing a man, woman and three or more children, where the occupational status of the breadwinner is that of unskilled manual worker, no less than 93 per cent are in poverty. Similarly, 82 per cent of individuals aged 80 or over are in poverty; as are 82 per cent of those having a disability and being of pensionable age; 77 per cent of children under 14 having unskilled manual parents; 74 per cent of those having an appreciable or severe disability; and 70 per cent of persons aged 60 or more who live alone. Townsend's research also shows that many of the households in poverty – indeed a much higher proportion than is officially believed to be the case – do not receive the means-tested benefits for which they are eligible. For example, only 65 per cent of those entitled to supplementary benefits actually obtain these, while the percentage take-up figure for educational maintenance allowances is under 15 per cent. For rent rebates this figure is 30 per cent, for rate rebates 25 per cent, while in the case of school-uniform grants it falls to below 5 per cent. Several case studies of individuals and families suffering severe hardship are included in the text and, especially when compared with similar examples drawn from among the relatively rich interviewees, these provide a moving account of the many ways in which material deprivation diminishes the lives of the poor in our society.

Finally, in order to explore the possible changes that may have occurred during the ten years between researching the national poverty survey and publication of its results, Townsend conducts a thorough review of official statistics, comparing those from the late 1960s with their counterparts for the mid and late 1970s. He finds that this period saw a fall in the percentage of wealth owned by the top 1 per cent of the population, but otherwise very little change in the distribution between the top 20 per cent and the rest. Although a number of new allowances were introduced during these years, including new benefits for the disabled and a family income supplement for the low-paid with children, the general picture is of benefits declining in real value because of inflation and rising living costs. The government's own estimates of numbers of poverty (taken from the Family Expenditure Survey) suggest that those living at a level below the supplementary benefit standard grew from 1¾ millions in 1972 to 2¼ millions in 1976. Townsend's estimate would, of course, be much higher than this, for if one looks at changes in the social structure of the United Kingdom between the years 1968 and 1976 (as shown by the indicators in Table 4.4), it is clear that most of the social minorities at greatest risk of poverty actually expanded as a proportion of the total population. There was, for example, a 143 per cent growth in the numbers unemployed (although the population as a whole grew by only 2 per cent). In 1968 there were half a million unemployed. By 1976 this had grown to 1⅓ millions. Presently, at the time of writing, there are 2½ million people officially registered as jobless. Meanwhile, the real value of unemployment benefit has been greatly diminished, both by its failure to match rises in living costs and by restricting eligibility for payments. Townsend's well-documented judgement is, therefore, that there was an underlying growth in the numbers in or on the margins of poverty between the 1960s and 1970s.

All the evidence suggests that during the 1980s this growth has continued unabated. For example, the Child Poverty Action Group estimates that between 1979 and 1985 the number of people in Great Britain living in or on the margins of poverty (140 per cent of supplementary benefit level or below) grew from 11,570,000 to 15,420,000 – in other words from 22 per cent to 29 per cent of the total

Table 4.4 Selected indicators of change in social structure of the United Kingdom, 1968–76

Social category	1968	1976	1976 as % of 1968
Total population	55,049,000	56,000,000	102
Retirement pensioners (incl. others with pensions, aged 60 and over)	7,133,000	8,617,000	121
People aged 75 and over	2,491,000	2,847,000	114
Families receiving family allowances	4,257,000	4,592,000	108
Families receiving family allowances with 3 or more children	1,766,000	1,631,000	93
Supplementary benefit recipients	2,736,000	3,050,000	111
1-parent families receiving supplementary benefits	(185,000)[a]	310,000	168
Unemployed	560,000	1,359,000	243
Unemployed receiving supplementary benefits	235,000	684,000	291
Unemployed receiving unemployment insurance benefit	331,000	617,000	186
Unemployed receiving neither supplementary nor unemployment benefits	110,000[a]	200,000	182
Recipients of supplementary benefits not eligible for long-term addition or long-term (higher) scale rate	550,000[b]	572,000[b]	104
Recipients of invalidity benefits for more than 6 months	416,000	431,000[c]	104

Notes: [a]Estimated.
[b]Britain only.
[c]For the year 1975.
Source: Poverty in the United Kingdom, Table 26.4.

population. Of these 15 million plus individuals, 9,380,000 (17 per cent of the population) were living on or below a level of income equivalent to supplementary benefit, while 2,420,000 (5 per cent of the population) were living on incomes actually below the government's own poverty line. Needless to say, the authorities themselves refuse to accept these figures as reliable. At a bare minimum, however, one might say that the social policies of Conservative governments since 1979 will have done nothing to undermine Townsend's general conclusion that poverty in Britain is a national phenomenon which is 'structurally pervasive and of major dimensions'.

IV

Of course, many observers were sceptical of Townsend's findings when they were published. *Poverty in the United Kingdom* was subject to a good deal of immediate critical attention in the press and media generally. Much of the response was promoted by political considerations, and saw Conservatives challenging Townsend's estimates of the numbers in poverty, and socialists using these same estimates as a stick with which to beat social democratic welfarism. Townsend's own political motives were often questioned. These arguments have continued unabated in academic circles.

Some of the criticism has been of a rather technical nature and is directed at aspects of Townsend's methodology. Much of it has centred on the index of deprivation. Why were these particular twelve items selected from the initial list of sixty? Other forms of deprivation, such as being unable to buy new clothes, would seem to be equally appropriate. Indeed, three of the features included in the index are lacked by over 50 per cent of the population, so that want of them can hardly be said to exclude an individual from 'ordinary living'. One might ask, therefore, whether this particular selection of items represents a national style of life, in the sense that each is practised as custom, and by a majority of the population? Might the index not have more to do with taste than necessity? Vegetarians, for example, would presumably choose not to have a Sunday joint. I myself prefer not to have a cooked breakfast (though, fortunately, my income would be sufficient to allow me this meal if I wished to consume it). To chose not to go on holiday is one thing; to have no opportunity to do so is quite another. In short, for some critics at least, the style of living index was inadequate to define poverty or deprivation, since many of its indicators seemed to have as much to do with personal preference as with essential needs that went unmet. People might well have an income sufficient to meet the costs of all twelve indicators, yet misspend it on other less essential items, or simply forgo the items included as a matter of choice.

Others have argued that, even if the indicators are accepted as a valid operational definition of some national standard of living, the statistical exercise relating household incomes to the degree of deprivation is itself unconvincing. While there is a general tendency for deprivation scores to fall as household income rises, the use of modal (or most frequently occurring) scores as the basis for the calculation relating deprivation to income does tend to conceal the fact that some low-income households also had low index scores, while others with high incomes scored highly in terms of deprivation. In fact, 15 per cent of those on the lowest income levels scored two or less on the deprivation index, while 3 per cent at the highest income level had deprivation scores of more than six. There is clearly a good deal of variation among people at the same income level. Moreover, the threshold below which the deprivation index falls sharply (which Townsend uses as his poverty line), is said to be an artefact of his own superimposition of two straight lines on the diagrammatic plot of modal deprivation index scores against the logarithmic income scale. In reality, as Figure 4.1 illustrates, the scores follow a curve. The kink in the curve is therefore of little statistical or substantive significance. It is simply the point on the *continuum* from wealth to poverty at which Townsend has chosen, for his own reasons, to define the threshold of poverty in relation to what is, in fact, a wide variety of patterns of living.

The damage done to Townsend's argument by these sorts of criticism is rather difficult to assess without closely scrutinizing the original data. In his defence, it should be noted that other researchers, such as the economist Meghnad Desai, have applied different statistical tests (including the much more powerful technique of regression analysis) to the material, and found that Townsend's interpretation is quite sound. There is indeed a break in the relationship between deprivation scores and income levels at roughly 150 per cent of the supplementary benefit scale rate. (Indeed, Desai's study suggests that this same pattern is evident also in other and more recent surveys of poverty in the 1980s.) In the absence of further detailed investigation, therefore, it seems not unreasonable to give Townsend the benefit of the doubt, and accept his conclusion that the evidence from his survey is 'inconclusive, but suggests that such a threshold may exist'.

Many of those who challenged the particular significance of the index of deprivation nevertheless accepted the general principle that poverty is relative. Some critics, however, have expressed more broad-ranging reservations about the fundamental assumptions of Townsend's approach. The distinguished economist Amartya Sen published a long and highly philosophical defence of the idea that there is 'an irreducible absolutist core in the idea of poverty'. 'If there is starvation and hunger', Sen maintains, 'then – no matter what the *relative* picture looks like – there clearly is poverty.' The argument here is that Townsend has confused the issue of poverty with that of inequality. The existence of the latter need not imply the presence of the former – as is witnessed by my feelings of 'relative deprivation' at the 'inequalities' between myself and my wealthier yachting friends. Ths is not to say that Sen defends the supplementary benefit scale as a means of identifying absolute poverty, since it too is socially constructed and reflects such factors as economic feasibility (the strength of the national economy), the success of political pressure-groups in pushing particular claims, and policy objectives other than poverty removal (including the reduction of inequality itself). Rather, Sen argues that standards of living should be assessed by the criterion of 'capability', in the sense that particular resources are required before individuals become capable of achieving certain ends. One might ask, for example, what commodities are necessary for an individual to be capable of avoiding shame from his or her inability to meet the demands of social convention regarding, let us say, dress. In terms of commodities, escape from poverty in the sense of avoiding shame might require the purchase of new shoes, a new dress, new coat and so forth. These commodities and the resources needed to purchase them can, of course, be described in relative terms. (An expensive designer-label dress would be nice, but a new off-the-peg frock from a chain store will nevertheless serve for the purpose of avoiding shame.) But, according to Sen, the capacity to avoid shame is itself an absolute. It is not a case of feeling more or less shame than others, simply of not being ashamed, absolutely. And it is this capability which is a constituent of the standard of living and which must be met if one is to escape poverty.

Townsend replied to Sen at some length (prompting in turn a counter-reply) and, to my mind at least, clearly had the better of the exchange. As he rightly points out, Sen does not clarify exactly what is meant by 'absolute', since it is not clear how the capabilities that separate poverty from non-poverty are to be selected. Sen's examples of 'the most basic capabilities' ('to meet nutritional requirements, to escape avoidable disease, to be sheltered, to be clothed, to be able to travel, and to be educated... to live without shame, to participate in the activities of the community – and to have self-respect') are for the most part self-evidently social and therefore relative. The definition of adequate shelter, for example, embraces not only suitable protection from the climate (itself a relative notion), but also such culturally created concepts as privacy and appropriate segregation of space for cooking, washing, or sleeping. (Is the quality of shelter provided by a damp bedsitter in the inner-city really identical to that obtained from a large detached villa in the suburbs?) It seems that human needs – including the need for shelter – are essentially social. Any list of basic needs (or capabilities) would itself be socially constructed. (Is travel a basic need? And if so, how much, and by what means?) Poverty, as Townsend has always argued, is inescapably a relative concept.

However, rather more controversy surrounds both the explanation that is offered for poverty's occurrence and the policies prescribed for its elimination. Townsend himself is careful not to go beyond his data on either matter. These data suggest clearly that poverty results from the 'rules of access which govern the scope or exclusiveness of structures, and not just the rules which control their internal differentiation'. That is, there are rules controlling entry, defining and organizing queues and categorizing entrants, as well as those determining what resources are distributed to whom. The most important of these rules of access govern the system of waged work, which is broken down into a hierarchy of occupational classes, better and worse working conditions, primary and secondary labour markets, secure and insecure jobs, and so forth. Since these rules deny large sections of the population access to secure work under good conditions, 'the direct implication is that, if poverty is to be reduced, there must be less differentiation hierarchically of the employed population *and* a smaller proportionate share of total national resources by higher groups'. Moreover, since that section of the population excluded from formal employment is generally given access only to a very low standard of living, then it must be recognized that the rules governing the distribution of resources other than earnings serve also to create poverty. Those with high incomes must, therefore, be prevented from defining access to education, property, credit and health in ways which simply augment the unequal distribution of earnings. My own sailing activities, if I may be permitted to return to them yet again, offer a good example of this. Boats are expensive to purchase and maintain. Naturally enough, I do not in fact own mine, but my location in the occupational hierarchy as a professional makes me sufficiently credit-worthy to be able to borrow the money necessary to finance my North Sea adventures. In this way I can use my relatively privileged income as a basis for augmenting my standard of living in other ways – so reinforcing the inequalities of the occupational structure itself.

In short, Townsend offers a structural explanation for poverty, as originating in 'institutions perpetuating the unequal distribution of wealth and benefits and services in kind'. An effective assault on poverty would therefore require the abolition of excessive wealth, excessive incomes, and of unemployment; the introduction of an equitable income structure and breaking down of the distinction between earners and dependants; and reorganization of employment practices and community services (for example, industrial democracy to replace hierarchy at work, and restraints on managerial autonomy). He specifically rejects the idea that poverty is the result of individual or group deficiencies, created by either the psycho-pathological features of a 'sub-culture of poverty', or a cycle of deprivation transmitted from one generation to another via 'inadequate socialisation' in certain 'disturbed' families. It is not lack of motivation that causes poverty: it is lack of resources.

Rather predictably, this diagnosis has been criticized by those on the political Right, as being structurally deterministic, and as overly voluntaristic by those on the political Left. Both, ironically enough, assume (unlike Townsend) that poverty is inherent in a capitalist market economy.

The former maintain that a free market is the most efficient way of producing wealth for the majority. But in order to function effectively the system requires inequality. People must be attracted to jobs requiring different levels of ability by differential rewards which act as necessary incentives for encouraging hard work, risk, innovation and the acquisition of skills. Remedial welfare measures must not create disincentives to employment (for example, by making low-paid work financially less attractive than the income to be gained from welfare payments). Inequality (and poverty) is therefore inevitable, but is nevertheless functional in maintaining the smooth running of the system, and in any case is compatible with social justice, since it is the less able and less hard-working who will find themselves in poverty, because of low pay or unemployment.

Critics on the political Left, on the other hand, argue that Townsend errs by conceptualizing poverty in distributional rather than relational terms. He fails to recognize fully the implications of his finding that some people are poor *because* others are rich. Poverty is inherent in the operations of the free market because capitalist societies create class inequalities – and the poverty line is merely an arbitrary distinction drawn at a particular level in the hierarchy of class inequality. The poor are simply the most disadvantaged stratum within the working class. The definition and explanation of poverty cannot, therefore, be divorced from the analysis of class structures. In terms of practical politics, this means that there can be no consensus about a style of life to which all should have access, since the relationships between classes are inherently conflictual. The privileged will always seek to realize their interests at the expense of the poor. The social democratic solution of merely redistributing resources will fail to challenge the structures which actually create and sustain inequality; only a radical restructuring of class relationships can achieve this.

As always, I find these criticisms reassuring. Good sociology invariably attracts a predictable response from Left and Right alike. Often, as is the case here, the particular criticisms of one camp are merely the obverse of those made by the other: the causes of poverty are either wholly individual or entirely structural; classes have everything or nothing to do with its existence; the market economy is an unadulterated good or a thoroughgoing evil; welfare payments undermine individual initiative or are a calculated means of social control. Frankly, Townsend's arguments are much more complex than his political opponents allow, and it is only by a determined reading of their own socio-political objectives into these that one can arrive at simplistic endorsements of either the capitalist status quo or outright class warfare. It is simply perverse to maintain, as one critic has, that Townsend's insistence on seeing poverty as relative deprivation effectively drains the concept of its objective content 'and inadvertently contributed to the view that poverty no longer exists in our society'. However, this sort of challenge from the Left does prove one thing, namely, that those on the Right who maintain sociologists are unprofessional because they are anti-empirical and anti-capitalist are clearly mistaken in their assessment of the discipline. Like most good sociology texts, *Poverty in the United Kingdom* challenges undemonstrated assumptions about the way our society works, on both sides of the political divide, and by reference to an impressive programme of empirical research.

V

My own assessment of the significance of Townsend's arguments can be expressed in rather different terms. I want to conclude by pursuing two aspects of his work that appear to me to be of particular importance in the context of my own defence of sociology from its critics on the Right. These follow directly from the twin underlying themes which I earlier identified in his text: first, those of relative versus absolute concepts of poverty; and, second, the attempt to define poverty objectively rather than as a value judgement. The first of these issues raises the question of citizenship. The second leads us to the problem of 'essentially contested concepts' in the social sciences.

It seems to me that Townsend's attempt to institutionalize a relative perspective on poverty is itself an aspect of what the British sociologist T. H. Marshall (no relation to the author) commonly referred to as the 'realisation of citizenship'. In his classic lectures on 'Citizenship and Social Class', delivered at Cambridge in 1949, Marshall argues that in Britain the principle of citizenship has historically stood in opposition to the workings of the free market. He sees citizenship as having three elements: civil, political and social. The civil element comprises rights of individual freedom, such as freedom of speech, the right to own property and conclude contracts, and the right to trial by jury. Political citizenship consists of the right to participate in the exercise of political power, either as an elector of a governing body, or as a member of such a body. By the social element he means

> the whole range from the right to a modicum of economic welfare and security to the right to share to the full in the social heritage and to live the life of a civilized being according to the standards prevailing in the society.

Various institutions are connected with these dimensions of citizenship: courts of justice with the civil element, Parliament and local government with the political aspects, and the educational system and social services with social citizenship.

Citizenship is realized to the extent that the members of a society share these rights in common. Reviewing this process in Britain, Marshall observed that the various elements were independent of each other, with civil rights being fought for and largely secured during the eighteenth century, political rights contested and won (by men at least) during the nineteenth century, while social citizenship was (and has remained) a matter of dispute throughout the twentieth century. In general terms, however, the achievement of citizenship has been progressive. Moreover, and rather crucially, citizenship tends to determine the welfare of citizens independently of their market situation and in an inherently egalitarian manner. It thus acts as a barrier to the free play of the capitalist market economy. Indeed, the two spheres are in direct conflict. The free market has no moral component. Employers and employees simply attempt to maximize whatever advantages their market position puts at their disposal. The former seek to increase profits while the latter endeavour to raise wage-levels. Each party to the exchange pursues his or her own self-interest. However, citizenship is rooted in the moral, rather than the material order of societies. It comprises universal precepts oriented towards legal, political and social equality, so that (at least in principle) all are treated equally, irrespective of their market capacities. In Britain, for example, the institutions of the welfare state recognize that a measure of economic welfare and social security is the right of every member of the society, regardless of his or her ability to pay. The conflict between this principle and that underlying the capitalist market mechanism is evident in the fact that the rights of social citizenship have been much disputed throughout this century. For example, supporters of the free market have sometimes argued that unemployment benefits only encourage 'scrounging on the dole', while advocates of extended citizenship have seen these payments as a necessary corrective to the inefficient workings of labour markets.

Poverty in the United Kingdom, and particularly Townsend's principal thesis about relative deprivation, offers a clear demonstration of the continuing conflict in this society, between the logic of citizenship on the one hand and the class relations of market capitalism on the other. The attempt to define poverty in relative terms is a straightforward application of the principle of social citizenship – 'the right... to live the life of a civilized being according to the standards prevailing in the society'. Townsend's index of deprivation seeks to specify these standards; or, in other words, to map the parameters of citizenship itself. Indeed, his whole mode of analysis is strikingly reminiscent of Marshall's picture of the fundamental and unresolved conflict between social justice and market value. He writes, for example, of poverty as an absence or inadequacy of those 'diets, amenities, standards, services and activities which are common or customary in society'. Poverty deprives people 'of the conditions of life which ordinarily define membership of society'. The words could be Marshall's own although, as it happens, Townsend himself makes no mention of the essay on citizenship, and only rarely uses the term.

The similarity of the analysis extends also to Townsend's discussion of policy. As he notes, three distinct general principles have historically underpinned social policy in this country: conditional welfare for the few, minimum rights for the many and distributional justice for all. The nineteenth-century Poor Laws were premised on the first of these principles. A cardinal distinction was made between the deserving poor, who were in difficulties through no fault of their own, and the undeserving poor, whose impoverishment was due to such 'character defects' as drunkenness, laziness, or immorality. The former were permitted sympathetic aid, with a view to encouraging a recovery of independence, whereas the latter were subject to the deterrents of prison and workhouse. The second principle has provided the basis for much of British social policy between the turn of the century and the present. It is implicit in the various notions of a national minimum subsistence level, including that spelled out in the Beveridge Report of 1942, and subsequently implemented in the national assistance, supplementary benefit and other means-tested awards. Within this perspective, poverty is a problem of certain unfortunate minorities who cannot work and must therefore be accorded certain basic necessities of life. The final principle has been invoked in limited areas of policy, notably public health and medicine, but, as Townsend observes '[it] has not yet been clearly articulated or tried in Britain'. It would require a rather fundamental redistribution of wealth, property and other assets; the extension of public ownership and of individual rights to amenities; and a restructuring of the rules by which access to resources is restricted to the privileged few. No government has seriously attempted to modify market outcomes by implementing such a programme of principled redistribution. Conservative administrations have argued that a forced enlargement of access or equality of distribution merely undermines the economic efficiency of the market. Even Labour governments have failed, as Townsend puts it, to recognize that 'there is an in-built tension, and even a contradiction, in the application of a principle of a national minimum to a market economy'. The former implies some notion of social citizenship; the latter depends on a freely established wage-earning and property-owning hierarchy. Not surprisingly, therefore, successive governments from the late 1960s to the present, confronted with the seemingly intractable difficulties of maintaining Britain's international economic competitiveness, have attempted to restrict the sphere of citizenship by invoking the original principle of conditional welfare for the few. 'Scrounging', 'lack of motivation' and the supposed 'immorality of the poor' have been used as levers to push welfare benefits back behind some putative boundary separating the deserving from the undeserving poor. The analysis is by Townsend, but it could easily have come straight from the pages of Marshall's essay about the conflict between citizenship and social class.

This brings me to the question of values and the argument that poverty may well be an example of an 'essentially contested concept'. The philosopher W. B. Gallie has argued that there exist concepts whose application is inherently a matter of contention. They involve 'endless disputes about their proper uses on the part of users'. This is because the definition of these concepts is inextricably tied to particular sets of value assumptions which predetermine their range and applicability. In other words, they are necessarily situated within a given moral framework, so are implicitly evaluative as well as cognitive in function. For example, to describe something or someone as 'deviant' is not only to categorize the behaviour in question as 'different' from that of the majority, but also to evaluate it as 'improper' in terms of some standard of what is judged to be reasonable conduct.

Poverty may also be such a concept. To describe a situation as one of poverty (rather than merely inequality) is to imply that its persistence is unfair. As we have seen, inequality can be considered just if one starts from the assumption that the market mechanism rewards people in proportion to their endeavours, so that an unequal society can nevertheless be highly meritocratic. Poverty, on the other hand, is a term that embraces a moral imperative. It not only identifies a situation of deprivation, but suggests also that it is unjust. Unless one is prepared somehow to fall back on some distinction between deserving and undeserving poor, then the implication is that, because of lack of resources, certain individuals and groups are being prevented from participating fully in society: in other words, they are being deprived of their rights as citizens. To make such a claim is inevitably to invite controversy about the terrain of citizenship itself. The concept is therefore of an 'essentially contested' nature, since it carries with it the clear implication that something should be done to change things for the better.

In view of this one can hardly fail to be impressed by Townsend's determined efforts to exclude value-judgements from his analysis of poverty in modern Britain. He does not deny that there are many alternative ways of defining the phenomenon at issue. However, as he rightly maintains, it is the role of the social scientist to point to the (often latent) implications of different conceptions of the problem: to the causes presupposed by certain definitions and the policies inherent in particular explanations. Most definitions of poverty, because they contain an implicit prescription for policy, tend to represent the interests of some party to the dispute: they embody elitist, conventional, reformist, or radical value standpoints. The deprivation index, for all its weaknesses, attempts to circumvent this difficulty by establishing a standard of poverty which derives from the non-fulfilment of obligations that are generally shared and approved in our society. The 'kink in the curve', the point at which 'a significantly large number of families reduce more than proportionately their participation in the community's standard of living', is therefore an objectively given indicator of poverty.

As Townsend himself concedes, the index is provisional, and may well only succeed in pushing values one or two stages further back into the research process. Decisions have to be taken about the components of the national style of living, their relative importance, and 'the extent to which they can be reliably represented by indicators used as criteria of deprivation by social scientists'. Similarly,

> in the last resort the decisions which are taken to define the exact boundaries of the concept of resources and weight the value of the different types of resource have to be based on judgement, even if such judgement incorporates certain criteria of number and logical consistency.

Values have not been eliminated from social research. But, in the present context at least, that is not the point. Rather, what is striking is Townsend's awareness of the extent to which his own perceptions are shaped by normative concerns, and his strenuous attempts, despite this, to conduct his research according to the established canons of scientific method. Addressing a social problem which has attracted a great deal of public concern, and about which it would have been easy simply to express justifiable anger, he has instead sought at every stage to make his measurements reproducible and dependent on external criteria rather than subjective assessment. Rather ironically, given its controversial subject matter and direct policy implications, *Poverty in the United Kingdom* is a powerful example of sociology as a social science; neither anti-capitalist nor anti-empirical, but committed only to the demystification of our socially constructed reality, in order that we might better understand both our society as a political construct and ourselves as social beings.

5 Managing the new technology

Students new to sociology may be forgiven if, by this stage in the text, they have gained the strong impression that the principal concern of sociologists is to demonstrate to the world at large that nothing much changes over the years. Thus far, for example, we have seen John Goldthorpe argue that, irrespective of the absolute social mobility wrought by shifts in the occupational structure, relative mobility chances have remained more or less constant throughout the course of this century. Brian Jackson and Dennis Marsden found that changes in the formal procedures governing access to educational opportunities nevertheless failed to alter the middle-class ethos of the grammar schools, so that working-class pupils entering these institutions were still at a considerable disadvantage, but for cultural rather than financial reasons. Finally, in Chapter 4, I have attempted to show that Peter Townsend's findings about the incidence of poverty in our relatively affluent society are by no means as implausible as his critics have sometimes claimed. Again, as we have seen, the argument here is about relative and absolute measures of the phenomenon at issue. If the former perspective is adopted, then it is entirely reasonable to maintain that large-scale structural poverty has not been diminished by the social policies of the past forty years.

Is it the case, then, that sociologists are somehow predisposed to find social stability, even where there is apparent social change? Does their interest in social *structures* inadvertently bias them against the study of *dynamic* aspects of social life more generally? In fact, nothing could be further from the truth. Sociologists have always been drawn to the study of social action and social change. Indeed, some years ago I myself defined the subject in precisely these terms, pointing out that sociologists and historians actually pursue common objectives in their research: namely, to uncover the meaning of social actions and social relationships, as such meaning appears to the individuals participating in these transactions; and, via comparative analysis, to arrive at causal explanations of these actions, of social structures and processes, and of the course of social change in the development of civilizations.

My choice of texts thus far has perhaps disguised this concern for the dynamic elements in society. In order to remedy matters the next three selections, therefore, deal explicitly with the subject of social change. The present chapter looks first at the impact of technical innovation on different forms of business organization. What happens when a new technology is introduced into traditional British firms? How do managers react to rapid changes in the markets for their well-established products? One of the most illuminating attempts to answer these questions can be found, not as one might expect in an economics text, but in the mainstream of British empirical sociology.

II

The Management of Innovation was first published in 1961. The authors were Tom Burns, a sociologist based at the University of Edinburgh, and the psychologist G. M. Stalker. The book attempts to describe and explain 'what happens when new and unfamiliar tasks are put upon industrial concerns organised for relatively stable conditions'. Twenty companies were studied in depth, using a mixture of documentary, observational and interviewing techniques. Burns and Stalker began by exploring the industrial procedures, market situation and organizational structure of each of the firms. They then moved on to conduct lengthy interviews (lasting anything from one hour to a whole working day), initially with the head of each enterprise, and subsequently with 'as large a number of persons as possible in managerial and supervisory positions'. Finally, they took part in numerous casual conversations and made systematic observations of 'how people dealt with each other' during the course of the working day and week.

The fieldwork was carried out in three phases during the 1950s. Burns's early observations of a rayon mill and an engineering factory had drawn his attention to two features of interest that were to become central to his subsequent research. One was the contrasting management practices of the firms themselves. In the case of the rayon mill, the functions of every manager (and worker) were precisely specified, and each was expected simply to execute the detailed instructions which flowed from the chief executive down the hierarchy. The 'organization chart' provided a clear blueprint to which the enterprise actually corresponded. Despite the obviously restrictive characteristics of this system, it seemed to work rather well, and Burns could find no real evidence that managers felt aggrieved by it. The firm was prospering. At the engineering factory, on the other hand, the managers and supervisors had very ill-defined functions. Most were performing tasks which had been created by some pressing emergency or reorganization. The company was expanding into new fields so the scope and responsibilities of the various posts were, at the time of the research, a matter of extreme uncertainty. Moreover, the head of the concern was strongly committed to the ideal that management should exploit to the full the specific capabilities of every individual, believing that a person's job should expand or contract according to his or her particular abilities. Minimal rather than exhaustive job descriptions were, from his point of view, not only appropriate but also desirable. This firm too was commercially successful, although the managers were insecure, grouped into cliques and cabals, and expended a good deal of their energy in internal politicking rather than in pursuit of organizational objectives.

In the light of this contrast, the possible connections between rapid industrial change, commercial success, organizational effectiveness, and individual anxiety seemed worthy of further exploration. But the rayon mill had also proved interesting in another respect. Although it had a research and development (R&D) laboratory which was supposed to be active in creating new products and improving techniques, its staff were viewed with hostility by the production managers, who had succeeded in making its activities entirely peripheral to their own. At the time of Burns's study, R&D had been rendered largely impotent, reduced to repetitive testing in response to an avalanche of routine and often trivial inquiries, most of which might reasonably have been dealt with by the production supervisors on the spot. Again, Burns's attention was drawn to the social relationships between individuals at work, and especially the adaptation of these to the technical and commercial objectives of the firm. In this case, however, it seemed to be initiative rather than stress that was dependent on the way in which management organized itself.

In order to pursue these insights Burns, in collaboration with Stalker, next analyzed the experience of ten firms which had participated in the Scottish Council's electronics scheme. The Council had been founded in 1947 as part of the government's attempt to introduce new industries – automobiles, plastics, pharmaceuticals, and such like – north of the border, in order to replace traditional heavy engineering, metal manufacture and shipbuilding which were then in decline after the wartime boom. Its first project was to promote the electronics industry in Scotland by persuading established engineering firms to apply new technology to existing processes. Government ministries encouraged companies to recruit R&D staff by awarding small development contracts to those with a possible interest in electronics. Thereafter, firms were expected to employ the new laboratory teams for their own purposes, thus exploiting whatever potential existed for the application of new electronics techniques in their particular sectors. The government hoped in this way to encourage 'electronic-mindedness' throughout Scottish industry. The companies, for their part, were attracted by the prospect of gaining new technical resources and exploiting such competence in markets already familiar to them.

In fact, most of the concerns participating in the scheme failed to realize their ambitions. Half simply abandoned their laboratory groups after completing the initial government contracts. Others converted R&D into a routine test facility or production department. Burns and Stalker attributed these failures to 'an inability to adapt the management system to the form appropriate to conditions of more rapid technical and commercial change'. They identified two divergent systems of management in the companies involved in the project. One, the 'mechanistic' system, was judged to be appropriate to firms operating in relatively stable market and technical environments. The other, the 'organic' system, was particularly suited to unstable business conditions. In broad terms the differences between the two simply echo the findings of Burns's preliminary study. The mechanistic system corresponds to management practice in the rayon mill whereas the organic is similar to that which prevailed in the engineering factory. The Scottish companies failed to change from the former to the latter, despite the technical and commercial changes occasioned by their entry into the rapidly expanding electronics field, because the internal political system and status structure of each firm were threatened by the new laboratory group.

These twin theoretical postulates – the typology of mechanical and organic systems of management, and the insistence that each working organization was a plural structure, containing political and status systems alongside the procedures oriented to strictly technical and commercial objectives – are central to the argument of the book. They have also been the most popular subjects of critical scrutiny. Both the original thesis and the subsequent criticisms will be pursued in some detail below.

Finally, in the third phase of the research, Burns studied eight English firms which had a more longstanding commitment to the development and manufacture of electronics. Their product ranges included radio and television equipment, laboratory instruments, radar and navigational aids, computers, machine-tool control gear, telecommunications, and guided weapons. By this stage in the project, Burns was specifically interested in two aspects of the management of these companies: namely, difficulties which seemed peculiar to firms engaged in rapid technical progress, and the problems of getting laboratory groups involved in research and design to work effectively with staff responsible for production and sales. The greater variety of responses to technical change on the part of the much larger English firms allowed Burns to explore in some detail the differences between the two types of management system outlined in the earlier studies. In particular, he identified both the code of conduct in each concern as the most important element in defining the kinds of relationships which came to prevail within the organization, and the head of the concern (the managing director or chief executive) as the key figure in determining which code of conduct was adopted.

Again, as in the preliminary studies, the code of conduct that is characteristic of organic systems, and which makes a company better able to cope with changing market and technical conditions, is found to levy a considerable charge on the individual. Organic systems set the limits of feasible action rather widely and require total commitment to organizational objectives on the part of employees. People are expected to assume responsibilities far beyond the boundaries of their formal obligations. As a result, the 'occupational self' comes to dominate the manager, with work gradually becoming central to his life. (So far as one can tell all of the respondents interviewed were male.) His existence is governed by the demands of his occupational role. In short, Burns concludes that 'developing a system of organised industrial activity capable of surviving under the competitive pressures of technical progress . . . is paid for by the increased constraint on the individual's existence'. Or, more succinctly, 'technical progress and organisational development are aspects of one and the same trend in human affairs; and the persons who work to make these processes actual are also their victims.' Obviously, these arguments carry important implications for the management and commercial success of British industry, so it is necessary to examine them in some detail.

III

Far from being anti-capitalist, Burns and Stalker accept that the principal objective of any commercial enterprise is to survive and grow, so that success in the marketplace is simply an uncontested premise on which their study is founded. They explain in some detail how, after the Second World War, the particular market for electronics equipment changed dramatically. There was a rapid decline in government contracts and an increasing dependence on sales won in open competition. Most of the eight English concerns they investigated during the late 1950s had initially been 'relatively unfit' to respond to this change, although all had adapted to the new circumstances with varying degrees of success.

The most important determinant of commercial prosperity was the perception of the market which held sway within the firm. Some treated it as a sink into which were poured endless applications of every technique made available to the production managers. Others, the most profitable companies, viewed the market as a source: an expanding pool of needs, actual and potential, which could be systematically identified and satisfied. In the latter case a firm was driven by the market to the extent that every design and production decision was oriented to potential sales. Even its R&D technicians would cite salesmanship as the principal quality of a good industrial scientist. There was easy and frequent consultation between laboratory staff, production managers and sales directors, during which the need for co-operation and awareness of the market were constantly reaffirmed. Companies that treated the market as a sink, on the other hand, tended to have independently organized sales, design and production facilities. Contact between departments was restricted to infrequent formal meetings. Technicians therefore designed components with no thought for the requirements of competitive selling. Sales managers chose styles from catalogues regardless of the technical consequences for design and production. Needless to say, these companies were not as commercially effective as those in which all technical and production decisions were harnessed to the focal task of determining sales policy, since the rapidly changing market for electronics equipment demanded quick and accurate decisions about the saleability of what was produced.

Clearly, the less successful firms had structured their management systems largely according to mechanistic principles, which were entirely appropriate to stable business conditions but not to the market situation and technological basis of the postwar electronics industry. Burns and Stalker give an exhaustive list of the organizational principles of such systems and this has been reproduced in Table 5.1. These maxims were all well suited to managing the rayon mill included in Burns's preliminary study. The market for the product was clearly defined, the techniques for producing it well-established and the resources of the company fully documented. Yarn could therefore be produced efficiently according to the rules, procedures and permitted tolerance levels ('limits and constants') laid down in the all-embracing rule-book or 'Factory Bible'. Each individual worked on his own, 'knew his job', and was 'responsible for seeing it done'. Decision-making took place within a tightly controlled and familiar normative framework – indeed, substantial spheres of production management had become so routinized that they could be formulated numerically as a programme for appropriate action under predictable circumstances. This ensured minimal loss of materials or time and maximal control of the process and staff. As a result, the company was a commercial success. Crucially, however, this structure of management is only suited to 'a concern for which technical and market conditions approximated very closely to stability'.

Changing conditions, which create unforeseen problems and tasks which cannot therefore be described functionally or distributed automatically throughout a clearly demarcated structure, require an organic system of management. The characteristics of this system are also conveniently listed by Burns and Stalker and are again shown here in tabular form (see Table 5.2). It is easy to see how firms applying these sorts of principles, of which successful electronics companies were typical, will better be able to meet the contingencies of a fast changing market than will those organized along mechanistic lines. The endless redefinition of occupational roles means that new tasks

Table 5.1   Characteristics of a mechanical management system

---

(a) The specialized differentiation of functional tasks into which the problems and tasks facing the concern as a whole are broken down.

(b) The abstract nature of each individual task, which is pursued with techniques and purposes more or less distinct from those of the concern as a whole; i.e. the functionaries tend to pursue the technical improvement of means, rather than the accomplishment of the ends of the concern.

(c) The reconciliation for each level in the hierarchy of these distinct ·
performances by the immediate superiors, who are also, in turn, responsible for seeing that each is relevant in his own special part of the task.

(d) The precise definition of rights and obligations and technical methods attached to each functional role.

(e) The translation of rights and obligations and methods into the responsibilities of a functional position.

(f) Hierarchic structure of control, authority and communication.

(g) A reinforcement of the hierarchic structure by the location of knowledge of actualities exclusively at the top of the hierarchy, where the final reconciliation of distinct tasks and assessment of relevance is made.

(h) A tendency for interaction between members of the concern to be vertical, i.e. between superior and subordinate.

(i) A tendency for operations and working behaviour to be governed by the instructions and decisions issued by superiors.

(j) Insistence on loyalty to the concern and obedience to superiors as a condition of membership.

(k) A greater importance and prestige attaching to internal (local) than to general (cosmopolitan) knowledge, experience and skill.

Source: The Management of Innovation, p. 120.

and problems are acted on rather than passed over. The common purposes of the organization are constantly reiterated at the numerous meetings during which individual tasks are reallocated and linked to the objectives of the whole concern. Individuals are expected to be – and are – more extensively committed to the firm than would typically be the case under the mechanistic system. There is effective and speedy communication between all departments and levels of management. The organizational chart or manual does not get in the way of interactions between superiors, colleagues and subordinates – indeed, Burns and Stalker often found that a formal organizational chart did not exist. At any one time, necessary authority was settled by consensus, and vested in whomever was best able to do the job in hand. This system of management is therefore well adapted to a rapidly changing commercial and technical environment. The appearance of novelties – new discoveries or market opportunities – will pose many fewer difficulties than would be the case under the more rigid mechanistic type of management structure.

The two types of bureaucracy are clearly appropriate to different

Table 5.2 Characteristics of an organic management system

(a) The contributive nature of special knowledge and experience to the common task of the concern.

(b) The 'realistic' nature of the individual task, which is seen as set by the total situation of the concern.

(c) The adjustment and continual redefinition of individual tasks through interaction with others.

(d) The shedding of 'responsibility' as a limited field of rights, obligations and methods. (Problems may not be posted upwards, downwards, or sideways as being someone else's responsibility.)

(e) The spread of commitment to the concern beyond any technical definition.

(f) A network structure of control, authority and communication. The sanctions which apply to the individual's conduct in his working role derive more from presumed community of interest with the rest of the working organization in the survival and growth of the firm, and less from a contractual relationship between himself and a nonpersonal corporation, represented for him by an immediate superior.

(g) Omniscience no longer imputed to the head of the concern; knowledge about the technical or commercial nature of the here-and-now task may be located anywhere in the network; this location becoming the *ad hoc* centre of control authority and communication.

(h) A lateral rather than a vertical direction of communication through the organization, communications between people of different rank, also, resembling consultation rather than command.

(i) A content of communication which consists of information and advice rather than instructions and decision.

(j) Commitment to the concern's tasks and to the 'technological ethos' of material progress and expansion is more highly valued than loyalty and obedience.

(k) Importance and prestige attach to affiliations and expertise valid in the industrial and technical and commercial milieux external to the firm.

Source: *The Management of Innovation*, pp. 121–2.

economic circumstances. It follows, as Burns and Stalker note, that 'there is no single set of principles for "good organisation", an ideal type of management system which can serve as a model to which administrative practice should, or could in time, approximate'. In their view, the management system is a dependent variable, related in the first instance to the rate of environmental change. The principal task of chief executives should be to interpret correctly the market and technological circumstances under which a company will operate and then design a management system to suit the likely rates at which conditions are changing. It also follows, therefore, that the firms participating in the Scottish Council's electronics scheme – having lost the stability guaranteed by government wartime contracts, and then made attempts to counteract this by implementing the new technology of the fast-changing electronics industry – should also have made corresponding adjustments in the management structures of the companies themselves. In fact, Burns and Stalker could find no evidence of such changes, and instead observed sustained efforts at maintaining and reimposing the existing mechanistic order. Why were the Scottish companies so intransigent?

The research suggested that two other independent variables (besides the rate of environmental change) directly affect the form taken by management systems. As was earlier observed, these are

> the relative strength of individual commitments to political and status-gaining ends, and the relative capacity of the directors of a concern to 'lead' – i.e., to interpret the requirements of the external situation and to prescribe the extent of the personal commitments of individuals to the purposes and activities of the working organisation.

The first of these refers to the existence of 'plural social systems' within any industrial concern. Employees – even at the senior managerial level – can seek to realize purposes other than those defined by the organization. Some of these may be irrelevant to, or even incompatible with, the formal objectives of the business. In particular, Burns and Stalker found that the 'informal organisation' of the political system and status structure within each concern exerted a powerful influence on its economic efficiency, and helped shape the form taken by the management system. In organic systems the high level of commitment inculcated in managers made it difficult to distinguish the informal from the formal organization of the firm. However, in the case of the mechanically organized Scottish engineering firms, the introduction of R&D laboratories had threatened to disrupt the established order of rank and privileges in each concern. 'Men with white coats and long hair', wielding high technical qualifications, speaking a private language, doing indeterminate tasks at their own speed, and for atypically high salaries, posed a direct challenge to the authority and status of other senior staff. The market context and technical basis of each firm were changing; so that the situation was 'alive with opportunities for advancement and transfer'; and alive also, 'with actual or potential threats to the status, power, chances of success or actual livelihood of some of the members of it'. The incoming R&D staff simply aggravated this problem. As a result, production and sales managers made strenuous attempts to entrench the mechanistic system, by demanding increased resources for their sections, additional rewards for themselves and status enhancement for their staff. This sort of empire-building, careerism and obstructionism undermined the economic efficiency of the concern as a whole and prevented the integration of the design and production sides of the business. A good deal of managerial energy was expended, instead, on disputes about the floor-space of offices, the size of desks, comfort of furnishings, and access to separate dining rooms and lavatories.

At this juncture the second determining element – the role of the chief executive – enters into the equation. The heads of the Scottish concerns, encouraged by their increasingly apprehensive managerial staff, effectively undermined the electronics initiative by separating the R&D laboratory, administratively and physically, as far as possible from the existing establishment. Special intermediaries – committees and liaison groups – were set up since these offered 'the possibility of retaining clear definition of function and of lines of command and responsibility'. Whole new departments were created to deal with the 'problem of communication' between the design and production sides of the enterprise. Burns and Stalker note ruefully that these then depended for their survival on the perpetuation of the very difficulty they had been created to solve. In this way R&D was effectively isolated from production and design. The inevitable technical difficulties associated with marrying the new technology to existing processes were then easily translated into personal shortcomings. Production managers saw the design engineers as snobbish and arrogant; the cohesiveness, loyalties and shared interests of the design staff meant that they, in turn, looked down on the production managers, and attended to the particular interests and status of the laboratory rather than those of the organization as a whole. So far as Burns and Stalker could determine, everything pointed 'to there being very solid social barriers of status distinction between production and design', and this led them to conclude that 'what is first of all needed is not supersession of the existing production management by more accomplished engineers so much as a means of overcoming the social inhibitions to effective communications'. In the last resort, it was the responsibility of the chief executive to provide the necessary means of transcending these barriers, by 'defining the situation' – the organizational structure and degree of commitment – in a manner appropriate to the economic environment and staff around him. The Scottish managing directors singularly failed to provide such leadership.

The final section of *The Management of Innovation* attempts to explain why this was so by exploring in some depth the role of 'the man at the top'. Burns and Stalker argue that, as the ultimate authority in any concern, it is the chief executive who sets its managerial tone. He defines the commercial objectives, sets the parameters of occupational roles, and determines the rewards and privileges pertaining to these. Naturally there are various recognized styles which can be adopted in relationships with subordinates: authoritarian, charismatic, isolationist, and so forth. Changes in the technical and market circumstances of the firm make the role and style of the chief executive crucial, since 'as the rate of change increases . . . so does the number of occasions which demand quick and effective interpretation between people working in different parts of the system'. The managing director must, therefore, see to it that a code of conduct appropriate to managerial roles under rapidly changing conditions of business is quickly institutionalized. Organic systems of management, as we have seen, hinge on effective lateral as well as vertical communications. It is essential for these systems that 'nothing should inhibit individuals from applying to others for information and advice, or for additional effort'. This, in turn, depends on 'the ability to suppress differences of status and of technical prestige on occasions of working interaction, and on the absence of barriers to communication founded on functional preserves, privilege, or personal reserve'. The use of first names, conduct of conferences in a well mannered and friendly atmosphere, and insistence on mutual respect of the other person's skills, up and down the entire social hierarchy, all facilitate such communication. This is especially important since the lack of clearly defined lines of responsibility which results from organic procedures requires an abnormally high level of commitment to the firm on the part of the employee – all the more so since he or she will be under considerable emotional stress due to the insecurities induced by constant changes of task and authority. The Scottish managing directors failed to implement such a code of conduct because, quite simply, *they themselves* felt threatened by the dilution of the formal hierarchy and the introduction of the new laboratory-based technology. They therefore colluded with senior production and sales staff in resisting the necessary changes.

Burns and Stalker must have collected some truly remarkable interview and observational material in order to arrive at this conclusion. Their argument is tantamount to an admission, on the part of the chief executives in question, that they felt their own power and status to be threatened by the new arrangements. The social relationships appropriate to making the new technology work effectively were perceived as a threat to the authority and autonomy of the boss. Most managing directors had worked their way to the top by playing the system – by accepting the existing procedures and norms. Now they were being asked to rewrite the very rules by which they had so obviously benefited. Many simply refused to do so. While they were attracted by the economic advantages of the new technology, they were nevertheless incapable of surrendering the command which it had taken them so long to acquire, and for this reason refused to alter the existing social arrangements within the firm. In most cases (and here perhaps one can see the influence of Stalker, the psychologist, at work), this refusal was implicit rather than explicit. Be this as it may, the latent resistance to change, as a mechanism for the defence of the self, had one rather crucial manifest consequence: the new technology was organized out of the firm and its economic benefits duly lost.

IV

These arguments were quickly assimilated to the sociological litera-
tures on bureaucracy, industry and technological change. On the
whole, they were enthusiastically received. A number of limited
criticisms were voiced, particularly with regard to the ideal types of
mechanistic and organic management, since some observers argued
that these were not necessarily mutually exclusive. Others maintained
that Burns and Stalker were attempting to give the (misleading)
impression that organic systems were not stratified – and, therefore,
that hierarchical control was not a universal feature of organizations.
(Thus, for example, the sixth characteristic of mechanistic systems is a
'hierarchic structure of control, authority and communication',
whereas the corresponding feature of organic management empha-
sizes the 'network structure' for organizing these matters.) The
objection here is that 'democratic consensus' can never be an effective
substitute for a 'controlling hierarchy'. In any case, some critics have
argued, it is simply not true that classical bureaucracies of the
mechanistic type are necessarily devoid of lateral communication,
since a professional employee's attitude may be determined as much
by his or her technical knowledge, and the ethics and mores of the
profession itself, as by the structure of the particular organization.
'Second opinions' may be sought routinely as part of an occupational
subculture.

These criticisms would seem to be misplaced since Burns and
Stalker take great pains to emphasize the 'ideal-typical' nature of their
schema. They insist, for example, that the listed items describe only
'the two polar extremities' of the forms which management can take,
and are not intended to be dichotomous, since 'there are . . . intermediate stages between the extremities empirically known to us'.
Indeed, 'a concern oscillating between relative stability and relative
change may also oscillate between the two forms', so that a single
organization 'may (and frequently does) operate with a management
system which includes both types'. They also state explicitly that
'while organic systems are not hierarchic in the same sense as are
mechanistic, they remain stratified', with positions still differentiated
'according to seniority'. It is difficult, therefore, to accept as valid the
criticism that Burns and Stalker make informality and democratic
consensus unconditional virtues and hierarchy an absolute vice.

However, the sorts of objection which can be levelled against the
analysis proffered in *The Management of Innovation* are, in fact, rarely
directed specifically at this text alone. More commonly they embrace
other examples of the general perspective which the argument is said
to exemplify. This is because Burns and Stalker, together with Joan
Woodward, Alvin Gouldner, Paul Lawrence, Jay Lorsch, and several
other British and American researchers, are popularly credited with

having initiated a minor revolution during the late 1950s and early 1960s in that branch of sociology known as organization theory. Collectively, these writers developed an approach to the study of social organizations that has since come to be known as the rational systems perspective, or more commonly the contingency theory of organizations. Needless to say, my own view is that the contribution of Burns and Stalker was fundamental to this enterprise, although it must be admitted that the work of several others (especially that of Woodward and Gouldner) is better known. In order to appreciate fully the critical response to *The Management of Innovation*, it is necessary therefore, to make a brief sojourn into the history of organization theory itself.

Organization theory, of which industrial sociology forms a substantial part, embraces the topics of organizational structure and strategy, organization–environment relationships, power and influence, and managerial psychology. It is widely taught on business and management courses in Britain and North America. There is little unity to the field, and almost no agreement as to how best to characterize the various schools of thought which have evolved over the years. However, a relatively uncontroversial distinction which can be drawn is that between the scientific management and other classical administrative approaches; the human relations perspective; sociotechnical and contingency theories of organizations; and, finally, the various radical critiques. This classification does not exhaust the current lines of analysis, but it does include the most popular approaches and research programmes.

The first of these, the scientific management movement, was founded by Frederick Taylor at the turn of this century. Taylor set himself the objective of organizing work, within the context of ever-increasing complexity in the manufacturing process, so as to obtain the highest possible profits and wages for owners and employees respectively. Both goals pointed to 'the importance of obtaining the maximum output of each man and each machine'. Taylor felt this could be achieved by breaking work down into a large number of routine tasks, to which incentive systems such as piece-rate payments could be applied, thus providing the greatest motivation for workers to meet production targets. Systematic time-and-motion studies could be used to discover the most efficient methods of designing jobs; namely, those which maximized both labour productivity and managerial control over the workforce. By fragmenting and deskilling work in this way, Taylor hoped to prevent 'soldiering' (deliberate restriction of output), since anything less than the theoretically optimum performance would incur loss of earnings as a 'just reward' for inefficiency or laziness on the part of the worker. From this point of view, which nowadays tends to be frowned on as unwarrantably inhuman (though it still has its advocates), labour is simply an homogeneous input which can be governed purely by economic controls. Other motivations (such as preferences for work satisfaction), and all other factors affecting the worker's capacity to match the set rate (fatigue, boredom, differential physical and intellectual abilities), are simply intrusions which diminish unnecessarily the optimum efficiency of the system.

An equally one-dimensional and mechanical view of work has been taken by the various administrative theorists writing about organizations over the years. Taylor's contemporary, Henri Fayol, together with more recent exponents of the classical approach, such as Lyndall Urwick and Peter Drucker, was principally concerned with achieving the 'most rational' organization for co-ordinating the various tasks specified within a complex division of labour. He identified the key functions of management as being those of forecasting and planning business activity. The most rational and efficient organizations are those which implement a plan that facilitates 'unity, continuity, flexibility, precision, command and control'. Certain universal principles of administration have been distilled from these objectives. Most notably, these include the key elements of the scalar chain (authority and responsibility flowing in an unbroken line from the chief executive to the shop-floor); unity of command (each person has only one supervisor with whom he or she communicates); a pyramid of prescribed control (first-line supervisors have a limited number of functions and subordinates, with second-line supervisors controlling a prescribed number of first-line supervisors, and so on up to the top executive); unity of direction (people engaged in similar activities must pursue a common objective in line with the overall plan); specialization of tasks (allowing individuals to build up a specific expertise and so be more productive); and, finally, subordination of individual interests to the general interest of the organization. This list is not exhaustive, but is sufficient to illustrate the key proposition of administrative theory, which is that a functionally specific and hierarchical structure offers the most efficient means of securing organizational objectives.

Both the scientific management approach and classical administrative theory rest on the premises that organizations are unproblematically rational and operate as more or less closed systems. That is, organizations are assumed to have unambiguous and unitary objectives, which the individuals within them pursue routinely, by obeying the rules and fulfilling their role expectations, according to the prescribed organizational structure. Moreover, in the attempt to maximize efficiency, it is only variables within that structure which need to be considered and manipulated. The interaction of the organization and its environment, together with the various factors which are external to the organization but nevertheless have consequences for its internal functioning, are systematically ignored. Clearly, both perspectives take a rather deterministic view of social action, since each assumes that individuals will maximize organizational efficiency, independently of their own welfare, and with no thought for the relationship between the collective goal and their own particular purposes. The human relations (or human resources) school of organizational analysis, an otherwise diverse group of writers and approaches, is united by its opposition to precisely this assumption.

It is difficult to summarize the human relations approach in simple terms, since it draws on several disciplines and has been subject to periodic revision. Most authorities accept that it grew out of the industrial sociology studies of Roethlisberger, Dickson and Mayo, carried out at the Hawthorne plant of the Western Electrical Company in Chicago during the 1930s. Major contributions have also been made by social psychologists such as Rensis Likert, Douglas McGregor and Chris Argyris, and industrial relations experts such as Frederick Herzberg and Victor Vroom. Whatever their particular concerns, these authors have commonly rejected the assumption that individuals are motivated exclusively by economic incentives, and that all organizations can (and ought to) correspond to a single ideal structure. Instead, they have concentrated their research on differences in the ways in which individuals interpret similar organizational roles, and on how people perceive and respond to noneconomic inducements. This has shown that human behaviour within organizations rarely corresponds to the model set down in the formal structure. The Hawthorne Studies, for example, demonstrated that social factors were significant in determining levels of productivity: that non-economic rewards and sanctions (such as the respect of fellow employees) could be more important to the individual than any economic incentives; that people behaved *socially* at work, and not merely as *individuals*, so that the work group (for example) could exert important influences on behaviour in organizational roles; and, finally, that organizations tended to have informal cultures (embracing actual leadership and communication) that could be clearly distinguished from the formal relationships and activities specified in the organizational chart. Subsequent studies embellished these findings by discovering a host of noneconomic factors – leadership styles, social relationships, subcultural preferences, individual needs – which were associated with work satisfaction, labour productivity and organizational effectiveness. The crucial significance of these results was that they challenged the twin assumptions that organizations were 'closed systems' and that they were peopled by 'economic men'. Instead, it was argued that people brought to the organization their own purposes, attitudes and values, and that these did not necessarily correspond to those of the organization. Consequently, in modelling organizational structure, one could not simply assume that members carried out their prescribed tasks in an entirely mechanical fashion.

However, although the human relations perspective goes some way to providing a corrective to the economic and organizational determinism of classical and scientific management theory, there are several aspects of individual behaviour in an organizational setting which continue to be routinely omitted from these accounts. There is, for example, very little mention of conflict, class, or power relationships within the concern. Instead, it is assumed that, given appropriate manipulation of the human and social environment, labour productivity (and therefore profit) can readily be maximized – albeit by means of a more humanistic control system than hitherto. Consequently, little thought is given to the possibility that the various external factors which affect behaviour in organizations might have systematic and conflicting societal origins, and might not therefore be easily reconciled to the unified formal workings of the organization. Perhaps, as one critic has suggested, this is because 'it is far easier and less politically portentous to make the worker feel that he belongs and is important than it is to tamper with the structure of industrial authority'. In any event, whatever its normative implications, human resources theory fails to address the possibility that there might exist a genuine conflict between organizational efficiency on the one hand, and what the individual considers to be good or desirable, on the other. Contingency theorists explored precisely this possibility.

The leading practitioners of this approach were united in their belief that no single organizational structure was inherently more efficient than all others. Instead, organizations differed in the tasks they performed and environments they faced, so that the appropriate organizational structure was in each case a function of such factors as technology, market, the predictability of tasks, and so forth. For example, Lawrence and Lorsch, in a study parallel to that of Burns and Stalker, also found that the degree of uncertainty in the task environment of firms was strongly related to their internal organizational arrangements. The greater the uncertainty, the greater the need to differentiate the sales, production and R&D departments. However, the greater the degree of internal differentiation, the greater the need for appropriate methods of integrating and resolving conflicts between the various segments. In fact, the various integrative devices which were found to be effective in highly differentiated organizations are rather reminiscent of those associated with organic management as described by Burns and Stalker. Similarly, in her research into manufacturing organizations in south-east Essex, Joan Woodward established that different production processes (small batch, large batch, mass and continuous) were related to differences in organizational structure. In general terms, the more complex the technology, the more prolific the levels of authority that commanded it. Other factors also related to technology included the span of control accorded to supervisors, the degree of functional specialization of roles, and the means of exchanging information throughout the system.

The interaction between technology and social relationships was also observed at the level of individual behaviour. For example, Eric Trist and other members of the Tavistock School of industrial sociology found, in their research on mining and textile manufacturing, that technological demands placed constraints on work organization, but that organizational structures also constrained action in ways that were quite independent of technology. Moreover, the social relationships that developed at work, and the way in which jobs themselves were performed, were the outcome of a mutual interaction between technology and organizational structure, on the one hand, and the social–psychological characteristics of the workers, on the other. From this point of view, organizations can be seen as 'open socio-technical systems', since they both interact with their external environment and operate an internal conversion process that mediates structural influences and those emanating from individual projects or purposes.

These analyses, together with that of Burns and Stalker, go beyond the earlier approaches in two important respects. First, organizations are not considered to be closed systems, but are instead situated firmly in particular economic and social environments. Second, there is no assumption that individuals within organizations act solely in accordance with the formal purposes of the enterprise, since they may well be motivated by concerns that conflict with those of the larger organization. These insights were a major advance in organizational theory in the 1960s.

In due course, however, contingency theory itself came under sustained criticism from a number of radical writers who, in the 1970s, launched a series of attacks on the entire corpus of existing organization theory. Some, such as David Silverman and Jill Jones, suggested that a 'social action' perspective was more fruitful than previous versions of organizational analysis. Others, including Stewart Clegg and David Dunkerley, argued for a Marxian approach to organizational issues. Although the solutions envisaged by these critiques are rather different, their diagnoses of the problems are not dissimilar and can be summarized in two related charges. The first is that organization theory is too structural, since it pays insufficient attention to explanations in terms of the actions of individuals and the diverse meanings they attach to these. Human resources and contingency theorists may acknowledge that individuals in organizations have their own needs, wants, feelings, and so forth, but they nevertheless treat interpersonal behaviour as relatively unimportant. No attention is given to the complex processes by which organizational reality is defined and sustained. Research interest in 'rational behaviour' has tended to preclude investigation of 'negotiated action'. The other charge is that organization theory reifies the organization *per se*, and fails to situate it clearly in its societal and political context. Marxists, in fact, treat conventional organizational analyses as little more than bourgeois ideology, since (allegedly) they merely help legitimate the structures which control and oppress labour. Established perspectives fail to reveal the larger role of organizations as key elements of domination within the capitalist economic system.

This is not the place to debate the cogency of these rather complex and fundamental criticisms. What is striking, in the present context, is the obvious sophistication of *The Management of Innovation*, when placed alongside the classical and human resources texts, and how much it also anticipates the radical critiques of Silverman and the neo-Marxists. Burns and Stalker's central argument is that the internal features of business firms are intimately related to their socioeconomic environment. The opening sentences of their book proclaim that the research 'arose out of an attempt, some years ago, to study an industrial concern as a "community of people at work", that is, in much the same terms one would use in a study of conduct and relationships in a village, an urban neighbourhood, or a small primitive community.' However, 'this aim was never realized, because it soon became evident that the social structure of the factory interlocked with, and often mirrored, that of the small isolated town in which it was situated'. Clearly, the authors were not fated to make the mistake, common to many community studies during the 1950s, of reifying the locality by treating it as a self-contained microcosm of the larger order. They take it as axiomatic that firms exist to survive and make a profit, not because they as individuals wish to endorse these objectives, but simply because the companies concerned are situated squarely within the context of an advanced capitalist economy. Why pretend, as some radicals seem to, that these goals are somehow immediately negotiable? The normative implications of *The Management of Innovation* are never, in fact, made clear, presumably because Burns and Stalker would wish to treat these as a proper subject for political, rather than sociological dispute.

Regarding the negotiation of order within organizations, it is true that Burns and Stalker do not describe in detail the precise steps by which individuals arrive at particular decisions, when faced with uncertainty and a changing business environment. But it is certainly implicit in their argument that the process of 'negotiating' organizational order is both complex and real. They themselves identify only the most important influences on the individual's perception of the situation: namely, organizational, political and status concerns. But this is scarcely tantamount, as some critics have claimed, to a reification either of the organizational structure or of individual goals. The importance that Burns and Stalker attach to 'purposive human action' and 'interpersonal behaviour' as determinants of organizational outcomes, is clearly evident in the central role given to sectional struggles between groups or departments, especially in their explanation of the failure of the electronics initiative in the Scottish firms. Individuals can and do pursue objectives, and adopt strategies to realize these, that may entirely contradict whatever ideas of rationality or efficiency inhere in the formal organization, or the various classical models of its structure. A 'plurality of action systems' are available to the employee, who 'may invoke any of them as the dominant reference system for this or that action, decision or plan, even though an outside observer, or the individual himself, for that matter, may see other manifest relevance of what he is doing to all or any of the other systems'.

It follows, therefore, that many of the criticisms applicable to other contingency theorists are inappropriate when levelled against Burns and Stalker. It is often claimed, for example, that 'rational systems theorists have acknowledged the existence of conflict and incompatible goals in organisations but have paid little attention to political processes'. Similarly, they are said to have explored extensively the nature and impact of authority, 'but have paid little attention to other forms of power'. These charges are scarcely legitimate when directed towards a text which describes the 'political system' of the business concern in some detail, and is particularly concerned with 'political activity which has to do with the amount of say which individuals or groups have in the destiny of the firm as a whole', especially in so far as this involves 'conflict . . . about . . . the degree of control one may exercise over the firm's resources, the direction of the activities of other people, and patronage (promotion and the distribution of privileges and rewards)'. Power and conflict are at the heart of Burns and Stalker's analysis. I am, therefore, prepared to go so far as to say that a systematic search of the literature suggests that the central arguments of *The Management of Innovation* remain to this day largely unscathed by subsequent research and critique, which is surely no mean feat for a social scientific analysis penned almost thirty years ago.

V

However, my own enthusiasm for this text is not simply a function of its importance within sociology, as a touch-stone for good organizational analysis. It stems also from the fact that, in the present climate of antipathy towards sociological research, *The Management of Innovation* shows clearly the relevance of mainstream sociological concerns to practitioners of more popular disciplines such as economics and business studies. One is struck, for example, by how much of what currently passes for management science in Britain is, in fact, derived from the established sociological literature. Standard words such as Rosemary Stewart's *The Reality of Organisations*, like most other business studies and management science textbooks, draws heavily on organization theory in particular and industrial sociology more generally. Perhaps surprisingly, such texts are full of references to the human resources, contingency and radical perspectives on behaviour in organizations; to the work of sociologists such as Max Weber, Alvin Gouldner and William F. Whyte; and full also of sociological theories about bureaucracy, power, conflict, professionalization, work satisfaction, nonrational and rational action, among many other things. The work of Burns and Stalker itself often looms large in the discussion. Stewart's book is no exception in this regard. In some cases the terminology and the implications for social practice have been changed from the originals. But sociology under any other name is still sociology.

Even more obvious is the connection between Burns and Stalker's analysis of management in the immediate postwar business climate of technological restructuring, and the 'new management' texts of the 1980s, which have attempted to explain the difficulties faced by British and American managers in coping with the economic pressures of recent years. Many of these recent studies – including the best-selling accounts by William Ouchi, Richard Pascale and Anthony Athos, and Frank Gibney – identify potential solutions for ailing Western businesses in the managerial strategies of the economically more successful Japanese. Ouchi, for example, argues in his *Theory Z* that the strongest American companies have developed a functional equivalent of the Japanese management system by implementing a mixture of strategies to build up loyalty to the firm. In fact his description of Theory Z organizations embodies many of the central insights of the human resources approach:

> Of all its values, commitment of a Z culture to its people – its workers – is the most important ... Theory Z assumes that any worker's life is a whole, not a Jekyll-Hyde personality, half machine from nine till five and half human in the hours preceding and following ... Up to now American managers have assumed that technology makes for increased productivity. What Theory Z calls for instead is a redirection of attention to *human* relations in the corporate world.

The most basic element for developing this commitment and loyalty is a strong 'corporate philosophy and culture' or, in the terminology earlier used by Burns and Stalker, an organizational code of conduct. Other components, also reminiscent of the analysis in *The Management of Innovation*, include open communication encouraged by job rotation and a strong emphasis on groups; the assignment of tasks to work groups who then decide collectively on the best way of achieving specific objectives; and consultative decision-making based on informal discussion with everyone who may be affected by any outcome. In short, what Ouchi calls 'participative management' is rather similar to the organic management system identified by Burns and Stalker, as also is his observation that such a system is not a panacea for all organizational problems, but simply one approach (among several) that is appropriate to certain environmental circumstances.

Others have opted for more conventionally Western solutions to the managerial problems behind the declining international competitiveness of Britain and the United States. Studies such as Thomas J. Peters and Robert H. Waterman's *In Search of Excellence*, or Walter Goldsmith and David Clutterbuck's *The Winning Streak*, have attempted to identify the 'formulas for success' used by top American and British companies. The latter study sampled twenty-three particularly successful concerns based in Britain, each of which was a market leader in its sector, with a solid public reputation and a high growth in assets, turnover and profits. One key factor that seemed to be common to Allied-Lyons, Marks & Spencer, Racal Electronics and the twenty other enterprises in question, was 'an ability to ... adapt management styles to their own circumstances – both the circumstances of the marketplace and how mature their organisation is'. Another was the 'organisational culture'. The most important elements in this culture are said to include, first of all, a strong 'market orientation'. ('Successful companies understand and inter-react closely with their market .. That "the customer is king" is axiomatic in their operations. Every function of the company has as its prime objective the satisfaction of customer requirements ... they go to great lengths to gather detailed market information'.) The 'involvement factor' is also important, since all of the successful companies had generated 'a remarkable level of commitment in their management levels', most notably by ensuring that there was 'a high level of consultation and discussion' and by stressing 'the importance of information'. Leadership too is identified as a key factor, 'particularly through visible top management ... and ... top managers [who] have a clear sense, a vision, of where their company is going and communicate that vision down the line'. In other words, a perception of the market as a source rather than a sink, a strong organizational code of conduct and a clear definition of the situation imposed by the chief executive, are all identified as crucial to economic success in the rapidly changing international markets of the late-twentieth century. One is struck, then, in reading this material, not only by the obvious fact that Burns and Stalker said all this (and more) almost thirty years ago, but also by the realization that they said it so much more convincingly.

Indeed, if there is a single common theme that has emerged among business consultants and experts from all their soul-searching about managerial strategies during recent years, then it is the (belated) realization that corporate enterprises are in fact plural, rather than unitary social systems. They therefore embody a complex 'organizational culture' which, from the corporate point of view, has to be harnessed to the overtly profit-making activities of the enterprise in question. Terrence Deal and Allen Kennedy's recent *Corporate Cultures* is typical in this regard. They conclude that 'a combination of forces – from the rapidly changing business environment to the new work force to astonishing advances in technology – is forging a breakdown of the large, traditional, hierarchical organisations that have dominated in the past'. In the wake of these changes, the most appropriate structure is that of the 'atomised organisation', consisting of small, task-focused work units, of ten to twenty persons; each with economic and managerial control over its own destiny; interconnected with larger entities through benign computer and communications links; and bonded into corporations by means of strong cultural ties. The role of organizational culture is crucial, and the chief executive, as 'organisational hero', exerts the most important influence on this by means of the managerial philosophy he or she imposes: 'The people who built the companies for which America is famous all worked obsessively to create strong cultures within their organisations.' It follows, therefore, that 'the winners in the business world of tomorrow will be the heroes who can forge the values and beliefs, the rituals and the ceremonies, and a cultural network of storytellers and priests that can keep working productively in semi-autonomous units that identify with a corporate whole.' This analysis may, as Deal and Kennedy hope, 'provide business leaders with a primer on cultural management'. It may even introduce them to 'a new law of business life', namely, that 'in culture there is strength'. But it is scarcely news to those of us who are familiar with the sociology of postwar Britain. It seems, instead, to be just so much rediscovering of Burns and Stalker's sociological wheel.

6 Workers and their wages

I

I argued, in the previous chapter, that the principal findings of Burns and Stalker still seem robust after more than a quarter of a century of research into behaviour in organizations. However, it has to be conceded that *The Management of Innovation* is not an easy read, even for the professional sociologist. For example, as Burns himself subsequently recognized, the causal structure of the explanation is not reproduced in the narrative of the argument; indeed, rather confusingly, the principal determinant of management practice (the code of conduct imposed by the chief executive) is introduced only towards the end of the text. Not surprisingly, therefore, the book has not proved to be very popular among sociology teachers and examiners. Experience suggests that Joan Woodward's work offers students a more accessible introduction to the rational systems perspective.

The fifth of my chosen texts focuses on the industrial behaviour of rank-and-file workers, rather than managers, and has had a quite different reception among those involved at all levels in the discipline. The *Affluent Worker Study*, published as a series of articles and monographs during the 1960s, is probably the most famous product of postwar British sociology. Its final reports have been translated into several languages; the results are, even today, widely referred to in work by other authors; many additional research projects have been derived from the original ideas and data; and, here in Britain, the study is extensively used in teaching sociology both in schools and higher education.

The project was devised by John Goldthorpe (whose subsequent work on social mobility was discussed in an earlier chapter), and David Lockwood, both at that time based in Cambridge. Jennifer Platt and Frank Bechhofer acted as principal research officers. At various times a number of other individuals, some of whom are by now well-known sociologists in their own right, provided assistance with interviewing, coding, computing and data analysis. The research was funded from 1961 to 1965. In total, perhaps a dozen or so articles associated with the project appeared in journals from 1960 onwards, culminating in three books published towards the end of the decade: *The Affluent Worker: Industrial Attitudes and Behaviour*, *The Affluent Worker: Political Attitudes and Behaviour*, and *The Affluent Worker in the Class Structure*.

The context of the study was originally set by the liberal theories of industrial society previously discussed in Chapter 2. These, it will be remembered, came to popularity during the period of sustained economic growth in the 1950s. Observing the industrial and political developments of the immediate postwar years, Bell, Lipset, Kerr and others concluded that violent clashes between capital and labour were becoming less common; that revolutionary parties had gradually abandoned their programmes for radical change; that trades union membership had more or less ceased to expand; and that the relative size of the working class was gradually decreasing. As we have seen, these changes were commonly attributed to structural shifts in the occupational order, making for greater upward social mobility; to the egalitarian social policies of welfare–reformist social democratic states; and to the institutionalization of class conflict within an overarching consensus based on an acceptance of the basic premises of market capitalist societies.

A certain amount of survey and other research of the period, both in America and Western Europe, appeared to confirm this interpretation of postwar social changes. Technologically advanced production methods, combined with progressive personnel management, were gradually breaking down the distinction between staff and works. The skilled workers employed in the automated factories and new service industries of the mid-twentieth century enjoyed employment that was less stressful and, it was generally assumed, more meaningful than hitherto. Their specialist knowledge, improved working conditions and high wages effectively integrated them into the employing organization. Seemingly, therefore, decreased alienation, combined with increased collaboration between labour and capital, was generating industrial workforces which identified with management rather than viewing it in terms of an oppositional 'us and them' relationship. Similarly, in the sphere of consumption, official statistics and other evidence pointed to a general improvement in living standards. The numbers of middle-income families had greatly expanded. Many manual workers now had wages roughly equivalent to those of white-collar employees. Class differences were further blurred by an homogenization of life-styles, due to expanding demand for relatively new consumer durables such as washing machines, television sets and refrigerators. Better-paid manual workers were also becoming car-owners and home-owners. Extensive rehousing programmes had demolished the worst of the working-class slums and replaced these with modern private or publicly owned estates.

This evolutionary and benign perspective on social change in the industrialized West was especially influential in the United States, but gained considerable impetus in Britain after the General Election of 1959, on which occasion the Labour Party was not only defeated for the third successive time, but saw its share of the total vote fall to 44 per cent, from the 49 per cent it had polled on being removed from office in 1951. A number of influential commentators drew the seemingly obvious conclusion that events in the economic and political spheres were connected in a relationship of cause and effect. Increasing affluence in the community, and decreasing alienation at work, had combined to re-orient large sections of the British working class towards a middle-class style of life and middle-class attitudes. This, in turn, explained the apparent drift of manual workers away from the Labour Party and trades unions. Conclusive proof of this, if it were needed, lay in the psephological (voting) data, which appeared to show that the decline in Labour support was greatest in the economically prosperous areas of the country, and in the New Towns and suburbs created by the housing developments of the 1950s.

All of this seemed to portend the likely embourgeoisement of the British working class. Academics and politicians alike routinely connected the growth of working-class affluence to a spread in middle-class norms and values and the decline of the Labour Party in Parliament. For example, David Butler and Richard Rose concluded of the 1959 General Election that 'The swing to the conservatives cannot be dismissed as an ephemeral veering of the electoral breeze. Long-term factors were also involved. Traditional working-class attitudes had been eroded by a steady growth of prosperity.' Labour politicians, worried about the 'new working class conservatism', debated controversial strategies for 'updating' the party's policies and revamping its 'cloth-cap' image. Several contemporary studies of manual workers and their families actually took the embourgeoise-ment thesis as a proposal for direct investigation. Probably the best known of these is Ferdynand Zweig's *The Worker in an Affluent Society*. Zweig's interviews with manual workers in five British firms led him to surmise that large sections of the working class were 'on the move towards new middle class values and middle class existence'. The 'new mode of life' and 'new ethos' of the affluent manual workers embraced a long list of attitudinal and behavourial changes, including 'a considerable rise in security mindedness'; a 'revolution of rising expectations' and 'steep rise in acquisitive instincts'; growth of 'family-mindedness and home-centredness'; 'greater individualisa-tion'; the decline of class divisions, class feelings and the ethos of class solidarity; and a new 'quest for respectability'. Similarly, after review-ing the literature on family and community in modern Britain, Josephine Klein concluded that 'the white collar is ceasing to be the easily identified distinguishing mark of the middle-class man... manual workers themselves are also adopting a middle-class way of life'.

Not all of these studies made the same strong claims about the processes allegedly in train. Lipset, one of the most enthusiastic proponents of the liberal perspective, concluded unequivocally that throughout the Western democracies, 'representatives of the lower strata are now part of the governing group, members of the club. The basic political issue of the industrial revolution, the incorporation of the workers into the legitimate body politic, has been settled'. Zweig, on the other hand, was more circumspect: 'It took the employer a long time to imbue the worker with his own values and turn him into a full and willing partner in the acquisitive society.' True, 'he has finally succeeded, and the results seem to reinforce the working and the fabric of the society and to make it more secure from inside.' But, he adds cautiously, the impact of higher living standards, new standards of values and conduct, and the new social consciousness on the social, political and economic life of the future 'can hardly be foreseen'. Moreover, and rather crucially, these tendencies are still in progress. They mark the direction rather than the completion of a trend, and are still 'battling against the older forces of the traditional code, ethos and mode of living, and against strong group resistance all round'. The final outcome of this battle 'may depend on the future of the economy, whether it will continue in the new ways of full employment and prosperity'.

Clearly, then, the many advocates of embourgeoisement were not all of one mind. Some rooted their accounts in the sphere of production while others stressed changes in consumption. A few simply deduced a trend towards middle-class values from changes in voting patterns. Among political scientists, the principal significance of working-class affluence was seen to lie in its effect on electoral behaviour, while in sociology it was the putative changes in family and community life that were emphasized. Nevertheless, in their enthusiasm for the thesis as a convenient shorthand explanation for the many social changes taking place in Britain at that time, politicians and semi-popular writers alike tended to ignore these differences of interpretation, and to describe the various processes as if they were self-evidently interconnected and part of some long-term and perhaps irreversible trend. Goldthorpe and Lockwood were highly sceptical of these assumptions and so set out to ascertain their empirical validity.

II

Their study eventually took the form of a critical test-case. Manual workers and their families were to be interviewed in 'a *locale*... which would be *as favourable as possible* for the validation of the *embourgeoise-ment* thesis', the authors reasoning that 'if, in the case we studied, a process of *embourgeoisement* was shown *not* to be in evidence, then it could be regarded as extremely unlikely that such a process was occurring to any significant extent in British society as a whole'. The town of Luton, in south-west Bedfordshire, was selected as an appropriate site for the research because it was at the centre of an economically buoyant area of the country; contained a high proportion of geographically mobile workers who (presumably) had come to Luton in search of higher living standards; was isolated from the older industrial regions of the country and thus not dominated by traditional patterns of working-class life; boasted several firms which had reputations for paying high wages, for advanced personnel and welfare policies, and for industrial peace; and, finally, because a high proportion of Lutonians lived in relatively new housing areas which included substantial private developments. (Zweig had also been attracted to Luton for rather similar reasons.)

Having settled on this location, the researchers then interviewed a sample of 229 married men aged 21 to 46, who were resident in (or lived close to) the town, and who regularly earned at least £17 per week gross (at 1962 values) – again reasoning that these would be the most affluent, physically mobile, consumption-minded manual workers, with the minimum experience of employment insecurity. In order to examine the effect of different technologies on attitudes and behaviour, interviewees were selected from three firms, which between them utilized all the major types of production system – small-batch, large-batch and mass, and continuous process. These were Vauxhall Motors, a subsidiary of the General Motors Corporation, where the research was concentrated on assembly-line workers; the Skefko Ball Bearing Company, part of the SKF organization, where machine operators, machine setters and craftsmen were interviewed; and Laporte Chemicals, a member of the Laporte Group, where craftsmen and process workers were contacted. Respondents were interviewed twice: at work, about largely employment-related matters (work history, attitudes to their jobs, perceptions of labour markets, union activities, and such like); and ('together with their wives') at home, about their leisure activities, contacts with neighbours and kin, conjugal roles (who was responsible for what about the home), friendship patterns, childbearing practices, political views, images of class, and household expenditure. For comparative purposes, fifty-four lower-level (nonmanagerial) clerical employees were similarly questioned, although the results of these interviews feature only intermittently in the group's publications since, on the whole, they merely confirmed what was already known about white-collar social attitudes and behaviour.

This research design seems relatively uncontroversial and certainly provides for an adequate test of the embourgeoisement thesis as it was generally understood at the time. However, before I move on to consider the findings themselves, there are three complications that must be introduced. The first concerns the historical context of the overall project. The Affluent Worker Study was conceived around 1960 – at the end of a decade of (relative) social stability and economic growth. The major publications appeared around 1970. By that time the economic and socio-political climates in the West had changed dramatically. In Britain, for example, the psephological support for the embourgeoisement thesis vanished with Labour election victories in 1964 and 1966. Here, and elsewhere, there was an upturn in union membership (largely attributable to increased recruitment among white-collar employees) and in levels of industrial unrest. In France this culminated in the General Strike of May 1968. The assertion of civil rights and black power in the United States caused turmoil in many major cities. Demonstrations against involvement in Vietnam added to the already widespread social conflict. Student protests and a great value of 1960s-style counter-cultural activities (drug taking, youth subcultures, and the like) merely underlined the breakdown of the postwar consensus. Academia itself reflected the new mood with the revival, in the mid 1960s, of intellectual Marxism and radical perspectives in the social sciences generally. These developments had a significant effect on the major publications of the Luton team. Although the arguments about embourgeoisement still provide their central organizing principle, a number of Marxist themes also loom large in the various books and articles. These make the final reports more profound – but also a good deal more complex – than was envisaged at the outset.

To take but one example, much of the argument of the principal monograph, *The Affluent Worker in the Class Structure*, is oriented towards New Left arguments about alienation and class consciousness, and particularly the idea of the 'new working class'. During the 1960s, commentators such as Perry Anderson and John Westergaard in Britain argued that the disruption of long-established working-class communities did not cause a decline in class consciousness, but rather were a prerequisite for its appearance. By dissolving local and sectional identities the new housing estates and mass industries would finally make transparent to all proletarians their common class situation and interests. Rational class action would surely then replace parochial solidarity as the characteristic form of collectivism among British workers. French Marxists, including Serge Mallet and Andre Gorz, were equally optimistic, but on rather different grounds. In their view, traditional proletarians such as miners and steel workers were alienated from their work by the progressive fragmentation of job tasks, and so remained merely 'economistic' in their demands. They did not struggle for the overthrow of capitalism but concerned themselves instead – as individuals – with the issues of wage increases and material consumption. Unions in the traditional industrial sectors reflected this mentality by making reformist rather than revolutionary demands. By contrast, the new working class of 'autonomous production workers' in the technologically advanced industries (chemicals, electronics, and the like) were 'objectively integrated' within production, in that their specific skills, relatively secure incomes and high levels of job security tended to be linked to particular companies with which they therefore identified. Having their basic consumption demands satisfied, being 'placed in the centre of the most complex mechanisms of organisational capitalism' and so able to see the long-term interests of the enterprise, these workers reinstated the demand for control at the centre of union concerns. Moreover, the argument continues, the specificity of their skills gives the new working class an enhanced ability to coerce management, and therefore a greater consciousness of its collective power. In short, for Mallet and others, 'the objective conditions within which the new working class acts and works makes it the perfect avant-garde of the revolutionary socialist movement'. Lockwood and his colleagues felt that they were obliged to investigate these claims alongside those of economic and political liberals. Necessarily, therefore, the discussion in the published volumes goes a long way beyond the narrow concerns of the embourgeoisement thesis *per se*.

A second complication is introduced, rather ironically, by the project's own prolific output. The first monograph was an unintended by-product of the main research. The sheer volume of the evidence, plus the unexpectedly uniform 'orientation to work' which was found among the respondents, prompted the team to make a separate and lengthy statement about industrial attitudes and behaviour. In fact, the findings of this volume have proved sufficiently interesting and controversial to stimulate wide debate even today, although they have tended also to generate a perception of the project as somehow predominantly industrial in its concerns. Some of the wider arguments of the principal (third) monograph have been greatly overlooked because of this. Furthermore, certain crucial arguments and assumptions made by the team are only apparent in the more specialized journal articles, so that familiarity with these is a prerequisite for a full understanding of the monographs. Indeed, as has often been pointed out, the explanations proferred for changes in the class structure are sometimes altered between the different publications. It should also be borne in mind here that the study was carried out by a research team – and it is clear, even from the published accounts, that its various members did not always agree about the significance of their findings. Most obviously, Jennifer Platt wrote two dissenting commentaries under her own name, which help shed light on the sometimes rather inconsistent arguments proposed in the major co-authored volumes.

Finally, it is worth noting (as have many others), that the preliminary articles written by Goldthorpe and Lockwood so effectively undermine the embourgeoisement thesis that the subsequent research in Luton hardly seems necessary. In these early essays, the authors point to a host of conceptual and empirical deficiences in the argument, so that with hindsight one is left wondering quite why the thesis attained the prominence that it apparently did. For example, they point out that its opponents fail to distinguish the economic, normative and relational dimensions of embourgeoisement, with the result that the argument seems sometimes to be referring to the acquisition by manual workers of incomes comparable to those of nonmanual employees; elsewhere to be suggesting that the former are adopting middle-class values and norms; and, finally, on occasion to imply that all social barriers between the working-class 'community' and middle-class 'society' have effectively been dismantled. Moreover, in all three cases, information readily available from official statistics and ethnographic research clearly suggested that the thesis was demonstrably false. For example, arguments about economic levelling tended to ignore the many fringe benefits of nonmanual employees – including, for example, their superior working conditions and amenities, greater promotion chances, job security, and enhanced pensions. Similarly, there was no good reason to suppose that manual workers were increasingly being treated by their white-collar counterparts as social equals and being incorporated into middle-class status groups on this basis. Most industrial sociology and community studies confirmed that the manual/nonmanual distinction was as salient a line of social demarcation after the war as it had been before it. Indeed, as Goldthorpe and Lockwood made abundantly clear, there was in fact very little hard evidence to support arguments in favour of embourgeoisement, in whatever version these were advanced.

In one of these early papers, 'Affluence and the British Class Structure', Goldthorpe and Lockwood actually proposed an alternative interpretation which was rather more consistent with the available research findings. Briefly, they argued that far from suggesting the *assimilation* of manual workers to the middle class, these data pointed to 'a much less dramatic process of *convergence*, in certain particular respects, in the normative orientation of some sections of the working class and of some white-collar groups'. That is, there was some reshaping of values and aspirations, but very little change in social relationships or status hierarchies at work or in the community. Furthermore, these normative adjustments were the result of changes in middle-class, as well as working-class orientations. Full employment, the gradual erosion of traditional occupational communities and the institutionalization of industrial conflict had all served to undermine working-class solidarism and communal attachments. More and more, collective trade-union action was pursued by manual workers as a means of individual economic advancement, oriented towards the conjugal family and its fortunes as a 'central life interest'. Conversely, however, rising prices and the growth of large-scale administrative bureaucracies were persuading large numbers of routine clerical workers of the virtues of collective trade-union action, although of 'a deliberately apolitical and instrumental type'. In short, the economic, industrial and ecological changes in postwar Britain were weakening both the traditional 'collectivism' of manual workers and the traditional 'individualism' of nonmanual employees. ' "Instrumental collectivism" and "family-centredness [are] thus proposed as the major points of increasing similarity in the socio-political perspectives and life-styles of manual and nonmanual strata.'

But convergence was not identity. There were still certain obvious differences between the circumstances and orientations of blue-collar and white-collar workers. The authors were convinced that further research in Luton could usefully shed light on these. For practitioners of a discipline that is supposedly not much interested in empirical inquiry, the Affluent Worker team showed impressive determination actually to collect original data, by persisting with their project well beyond the point at which they might legitimately have rested their case. Lockwood and his colleagues had in fact effectively demolished the thesis of working-class embourgeoisement before they ever set foot in Luton.

III

The detailed findings of the whole project are too numerous and complex to be summarized here. They range across a great variety of substantive areas and give an almost complete account of working-class life in Luton. I propose, instead, to mention only the most important and controversial conclusions. Many of these were clearly anticipated in the team's earliest publications.

The interviews showed that the sample of affluent manual workers shared a predominantly 'instrumental orientation' to their employment, irrespective of differences in skill, occupational status, or the technology with which they were involved. By an instrumental orientation the authors mean that workers were attracted to their jobs because of 'extrinsic', i.e. mainly economic, considerations. For example, 87 per cent of skilled men and 82 per cent of those semi-skilled explained their work attachments wholly or partly in terms of the level of pay, degree of security, or extent of the fringe benefits available. Only 29 per cent of the former and 14 per cent of the latter mentioned 'intrinsic' attractions such as job satisfaction. Consistent with this, few participated actively in work-based societies or clubs, and few were members of solidary work groups. Nor did they base their social lives outside the factory on associations with workmates. Home and factory were psychologically and socially isolated from each other. Thus, for example, 76 per cent of skilled men and 66 per cent of the semi-skilled reported they would be 'not much bothered' or 'not bothered at all' if they moved away from their present workmates to another job.

However, almost two-thirds of the sample thought that few other companies could offer economic rewards comparable to those they obtained at present, and this was a major factor in persuading them to stay in their existing employment. It was clear to the researchers, then, that 'in the main, these workers saw their relationship with their firms as an almost exclusively contractual one, founded upon a bargain of money for effort'.

This pecuniary (or money-minded) orientation to work was reflected in the respondents' occupational aspirations. Few believed that they were favourably placed to obtain promotion at work. They concentrated their efforts instead on securing a continuing improvement in their standard of domestic living. Consequently, although amost 90 per cent of the sample were union members, few had joined as a matter of principle or duty. Of the craftsmen 61 per cent, but only one-third of the other workers thought that one of the objectives of a trades union was to give workers a say in management. The majority were convinced that unions should only be concerned with negotiating higher pay and better conditions for their members.

The authors explain this motivation to increase the economic returns from work and the inclination of the affluent workers towards a family–centred style of living in terms of their respondents' position in the life-cycle and their experiences of geographical and social mobility. As young husbands, the large majority of whom had dependent children, these men would be more likely to have strictly monetary interests in their work than those at an earlier or later stage in the life-cycle. Moreover, two-thirds of the sample had migrated to Luton, in the great majority of cases specifically in search of higher incomes and better living conditions. This, in turn, had tended to restrict social contacts outside the home. The town contained a particularly high proportion of geographically mobile people, most of whom were now physically isolated from their kin and were therefore led to adopt a style of life which militated against the communal sociability of established working-class districts. The workers' spare-time activities were centred instead on the home and the conjugal family. 'Their major emotional investments', the authors conclude, 'were made in their relationships with their wives and children, and these relationships were in turn their major source of social and psychological support.' Finally, a relatively high proportion of those interviewed had experienced downward social mobility, and the research team hypothesize that the attendant feelings of relative deprivation would have reinforced the motivation to acquire a high standard of living, already encouraged by the men's 'privatized' social lives.

In short, the privatized social life and instrumental orientation to work of the affluent workers are mutually supportive aspects of their life-style, which tend to encourage a more 'companionate' (or partnership-like) conjugal family: relationships between husband and wife and parents and children become closer, 'certainly more so than could generally have been the case under the economic and social conditions of the traditional working-class community'. Because the worker's central life interests are found in the home and family, his commitment to trades unionism is limited to his interest in improved working conditions and higher wages, or in other words expanding his consumer power. The authors anticipate, therefore, that 'while militancy directed towards such ends as greater workers control may well become more difficult to sustain... we would regard greater aggresiveness in the field of "cash-based" bargaining as a very probable development'. They also suspect that, as the traditional modes of working-class life are further eroded by urban redevelopment and geographical mobility, the tendency will increase for manual (especially semi-skilled and unskilled) workers to define their work in largely instrumental terms. For that reason, they regard the Luton workers as 'prototypical' of the 'new' working class in Britain, setting patterns and norms in their work and family lives which, at the same time, 'stand as inducements to others still to seek in their turn a road which leads to affluence'.

This shift from a traditional to a more privatized style of working-class life also had a significant impact on political attitudes and behaviour. While it was true that some 80 per cent of the affluent manual workers in the sample were strong Labour supporters, and that this support was most commonly justified by diffuse expressions of class loyalty, the next most important reasons for voting Labour were explicitly instrumental and calculative in nature: Labour was the party which was most likely to increase the living standards of the ordinary working man. The authors note that 'the sober calculation of such material advantages is not... incompatible with sentiments of "class loyalty"'. But, they continue, 'other evidence that we collected does suggest that our affluent workers' support for Labour is probably less solidaristic and more instrumental than that of the many traditional workers from whom the Labour Party has in the past received almost unconditional allegiance.' In this context they cite their findings that among intending Labour voters almost half were opposed to trades union support for the party. A quarter of these same men had contracted out of paying the unions' political levy. There was a quite widespread feeling that 'the unions should keep out of politics'. Nevertheless, collective action by class organizations (in this case the trades unions and Labour Party) still represented the principal means by which the affluent workers could defend or improve their material circumstances, so Goldthorpe and his colleagues concluded that the political beliefs and values of their Labour-voting respondents were best described as an ideology of 'instrumental collectivism'. Workers felt that their economic interests could most usefully be served by joining a union and voting Labour – but this support was conditional upon anticipated material pay offs. It was 'devoid of all sense of participation in a class *movement* seeking structural changes in society or even pursuing more limited ends through concerted class action'. In that sense, it is quite different from the 'solidaristic collectivism' of the traditional industrial worker, which is based on a consciousness of belonging to a working-class community.

Traditional working-class communities were, of course, usually associated with industries which isolated workers in solidary neighbourhoods. Normally, employees in the shipbuilding, mining, or fishing industries, for example, developed a distinctive work culture and an 'occupational community'. That is, they shared a high degree of involvement in their jobs, close attachments to primary work groups and a preference for workmates as leisure-time companions, neighbours and even kin. Indeed, as Lockwood and his colleagues observe, 'the existence of such closely knit cliques of friends, workmates, neighbours and relatives is... the hallmark of the traditional working-class community'. The values of mutuality expressed through these social networks allegedly foster a communal sociability and 'accentuate the sense of class identity that springs from shared work experiences'. As we have seen, this shared consciousness of class is said to make support for Labour and the trades unions 'natural' or 'instinctive', in contrast to the calculative loyalty of the instrumental collectivists in Luton. It also supports a worldview which poses a sharp distinction between 'us and them' – between ordinary working men and the all-powerful bosses or managers.

The manual workers in Luton did not share in this worldview. True, two-thirds continued to describe themselves as working-class, and only 14 per cent claimed a definite middle-class standing. However, these claims to class identity rested on a 'commodity consciousness' and a largely destructured image of the social hierarchy. That is, 'in so far as coherent images of the class structure were to be found, these most often approximated "money" models in which extrinsic differences in consumption standards, rather than relationships expressing differences in power or prestige, were represented as the main basis of stratification'. One-third of the sample distinguished only two major classes in Britain – but only two of these men actually subscribed to a power-based model of society. Nor did many respondents hold elaborate hierarchial images of society rooted in the idea of differential prestige or status – a typically middle-class perspective on social order. Instead, as many as two-thirds of those advancing a more or less coherent image of the social structure identified money as the major determinant of class inequalities, and a large central or majority class differentiated internally by only consumer preferences and purchasing power. In this way, most people discounted the manual/nonmanual distinction as a significant social boundary, and expanded their own class so as to include all but a few extreme groups. This perception is obviously consistent with the workers' preoccupation with economic advancement. It indicates neither a high degree of (typically middle-class) *status* consciousness nor (traditional) proletarian *class* consciousness. It suggests, rather, that liberal claims of embourgeoisement and neo-Marxist hopes for a revolutionary socialist 'new working class' are equally misplaced. More plausibly, these data support Lockwood and Goldthorpe's initial suspicion of 'normative convergence' between certain routine non-manual and 'affluent' manual groups, 'involving in the case of white-collar workers a shift away from their traditional individualism towards greater reliance on collective means of pursuing their economic objectives; and in the case of manual workers, a shift away from a community-oriented form of social life towards recognition of the conjugal family and its fortunes as concerns of overriding importance'. Always assuming, of course, that Luton provided a template for similar changes throughout the country as a whole.

IV

Covering, as it did, such a broad range of topics – friendship patterns, attitudes to work, images of class, conjugal roles, and so forth – it was to be expected that the *Affluent Worker Study* would attract critical attention on a large scale. In the event it has turned out to be probably the most widely discussed text in modern British sociology. Much of the subsequent discussion has, in fact, been generally favourable; understandably so, in my opinion, since it is difficult not to be impressed by the thoroughness of the research and the care taken in relating theory to data. Some derivative studies subsequently extended the major empirical findings and reported similar results among workers in other plants and locations. However, a number of criticisms have also been voiced repeatedly over the past twenty years or so, and it is worth recording the most important of these, briefly, before outlining my own assessment of the lasting significance of the research from the point of view of the present book.

Few commentators objected to the claim that the Luton results convincingly falsified the liberal thesis of working-class embourgeoisement. The socio-political perspectives of the affluent workers were far from middle class: there was no widespread concern to translate economic into status advancement; the majority were stable Labour voters; and, most importantly of all, the workers and their wives had not been assimilated into middle-class social networks. Very few had formed social relationships with white-collar employees, and not because of middle-class exclusiveness, but because they themselves were uninterested in developing such contacts. Instead, they followed a family-centred, relatively privatized pattern of social life. Since evidence of embourgeoisement was so obviously absent, despite the relatively favourable circumstances afforded by this critical test case, then there were good grounds for generalizing this negative finding to other British manual workers located in different kinds of industries and communities. On the other hand, a number of left-wing critics argued that instrumentalism and privatism amounted to a new form of embourgeoisement, because they effectively denied the possibility of manual workers developing a socialist or even a militant class consciousness.

The thesis of normative convergence in the middle layers of the British class structure has attracted rather more in the way of sceptical comment. The study of clerks in the three plants is said to be far too limited to demonstrate the necessary changes in white-collar attitudes and behaviour. More obviously still, a contrast is repeatedly drawn between the beliefs and practices of the 'new' privatized manual worker, and those of his 'traditional' working-class counterpart. However, no systematic evidence regarding the latter is ever offered, despite the fact that this comparison is crucial to the argument. As Leslie Benson puts it, 'the "proletarian traditionalist" remains an obdurately ideal-typical construction for the most part, and as a result there is no baseline against which to judge the alleged "deviation" of the privatised individual from his more class-conscious peers'. This seems to leave the argument about normative convergence stranded on the level of hypothesis.

On a narrower front, industrial sociologists have questioned the analysis offered in the first volume of the *Affluent Worker* trilogy, in particular the emphasis placed on orientations to work and the associated tendency to ignore in-plant experiences. Some have objected to the apparent stability given these orientations and pointed to research elsewhere which seems to show that attitudes to work generally are affected *at work* by such factors as the size of the factory, types of technology it utilizes, the organization of the work group, relationships with supervisors and managers, and the worker's autonomy in performing his or her tasks. Others have argued that the whole perspective of 'orientations to work' is simply too voluntaristic, since it implies that workers are free to make choices about their present employment, and so ignores the constraints imposed by the organization of production. Orientations – 'revealed preferences' – may be as much a reflection of what is concretely available in, let us say, a particular labour market, as of 'ultimate wants' freely expressed.

The attention given by the Luton team to workers' *perceptions* of employment, company and unions is also claimed by some to have prevented respondents from expressing their *feelings* about these matters. Studies of workers elsewhere, containing questions worded to elicit evaluation as well as those designed to determine cognition, seem to suggest that, had the researchers dug deeper, they would have found ethical judgements which indicated greater working-class solidarism, and a more complex involvement with jobs themselves, than appears to be the case from the strictly practical assessments taped in the Luton interviews. The fact that workers in a capitalist enterprise, when asked about their orientation to work, tend to answer in pecuniary and instrumental terms, should not, perhaps, come as a surprise to sociologists. After all, these same workers live in consumer-oriented societies and are exhorted at every turn to acquire goods and services which, to a large extent, are available only in exchange for money. The thesis of working-class instrumentalism may, therefore, do little more than state the obvious fact that the dictates of a modern market economy ensure that workers are with good reason interested in their pay packets. Consequently, more often than not, they will articulate their ambitions and preferences in pecuniary terms. Since money is increasingly the generalized medium of exchange in capitalist societies, people are constrained to think in monetary terms. What the Luton team fails to do, in the eyes of some critics, is to uncover the *meaning* of money to the individuals concerned. Jennifer Platt's most important dissenting comment concerns precisely this matter and points out that an instrumental orientation to work is imputed to the Luton respondents on the basis of indirect evidence from a variety of data which were collected for other purposes, rather than from direct measures designed specifically to test that proposition.

Similarly, at least one prominent left-wing commentator has argued at length that Lockwood and his colleagues (neo-Weberians to a man and woman), simply rediscovered (at last) Marx and Engels's 'cash nexus'. John Westergaard was not surprised by the *fact* of workers' pecuniary instrumentalism but by the *interpretation* that the Affluent Worker team placed upon it. He rejects

> the implication that the worker's monetary orientation to his job is somehow a new phenomenon, which is the trigger for developing 'privatisation' of the affluent workers' entire social outlook. For this 'monentary orientation' seems to amount to something remarkably like a recognition of the 'cash nexus', which Marx identified as the main residual binding force of capitalist society well over a hundred years ago.

If workers are tied to their jobs only by their wages then their commitment to labour, and to everyday co-operation with management, seems to Westergaard to be rather brittle. As he puts it, 'the "cash nexus" may snap just because it is *only* a cash nexus – because it is single-stranded; and if it does snap, there is nothing else to bind the worker to acceptance of the situation'. Westergaard therefore concludes that a strictly pecuniary orientation to work can potentially sponsor widespread militancy and, ultimately, socialist radicalism. Instead of deducting socio-political quiescence from instrumentalism, as the Luton team does by postulating privatism), Westergaard paints a picture of a working class precariously balanced between attitudes of co-operation or resignation, on the one hand, and a nascent class consciouness, held in check only by the tenuous thread of the cash nexus, on the other. Working-class instrumentalism is real enough; the dispute here is about its implications for the class struggle.

A number of other, more detailed criticisms, might also be mentioned in passing. One persistent worry over the years has concerned the alleged tendency of the Affluent Worker team to over-interpret their own data. To take but one example (already cited above), the finding that 52 per cent of workers agree 'unions should just be concerned with getting higher pay and better conditions' while only 40 per cent concur that 'they should also try to get workers a say in management' (the other 8 per cent could not decide between these options), scarcely seems to justify the conclusion that 'there is no very widespread desire among these men that their unions should strive to give them a larger role in the actual running of the plant'. The men's supposedly 'pecuniary' model of the class structure also sits uneasily alongside the facts that 72 per cent of them agreed 'there's "one law for the rich and another law for the poor"' and 60 per cent endorsed the statement that 'big businessmen have too much power in the country'. Problems are also created by the shift of emphasis in the arguments advanced by the team over the years. Some have claimed that occasionally these amount to outright contradictions. It is not clear, for example, how the traditional working-class community can support both a 'parochialism' which can be contrasted with 'class consciousness' (when Goldthorpe and his colleagues are discussing Marxist theories), and a 'universalism' that transcends the instrumental collectivism and privatism of the affluent workers, in those parts of the argument set against the background of liberal theories of embourgeoisement.

Some subsequent research, especially by feminists, has led several critics to conclude that the Luton team tends to romanticize the rewards of the companionate form of conjugal relationship. It is not at all clear, from these later studies, that either men or women find emotional and psychological compensation for boring employment in their homes, children and spare-time activities. On the other hand, to be fair to the original researchers, other studies have shown that it is precisely in the home and family that the greatest satisfactions of modern everyday life are to be found – hence the recent growth in such things as do-it-yourself home-improvement stores and all-day family theme parks.

Finally, there are a number of problems related to the site of the research itself and to the particular sample of workers chosen. The very factors that make Luton an ideal place to test the embourgeoisement thesis make it a correspondingly bad case from which to argue that privatism and instrumental collectivism have facilitated a normative convergence that is likely to become a lasting feature of the British class scene. The research was designed to prove a negative thesis and is therefore badly suited to substantiating a positive one: the Luton workers were, as the researchers themselves intended them to be, specifically selected for their (probably) high level of motivation towards material advancement. Margaret Grieco has also pointed out that the sample may have been biased in other respects as well. Since the major companies in Luton used recruitment practices which screened out union activists, and many newcomers had arrived in the town from areas of high unemployment, the money-mindedness and instrumental collectivism of the workers interviewed may simply be artefacts of the circumstances of their migration. For all of these reasons, the Luton workers could in fact be atypical, rather than prototypical of the British working class as a whole.

V

I do not want to dwell on these issues here. Some of the criticisms are certainly valid. The overall project clearly does suffer from a structural problem attributable to the changing socio-political and intellectual contexts of its origins and final publication: namely, that in so far as the Luton workers are seen as special, one's general interest in findings about them is necessarily limited; whereas, conversely, if they are treated as somehow prototypical then it can always be pointed out that, in various ways, the sample is highly unrepresentative of workers as a whole. It is also true, however, that the study has been subject to constant, sometimes bizarre misrepresentation. Most obviously, it continues, even today, to be cited as a demonstration of workplace alienation among car-assembly workers, when in fact the Vauxhall men constituted less than half of the blue-collar sample. This error has been so often reproduced that one cannot but suspect many critics of having become familiar with the findings through the now voluminous secondary literature, rather than through acquaintance with the original publications.

One thing that cannot be denied is that the project was a catalyst for an extraordinary number of derivative studies. Probably the best known of these were a direct response to David Lockwood's classic article on 'Sources of Variation in Working-Class Images of Society', one of the early position papers associated with the Luton research, and (in my view) probably the most significant publication to come out of the whole project. Drawing together the findings from a range of existing studies of social imagery, voting behaviour, industrial sociology, and community life, Lockwood derived an influential threefold typology of manual workers as 'traditional proletarians', 'deferential traditionalists', and 'privatised instrumentalists'.

As we have already seen, the first of these is associated with industries such as mining or shipbuilding, which typically gather their labour forces into solidary communities and isolate them from the wider society. These workers tend therefore to be members of occupational communities, characterized by a high degree of job involvement, strong attachments to primary work groups, and workplace relationships which carry over into leisure activities; to reside in 'traditional working-class communities', comprising closely knit ·cliques of workmates who are also friends, neighbours and relatives; to develop social networks emphasizing mutual aid, sociability, cohesion and collectivity; and, finally, to display a proletarian social consciousness centred on power-based models of society which distinguish 'us and them'. Deferential traditionalists, by comparison, adhere to a prestige or hierarchical model of society in which people are ranked according to status.. Characteristically, these workers defer to their betters both socially and politically, for example by voting Conservative on the grounds that the traditional elites in society can best be trusted to pursue national as opposed to sectional or class interests. This worldview tends to be characteristic of employees in small-scale family enterprises, or in other work situations where paternalistic forms of industrial authority are prevalent as, for example, they are among farm labourers. Typically, such workers live in small communities comprising a 'local status system', in which social standing is determined by 'interactional' rather than 'attributive' mechanisms. That is, because of close personal acquaintance, people tend to judge each other, both formally and informally, in terms of a few, readily observable personal criteria. Each person's qualities become well known, as does his or her membership of particular status groups, 'which operate to give the individual a very definite sense of position in a hierarchy of prestige, in which "each knows his place" and recognises the status prerogatives of those above and below him'. Finally, of course, there are the 'privatised instrumentalists'. These workers, of whom the majority in the Luton sample are typical, develop a pecuniary model of society in which class divisions are seen principally in terms of income and material possessions. As Lockwood notes:

> Basically, the pecuniary model of society is an ideological reflection of work attachments that are instrumental and of community relationships that are privatised. It is a model which is only possible when social relationships that might provide

prototypical experiences for the construction of ideals of conflicting power classes, or of heirarchically independent status
groups, are either absent or devoid of their significance.

Lockwood's typology, and the arguments underpinning it, acted as
a benchmark for literally dozens of subsequent studies of occupational
communities, of the impact of work and community life on social
consciousness, of working-class images of society, deference and
proletarian traditionalism. Indeed, for a decade or more these studies
constituted the core of mainstream sociological research in this
country, rooted consciously in Lockwood's highly imaginative
synthesis.

There is no need to summarize this research here. (I have, in any
case, already performed this task elsewhere.) It is sufficient merely to
note that Lockwood's article simply underlines one of the principal
unresolved problems of the Affluent Worker project as a whole. On
the one hand, it is claimed that the privatized instrumentalists of the
age of postwar affluence are prototypical of workers in general, and
that their pecuniary worldview is gradually replacing those of the
traditional proletarians and deferential traditionalists of earlier eras.
On the other hand, however, Lockwood also insists that these are
ideal types: that 'the "traditional worker" is, of course, a sociological
rather than an historical concept'; and that 'a purely pecuniary
ideology is, of course, just as much of a limiting case as a purely class
or purely status model of society'. Not unreasonably, the specific
historical context of these sociological types became a matter of some
dispute in subsequent research, which attempted to situate such
characteristics as privatism, instrumentalism and sociability much
more precisely in particular periods in the history of the British
working class. (The issues here are rather similar to those surrounding
the controversy about the 'cultural loss' of the 'organic' working-class
community, which Jackson and Marsden associated with the
grammar-school type of education.) Although this debate has still to
be resolved, the historical data thus far examined tend to suggest a less
romantic reality than is implicit in Lockwood's typology, since the
latter persistently contrasts the atomized and consumer-oriented
working class of today with a communitarian and solidaristic proletariat of some bygone era of class antagonisms. To take but one empirical
example, the well-documented privatism and instrumentalism of the
artisans and skilled workers of the mid-Victorian 'labour aristocracy'
suggest that these attitudinal and behavioural traits are not peculiar to
the postwar period, and may always have been close to the surface of
working-class life.

It is difficult, then, in the light of the prodigious amount of
commentary already available, and numerous unresolved empirical
issues generated by the Luton project, to say anything new about the

study. I propose, therefore, to conclude this account by drawing the reader's attention to only one aspect of the argument which, it seems to me, is particularly apposite in the present context. This is the thesis of instrumental collectivism, which was further developed by John Goldthorpe in an article on inflation published some years after the *Affluent Worker* volumes, and which provides a pertinent reminder of the relevance of sociological research to the formation of social policy. (That it does so by pointing to the limitations of economics as a social science makes it especially appealing as a stick with which to fend off some of sociology's many critics.)

Goldthorpe's paper on 'The Current Inflation' was written in the mid 1970s and is rightly not considered to be a part of the Affluent Worker project. However, his argument is so obviously a development of these earlier findings, that it can fairly be seen as an extended footnote to the study of Luton. In this later analysis, Goldthorpe attempts to provide a sociological explanation for the high rates of inflation that were the major economic preoccupation of governments during the 1970s, and at the same time to point to the limitations of merely economic accounts of this phenomenon. Two such accounts were influential in policy-making circles at that time. Monetarists argued that the main cause of inflation was simply excessive monetary expansion: too much money was being printed and issued. Since responsibility for the money supply lies with governments, then it follows that governments are chiefly to blame for inflation. Of course, the question then arises of *why* governments behave in this fashion, to which the answer was given that any government wishing to reduce inflation, but failing to control the supply of money, was simply acting 'irrationally'. This, in turn, was the result of bad economic advice, woolly-mindedness, or lack of political will. Alternatively, it might occur because governments sometimes ('mistakenly') seek to maximize their support among the political beneficiaries of inflation, such as, for example, home-owners who can enjoy soaring increases in the nominal value of their assets. The other economic explanation of inflation casts trades unions rather than governments in the role of villain. Cost-push theorists maintained that the main cause of inflation was leap-frogging demands for higher pay on the part of organized labour. Again, the question arises of *why* trades unions behave in this fashion, and again economists reply that the behaviour is simply irrational: it is due to error, ignorance, frustration, envy, a new mood of greed or acquisitiveness among members, or some combination of all of these. Union leaders and members alike simply fail to appreciate that, in the long-term, the adverse consequences of aggressive pay bargaining (that is, structural inflation) will be unfavourable for the whole community, including trades unionists, because the natural equilibrium of the national economy will be upset by escalating costs of production. Ultimately, this may lead to political crisis, or even wholesale social disorder. Unions, like governments in the monetarist accounts, are therefore behaving irrationally by making repeated, 'economically absurd' claims for higher wages.

Goldthorpe is struck, in reviewing these explanations, by the inability of economists to make sense of behaviour which does not seem to correspond to their own expectations of 'rational action'. If action is not 'economically rational' then it is simply 'irrational' – stupid or short-sighted. The fact that economists have to fall back on these 'residual categories' in order to account for the activities of certain governments and unions indicates the limits of their analytical scheme. They are faced with behaviour which is relevant to the phenomenon they wish to explain, yet they cannot make sense of it, at least in terms of the assumption of 'rational self interest' which underpins economic theory. They resort, therefore, to what Goldthorpe calls 'residual psychologism', moving 'from the assumption of rational actors whose motives are capable of being discussed in terms of the conditions, means and ends of action to the assumption of actors whose motives can rather be understood only in terms of impelling emotions'. That is, people are, for example, simply greedy, jealous, or stupid. Sociologists, by comparison, can offer an account of the practices of governments, unions and their members which renders their activities intelligible and therefore explicable. This is because the analytical scheme of sociology admits of the possibility of social action which is neither economically rational nor irrational, but is rather 'value-rational' or 'normative' in tenor. In other words, actors may pursue a particular strategy or goal because of some 'value commitment' to it, this being derived from a source other than their perception of economic self-interest. They may act out of loyalty to friends, respect for certain religious principles, or a host of other such normative concerns.

It is not difficult to explain why the two disciplines take such a different view of the same substantive issue. The reason is simply that they make contrasting assumptions about the capitalist economy. To quote Goldthorpe:

> economists tend to see this as having an inherent propensity towards stability or, at least, as capable of being stabilized through skilled management on the basis of the expertise that they can themselves provide. Sociologists, on the other hand, tend to view the market economy as being inherently unstable or... as exerting a constant destabilizing effect on the society within which it operates, so that it can itself continue to function satisfactorily only to the extent that this is offset by exogenous factors: most importantly, by the integrative influence of some basic value consensus in the society, deriving from sources unrelated to the economy.

This 'value consensus' (or, in the matter of pay-bargaining, value conflict) occurs in the normative realm of societies. Because economists can introduce normative elements into their analytical scheme only in an *ad hoc* way, they tend to dismiss as irrational ('stupidity', 'ignorance', 'greed') behaviour with which sociology is actually centrally concerned, and for which it can often provide adequate causal explanations.

In fact, Goldthorpe's alternative sociological explanation of inflation is rooted neither in some inexplicable rise in the greed of rank-and-file wage earners nor in the unaccountable stupidity of governments and unions, but in empirically documented changes in the social structure of modern Britain. It echoes David Lockwood's suggestions about the prototypicality of the new privatized instrumentalists in Luton by settling this mantle upon the British working class as a whole. Three developments of the postwar period are identified by Goldthorpe as crucial to the explanation of working-class 'pushfulness' in pay-bargaining. The first of these is the decay of traditional status orders based on deference, social acceptance and derogation. 'Urbanisation and the greater physical mobility of the population, which are concomitants of industrialism *per se*, largely eliminate the *local* status group structures.' In addition, the decreasing salience of precapitalist value-systems (such as those associated with religion), mean that present-day capitalism has a 'depleting moral legacy'. Moreover, 'within a growing market economy, market relations and the principle of "equal exchange" tend to enter into an ever-enlarged area of social life, as the dynamics of the "commercialisation effect" work themselves out'. All of this undermines status orders grounded in the moral acceptance of the world as it stands; relationships are increasingly formed, instead, about a 'cash nexus'.

The second development is the realization of citizenship. It will be remembered, from the earlier discussion of Townsend's work on poverty, that T. H. Marshall saw the achievement of citizenship as an inherently egalitarian undertaking. Citizenship, for Marshall, was realized to the extent that members of a national society enjoyed in common a body of civil, political and social rights. Goldthorpe, drawing on Marshall's analysis, argues that the growth of citizenship rights throughout the nineteenth and twentieth centuries has made for 'a progressively greater equality of conditions of conflict' between rank-and-file employees and their employers. The 'secondary system of industrial citizenship', whose key institutions are the trade union and the right to bargain collectively, has considerably enhanced the ability of labour to bargain for extensions to social rights ('a right to work', 'a right to a living wage', and so forth) and to diminish the role of the market in determining life-chances. Under these circumstances, therefore, 'it is scarcely surprising... that workers should react to redundancy and unemployment, or to the threat of these, with something more than the resigned or fatalistic acceptance which they may have shown in earlier periods'.

Finally, Goldthorpe observes that Britain possesses the demographically and socio-politically most mature working class in the Western world. The processes of urbanization and industrialization began earlier and proceeded more rapidly in this country than in, say, France or Germany. Furthermore, Britain has long had a relatively small agricultural sector, compared to all other Western industrial nations. The combined effect of these circumstances has been to generate a working class which, as can be seen from the relevant data on social mobility, is substantially self-recruiting. Its members possess 'a relatively high degree of homogeneity in their social backgrounds and patterns of life experience'. They are, for the most part, at least second-generation working-class. This demographic maturity has, in turn, sponsored socio-political maturity. That is, 'successive generations of a working class... have grown up alike within a stable national community, in which citizenship rights have been upheld and developed, and in which therefore workers have been able to pursue their industrial and political interests by means of their own organisations'.

The decline of locality-based status orders, extension of the sphere of citizenship, demographic and socio-political maturity of the British working class, have all tended, over the years, to encourage employees in this country to exploit to the full whatever market advantages they may happen to possess. Manual workers and their leaders have simply become 'more free of various constraints on their actions in pursuit of what they see as their interests'. As Goldthorpe notes, once this analytical context is established, 'it is possible for rank-and-file "pushfulness", distributional dissent, union militancy and "irresponsibility" etc. all to be viewed in a rather different way to that of the economists'. It is no longer necessary to invoke empirically unproven and implausible residual psychological elements, such as some wholesale current of stupidity that has engulfed governments, or new moods of envy and greed among workers. Rather, 'it is not so much that *new* influences on wage- and salary-earners and their organisations need to be recognised, but rather the disappearance of old ones – that is, the weakening of the inhibitions formerly imposed by the status order.'

Now, one would not wish to draw too many lessons from a single illustration of a sociologist venturing, rather successfully as it seems to me, into the terrain normally reserved for and by economists as their own. (All the more, in this particular case, since other sociologists have more recently argued that Goldthorpe's analysis is empirically suspect, and in any case ignores other more plausible economic explanations for the phenomenon, such as the export of inflation to the rest of the world by the USA at the end of the 1960s.) Nor am I arguing that economics is necessarily a dismal science. Nevertheless, this particular example does tell us something about the intellectual scope of sociology, and the boldness of many of its practitioners. Inflation has been a constant preoccupation of successive governments in this country throughout the past two decades. During that period I have probably read several hundred newspaper articles on the subject, and listened to at least that number of radio and television interviews with treasury analysts, government officials and other 'informed experts', all attempting to diagnose and suggest a cure for this particular social problem. Almost without exception the authors of these pronouncements have been economists. I do not recall a single sociologist ever being asked for his or her professional views on the subject. Of course, it is easy to see why this should be so. No discipline which starts from the assumption that free markets exert a constant destabilizing influence on society is likely to find itself popular with a social-democratic government of almost any political hue to the right of socialist. Nevertheless, the fact that scientifically sound sociological research often carries political implications which some (particularly governing elites) find uncomfortable, does not detract from the intellectual worth of the findings themselves. Gold-thorpe is not saying that inflation is incurable without a radical transformation of society. As a sociologist he is simply offering an analysis – not a prescription for political action. Curiously enough, however, and by way of contrast, the supposedly technocratic solutions for inflation proposed by economists *are* heavily value-laden, since these assume that, in the light of economic science, its practitioners can tell us how we *ought* to live our lives. In this particular case, we ought simply to summon up the monetarist (or Keynesian) institutional plumbers, place additional controls on credit, push up exchange rates (for example), and re-establish the supposedly politically neutral outcomes of the so-called 'free market'. It is, therefore, deeply ironic that, isolated as they have been from the policy-making processes in government, it is Britain's sociologists, rather than her economists, who have constantly had to defend themselves against charges of partisanship and covert political interference.

7 Race and housing in the inner city

The empirical setting of the Affluent Worker Study, the Bedfordshire town of Luton, was, as we have seen, central to the project's theoretical rationale. Lockwood and his colleagues devote almost a whole chapter of their principal monograph to justifying this choice of location. Luton's industrial, demographic, social and geographical characteristics are said to make it an ideal site for testing the thesis of working-class embourgeoisement. However, it is one of the ironies of the project that the published results convey remarkably little sense of the town itself, or of the flavour of everyday life in the local community and factories. The authors' survey technique tends to decontextualize the research. The setting is Luton – but the reader could scarcely guess this from the analysis of the interview materials. The text I will look at in this chapter, on the other hand, exhibits a pronounced sense of time and place. John Rex and Robert Moore's *Race, Community, and Conflict* is a study of Birmingham in the early 1960s. The specific features of this particular urban setting constantly intrude into their sociological analysis; locality is crucial.

This is not to suggest that Rex and Moore attempt to describe all aspects of life in the city. The argument of *Race, Community, and Conflict* hinges instead about two very obvious themes – those of housing and of race. The study was, in fact, financed by the Institute of Race Relations as part of a more general survey of race relations in Britain. By the early 1960s race had become a social problem in this country so the need for such a survey seemed obvious.

Why choose to study Birmingham in particular? The city had enjoyed a substantial economic expansion after the Second World War. Local engineering companies were quick to exploit the postwar new technology which, in turn, fuelled additional growth in the construction and service sectors. This created a sustained demand for labour during the mid 1950s and early 1960s, particularly in semi-skilled and unskilled employment, which could not be met locally. From the mid 1950s onwards, therefore, New Commonwealth immigrants began to join the already resident Birmingham Irish as a replacement labour force. Between 1951 and 1961 the numbers of Brummies born in the New Commonwealth rose from about 5,000 to 30,000. By 1971, some 10 per cent had parents born in the New Commonwealth, and the city had the largest black population outside

London. Although the local demand for labour meant that jobs were not an issue, housing most certainly was, because the postwar council building programme had remained obdurately modest, despite the fact that the city had suffered a good deal of bomb damage during the war. During the early 1960s the shortage of accommodation in the city had become chronic and exceeded 30,000 dwellings. The new coloured immigrants seemed only to be adding to the housing shortage, since they established themselves in reasonably sound dwellings in the inner city, which then quickly became overcrowded and were allowed to deteriorate physically. Locally, therefore, as Rex and Moore note, 'almost invariably the question of colour was discussed in relation to housing problems and in relation to the so-called "twilight zones", that is, areas where large, old houses, too good to be classified as slums, had become multi-occupied lodging-houses.' Predictably, whites in the adjacent areas (and those on the housing waiting-list) became extremely agitated about the damage being done by multi-occupation, blaming this on black tenants and landlords alike. Racial problems soon came to dominate public discussion in the city. Rex later observed that, by 1962 (the year in which immigration was first curtailed by the passing of legislation that deprived Commonwealth subjects of their traditional right of entry to Britain), Birmingham 'had got itself into a state of near-hysteria' over the problem of the twilight zones.

In short, Birmingham seemed to offer a particularly suitable site for investigating the 'implications for British society of the presence of a substantial number of Commonwealth immigrants', which was the declared aim of the Survey of Race Relations in Britain. Rex, fortuitously, was a lecturer at the local university. Moore joined him as a full-time fieldworker at the outset of the project. Additional research assistance was provided by Alan Shuttleworth and Jennifer Williams. During the years 1963–4 the team studied the Sparkbrook area of the city, which lies about 1½ miles from the centre on the south-east side, with the apparently straightforward objective of finding out 'who lives there, what primary community ties they have, what their housing situation, economic position and status aspirations are, what associations they form, how these associations interact and how far the various groups are incorporated into urban society as citizens'. Moore later wrote that it was his task, as the primary fieldworker, 'to find out these things by whatever methods were appropriate'. In fact, a quarter of a century later, one can only marvel at the tenacity of the research team in pursuing its goal. It was a relatively simple matter for Shuttleworth to do the necessary documentary research into the development of race relations and housing policy in Birmingham. Rex and Moore interviewed numerous 'key actors', including planning and housing officials, public health authorities and local politicians. Again this was a reasonably straightforward exercise, although the researchers were often called upon to contain their anger at the overt racism of some local government officers, most notably a senior official responsible for 'race integration' who described Pakistanis as 'a bunch of frustrated, shrivelled up little bastards'.

However, entering the local community was an altogether different proposition, since many of the typical actors and groups with which it was necessary to establish contact were elusive and in any case understandably suspicious about the purposes of the research. Notwithstanding the obvious fact that the researchers were white, whereas many of their respondents were black or Asian, it required considerable diplomatic skills to interview immigrants about 'where they lived and their housing status; how long they had lived there and what their previous movements had been; what family they had or where their closest kin were located; what, if any, organisations they belonged to; what work they did and how they spent their free time' – all set against a background of racial discrimination, public disquiet at the mores of coloured tenants and landlords, and political debate about the desirability of rigorous immigration controls and even repatriation. Moore did the usual things: contacted officers of the local clubs and societies, attended meetings and church services, and patiently hung around in pubs and on street corners. Eventually, he found himself being invited to visit private homes to meet and talk to 'ordinary' people.

As if the problems of informal observation were not enough, the team was also resolved to conduct a formal survey in the area, as a check on the reliability of their other data. (Again, giving the lie to the popular belief that sociologists will always choose the methodological soft option.) The survey itself raised many additional difficulties; for example, the population (especially the immigrant population) of the area was fluid, with tenants moving from house to house at very short notice. Not surprisingly, therefore, it was poorly enumerated and subject to widely different estimates. Most of the inhabitants worked irregular hours. Some single men effectively came home only to sleep. Many spoke little or no English. Indeed, population movements were so rapid that interviewers often arrived with the wrong interpreter. Interviews were conducted by student volunteers in no less than seventeen languages. Respondents had to be convinced that the researchers were not 'snooping' on behalf of the local authorities. Custom sometimes required that several evenings were spent in eating and drinking with the family before an interview was granted. The fact that the researchers managed to draw up an adequate sample and achieve a satisfactory response rate under these circumstances represents something of a methodological miracle.

Eventually, many gallons of sweet tea and not a few aggressive encounters later, the team had successfully interviewed more than half of the individuals they believed to be in their sample of 201 dwellings, containing 382 households, comprising 1052 persons (417 men, 315 women, 302 children, and 18 individuals of unknown status). In total, some 386 complete interviews were obtained (200 males, 186 females), of which 192 were with English respondents. The 194 immigrants were a mixture of Irish (89 interviews), West Indian (48), Pakistani (32), Indian (7) and others (18). Basic demographic information was also obtained for 346 additional individuals who might have been interviewed in more depth, but for the fact that the researchers ran out of time. The team failed to contact only 18 adults – less than 3 per cent of the sample. Under the circumstances, these figures are a truly remarkable research achievement. They also made it less easy to dismiss Rex and Moore's subsequent findings on the grounds that they·had spoken only to selected people and made no attempt to sample opinions generally in Sparkbrook. In due course this was to prove an important point in the researchers' favour as their argument came under sustained criticism from politicians and academics alike.

II

From the mass of information gathered by the interviews, survey and documentary research, Rex and Moore gradually built up a detailed picture of the Sparkbrook residents. Their ethnography is convincing, and readily conveys the flavour of everyday life in an area of the city rarely visited by outsiders, although the details do not lend themselves to easy summary. Nor, indeed, do the prolific statistics on household composition, migration experiences, kinship connections, church affiliation and attendances, employment patterns, and residential aspirations. Fascinating though this material is, the really interesting parts of the analysis occur towards the end of the book, where the authors use the insights gained in the research as the basis for a completely novel interpretation of race relations in the inner city. This new approach extends the work of the so-called Chicago School on the ecology of the city and fuses it to Max Weber's writings about social class.

The Chicago School is the name usually given to the distinguished group of sociologists who studied that city during the 1920s and 1930s. Its members published many graphic accounts of life in the various zones which formed more or less concentric circles around the Chicago Central Business District: the zone of transition, zone of working-class housing, middle-class residential zone, and commuter zone (see Fig. 7.1). These rings had been built up, one after the other, as the city steadily grew. They had also been successively invaded from the inside, so that as inner-city areas originally occupied by wealthy residents began to run down, large homes were taken over as

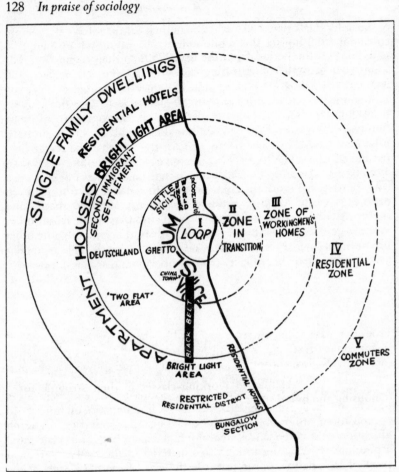

Figure 7.1   The urban areas of Chicago
   Source: Robert E. Park *et al.*, *The City* (University of Chicago Press, 1925), Chart II.

lodging houses. The hitherto middle-class area thus became a twilight zone as its former residents moved out to the newer and more attractive suburbs. The author of the concentric zone theory, Ernest Burgess, described this pattern of spatial segregation as a consequence of 'economic and cultural competition'. His associates were primarily interested in describing life in the various localities – for instance in Little Sicily, or Chinatown – and so were content simply to accept Burgess's rather vague explanation for the ecological structure that had emerged. Rex and Moore, writing some thirty years later, offer a much more specific interpretation of urban segregation in Birmingham.

Like the Chicago researchers, they begin their analysis with an historical account of the evolution of the city, concentrating in particular on the period from the mid 1750s to the present day. The industrial growth of Birmingham during the eighteenth and nineteenth centuries was accompanied by a residential segregation 'determined by position in relation to factories, civic buildings, and prevailing winds'. The upper-middle class lived in substantial family houses, with good access to the central facilities, but away from the industrial dirt. Their way of life was based on the independence of the family and on secure possession of capital and property. It is clearly expressed in the gracious architecture of their substantial dwellings. The rent-paying working class, on the other hand, lived in gridiron rows of red-brick cottages squeezed together in left-over spaces, and segregated both from the captains of industry and from other working-class communities by canals, railways, rivers, or some other obvious feature. No concept of family life was built into this architecture. Yet, because of shared adversity, these areas came to develop a strong extra-familial communalism, reflected in such things as the pubs and chapels, extended kin groups, neighbourhoods, trades unions and friendly societies. As Rex and Moore put it,

> mutual aid rather than property gave security to the inhabitants of this area and when that mutual aid was expressed in political terms in the socialism of the city hall it was greatly to enhance the power of the established working-classes in their struggle for housing and living space.

Finally, towards the end of the nineteenth century, a socially and economically intermediate group of lower middle-class people – shopkeepers, clerks and minor professionals – began to emerge. These white-collar workers aspired to the life-style of the upper-middle class but lacked equivalent resources. Nevertheless, they managed to establish themselves in rented accommodation that was noticeably superior to the workers' cottages, their status and aspirations being obvious in the servants' quarters that constituted their attics and cellars.

In the initial settlement of the modern city, then, 'three different groups, differentially placed with regard to the possession of property, become segregated from one another and work out their own community style of life'. The city's inner ring thus comes to contain three characteristic types of housing. Then, in the twentieth century, 'the great urban game of leapfrog begins'. In order to escape the expanding business area, the new trams and buses and the general increase in population density, the industrialists moved to elegant new detached houses in inner suburbia, seeking the quietness and privacy

of large secluded gardens. The white-collar workers, in turn, abandoned their town houses in the great interwar migration to the
cheaper suburban semis, retaining the private garden to one side, but
dispensing with the servants en route. Finally, the working classes
used their growing political muscle to secure their own version of the
new suburban ideal, modelled on that of the white-collar families and
distinguished only by the fact that once each week someone from the
local council called to collect the rent. Rex and Moore conclude,
therefore, that 'these three ways of life and housing are considered
desirable and normal in the city'.

Less desirable – and less normal – is the way of life of those who
now inhabit the inner zone. These include workers 'left behind' in
slum property, either because they have bought their own houses, or
because the council lacks adequate replacement public housing;
tenants seeking to rent a room or two in shared accommodation; and
those who have bought the larger old houses but must take in lodgers
in order to pay their way. The researchers also concede that 'there
will, of course, be some deviants, romantics and intellectuals who
actually prefer living in the inner zone'. But, they maintain, 'the
persistent outward movement which takes place justifies us in saying
and positing as central to our model that surburban housing is a scarce
and desired resource'. It seems to them, therefore, that 'the basic
process underlying urban social interaction is competition for scarce
and desired types of housing'. The ecological structure of Birmingham was not simply, as the Chicago sociologists might have assumed,
the result of some general economic competition. It was, rather, the
specific consequence of conflict over desirable suburban housing.

At this point, and in order to develop their argument further, Rex
and Moore turn to a quite different sociological tradition. They
suggest that in the competition for scarce housing, 'people are
distinguished from one another by their strength in the housing
market or, more generally, in the system of housing allocations'. Of
course, as we have already seen in our discussion of Goldthorpe's
work on social mobility, 'market situation' is the central feature of
Max Weber's classic theory of social classes. Classes, for Weber, are
groups of individuals sharing roughly equal life-chances as a result of
their economic power in labour markets. Rex and Moore simply
extend Weber's discussion by suggesting that any market situation,
and not merely the individual's labour market situation, can lead to
'the emergence of groups with a common market position and
common market interests which could then be called classes'. More
specifically, they modify Weber's notion of differential placement in a
labour market and develop it to include unequal chances of access to
housing. In the urban milieu, 'a class struggle between groups
differentially placed with regard to the means of housing develops,
which may at the local level be as acute as the class struggle in

industry'. Thus Rex and Moore arrive at the conclusion that 'housing classes' are central to the explanation of urban conflict. Being a member of one or other of these classes 'is of first importance in determining a man's associations, his interests, his life-style, and his position in the urban social structure'. In short, 'the class struggle over the use of houses . . . is the central process of the city as a social unit'.

Seven such classes are identified (and listed here in order of decreasing status): the outright owners of large houses in desirable areas; mortgage payers who own whole houses in desirable areas; council tenants in council-built houses; council tenants in slum houses awaiting demolition; tenants of private house-owners, usually in the inner ring; house-owners who must take lodgers to meet loan repayments; and, finally, lodgers in rooms. These classes follow a definite territorial distribution in the city, depending on the age and size of buildings, so that in Birmingham, for example, owners repaying mortgages will tend to be found in the outer suburbs. Council tenants of houses with long expectations of life tend also to be found here. Those in property scheduled for slum clearance, on the other hand, are usually situated in the inner city. Here, too, are the lodging houses occupied by their owners and tenants.

Since the housing market comprises the twin systems of cash purchase (of home-ownership) and bureaucratic allocation (to council property), then the class conflict in housing is primarily a struggle for either a mortgage or a council tenancy. Access to the first depends on possession of a sizeable and secure income. 'Housing need' and 'length of residence' are usually crucial to securing the second. Those whose housing situation does not include either of these types of resource will invariably be found in the 'twilight areas' of the zone of transition. This, finally, brings the authors to the question of ethnicity; and, in particular, to the highly charged racial tensions of Birmingham in the early and mid 1960s.

Coloured immigrants arriving in the city rarely possessed the necessary capital or security of income and employment to raise long-term credit for a house purchase. The building societies, who in large part controlled the allocation of these funds, effectively prevented the newcomers from achieving entry to the private owner-occupied sector. Nor did immigrants have the necessary qualifications for access to good council housing. Birmingham City Council operated a five-year residence rule which effectively rendered new arrivals ineligible for council housing. Those who, in due time, fulfilled this requirement were then interviewed by a housing visitor whose job it was to grade families on the housing waiting-list according to their 'suitability' for different qualities of council accommodation. Applicants who were regarded as 'undesirable' tenants for the newer or better houses were offered sub-standard short-life (slum) housing in inner-city areas. This placed immigrants in a vicious circle from which it was difficult to escape. For at least the first five years of their residence in the city they were forced, by lack of available alternatives, to rent accommodation in the cramped lodging-houses of the twilight zones. For reasons that will shortly become clear, the quality of housing here was low and tending to deteriorate. Housing visitors therefore took residence in the lodging-houses to be clear evidence of low domestic standards. As a result very few coloured applicants were ever offered tenancies of the sought-after low density prewar council houses, postwar flats, or other good dwellings taken into council ownership. Indeed, Rex and Moore could not find a single case of a West Indian or other coloured applicant being offered a council-built property during the entire period of the research in Birmingham. Those who were made offers of council accommodation invariably found that these were for 'patched' houses awaiting demolition. So, while the researchers do not claim to be able to prove that Birmingham Council operated a discriminatory policy to keep black people off its estates, they feel justified in concluding that 'it is quite possible... to discriminate without a policy of discrimination ever being publicly admitted'.

But what happens to those who do not qualify for council housing? Clearly, if they also lack the resources to become owner-occupiers of desirable suburban properties, they must become private landlords of less desirable properties – or, more probably, tenants of such landlords. The large, formerly middle-class dwellings of the twilight zones offered the most suitable accommodation for let in lodgings. These were the houses built in the second half of the nineteenth century for the white-collar workers and shopkeepers, structurally more sound than the older inner-city workers' cottages, but known to planners as 'twilight properties' because they were approaching, but had not yet reached, the night of slumdom. In Birmingham, in the 1960s, they were grouped in the north in the Soho, Handsworth and Aston areas, and in the south in Edgbaston, Deritend, Moseley, Balsall Heath, Small Heath and Sparkbrook. Some had already been converted to lodgings for Welsh and Irish immigrants in the 1930s. The arrival of coloured immigrants greatly accelerated the process of multi-occupation. Excluded, as we have seen, from access to long-term mortgages and council properties, the new arrivals were forced to borrow money from friends, relatives and moneylenders on a short-term basis. This was used to purchase property in which no one else had a long-term interest but which had sufficient rooms to ensure a high rental income, so that the borrowed capital could be repaid – the twilight properties of the zone of transition. The immigrant could afford to buy one of these houses only if he proceeded immediately to let rooms. And, as Rex and Moore discovered, 'once he did this, he found himself meeting a huge demand from other immigrants, black and white alike, from people who wanted accommodation with no questions asked, and from all those others who were at the back of the housing queue'.

By such means Sparkbrook had come to have three distinct areas by the early 1960s. These are shown in Figure 7.2. 'Sparkbrook 1', comprising the streets immediately to the east of the Stratford Road, was the lodging-house district at the heart of the zone of transition. More than 50 per cent of all immigrants in Sparkbrook lived here, in multi-occupation lodging-houses with remarkably mixed populations. Overcrowding was prevalent, amenities were often shared and the material standards of furnishing and such like were low. 'Sparkbrook 2', to the west of Stratford Road, was a network of artisans' cottages which, according to the researchers, still looked 'more like an urban working-class zone than any other part of Sparkbrook'. Many of the properties had been acquired by the Corporation for demolition and redevelopment. In the meantime tenancies were allocated to those families who had hitherto inhabited slums due for demolition who were judged to be unsuitable for new property elsewhere in the city. The picture was therefore one of 'mean, drab streets of terraced houses, small shops and corner pubs, indefinitely awaiting the bull-dozer'. 'Sparkbrook 3', to the south-east, was 'model' housing built by a residents' association from the 1890s onwards, for 'respectable' working-class tenants. The association, Corporation and tenants had maintained and improved these properties over the years. Almost all were structurally sound with long life-expectancy. Understandably, therefore, they were in high demand. Residents were strongly opposed to this area being used to house large and problem families and resented the implication that it formed part of a twilight zone. No coloured immigrants lived here.

But why should multi-occupation of the large, mid-Victorian terraced properties in the central district of Sparkbrook 1 seem to lead inexorably to the rapid physical deterioration of these houses? Rex and Moore found that most landlords in the twilight zone were in a very weak financial position. They had been obliged to borrow money at high rates of interest and over the short-term. Many were repaying several loans – to a bank, to friends and to relatives – at the same time. Moreover, as the researchers soon discovered, many (particularly Pakistani) landlords felt obliged to provide accommodation for their kin either rent-free or at a nominal charge. This further diminished their total income. In addition, few of the houses would have provided an adequate return on either the initial or any subsequent investment, had they eventually been resold. The majority were held on 99 year leases which, by the mid 1960s, were nearing their expiry date. So landlords had neither the money nor the incentive to maintain their property. Nor did the tenants. There was, for example, little or no security of tenure for those who leased the rooms. Moreover,

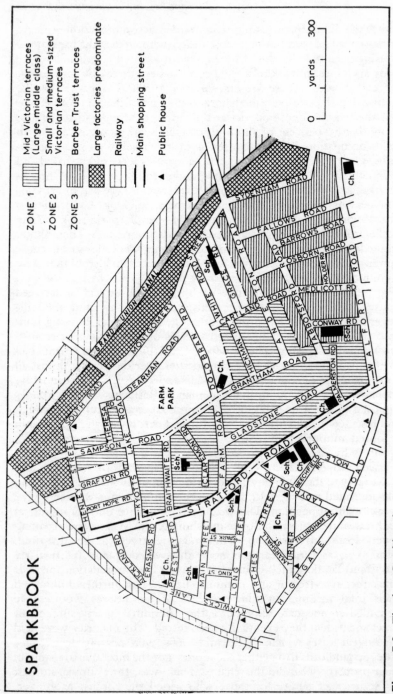

SPARKBROOK

ZONE 1 ▦ Mid-Victorian terraces (Large, middle class)
ZONE 2 ☐ Small and medium-sized Victorian terraces
ZONE 3 ▨ Barber Trust terraces
▩ Large factories predominate
▤ Railway
∥ Main shopping street
▲ Public house

0   300
yards

Figure 7.2 The three Sparkbrooks

Source: *Race, Community, and Conflict,* Map 2.

besides the immigrants, the zone of transition attracted deviants of various sorts – discharged prisoners, petty criminals, prostitutes, alcoholics, and so forth – who valued the anonymity of the area and the impersonal market relationship with the landlord. These residents were prone to give the fabric of the buildings hard use and invariably lacked the resources necessary for adequate maintenance. By the early 1960s, therefore, 'twilight zone' came to be a term that was applied, not simply to a certain age of housing, but to any area of multi-occupation and immigration that was experiencing a rapid physical deterioration.

This situation was made worse by the actions of the Birmingham Corporation. The pressure on housing in the city was so great that other areas besides the twilight zones seemed likely to go over to multi-occupation. The council therefore acquired (through appeal to the House of Lords) extensive statutory powers which allowed it to refuse planning permission to landlords seeking to establish additional subdivided properties. Lodging-houses were universally regarded – by property-owners, council tenants and Corporation alike – as undesirable because of their association with poor amenities and standards. Yet neither the free market nor the state was providing adequate housing for the whole population of Birmingham. Multi-occupation, and the lodging-houses of the twilight zones, were a visible indictment of the failure of the system of private property to produce a democracy of owner-occupiers; and, equally, of the failure of the welfare state to offer good-quality housing as a social service safety net for those who failed to enter the property-owning classes. The immigrant proprietors, therefore, were performing an essential service by providing housing for fellow citizens who would otherwise be homeless, yet they stood morally condemned in the eyes of the majority of the population. A pariah group of private landlords was needed to do the dirty work of the housing market, but in Birmingham at least, they were severely criticized for their efforts: 'The city, having failed to deal with its own housing problem, turns on those upon whom it relies to make alternative provision, and punishes them for its failure.' Naturally, the punishment cannot go too far, 'for the consequence of driving the lodging-house landlords out of business would be to leave large numbers of the population to sleep in the parks'. So multi-occupation is tolerated, but within carefully controlled areas, in order (as the Corporation sees it) 'to stop the evil from spreading to other areas where the property-owning democracy and the welfare state may be preserved intact'. But, as Rex and Moore conclude acidly, one thing makes calm debate of this housing problem unlikely: 'Since most of the tenants and some of the landlords are immigrants, the cause of poor living conditions in the lodging-house areas can be attributed to their culture or race'. In these circumstances, 'stopping the cancer of multi-occupation' from spreading becomes equivalent to a policy of creating black ghettos, and of 'stopping the cancer of immigration'.

In other words, Birmingham's own housing, planning and public health policies had created and then exacerbated the racial problems which dominated public discussion in the city during the 1960s. Immigrants were compelled to live in the zone of transition, alongside other 'deviants' and 'isolates' whose form of life was unacceptable by welfare state standards, and, perversely were then condemned for undermining these standards by their failure to find suitable alternative accommodation. In short, as is so often the case in our society, the victims had been cast as the culprits. And, as usual, a sound piece of sociological research was the instrument for uncovering the nature of the inversion.

III

Race, Community, and Conflict was launched at a lunch for top people in the Café Royal. Few sociological reports, before or since, have enjoyed such a conspicuous unveiling. Not surprisingly, therefore, the critical response to the book was almost immediate; unlike the text itself it was also highly political.

The Times, for example, argued that the results of the study showed the need for rigorous immigration control, incorporating a colour bar, which would exclude blacks but admit Commonwealth whites 'who bring nothing but benefits to British life'. Similarly, in the *Daily Telegraph* Enoch Powell suggested that the book simply added weight to his own views on the need for barriers to immigration into Britain. Birmingham Council made a determined (though fortunately futile) attempt to identify the key informants who had alerted the researchers to the various discriminatory elements in the city's housing allocation. Robert Moore, reflecting on the study a decade later, also gives details of some of the radio and television broadcasts that were associated with the research. It is quite clear from his remarks that open discussion of its findings was hampered by certain 'sharp editorial practices' on the part of producers and others. At least one television interview, featuring a local official who was publicly willing to endorse the project's findings, was simply suppressed. More subtle was the tactic of the *This Week* team, who consulted the researchers at length about their results, but then, as Moore notes wryly, broadcast

a programme featuring Roy Hattersley, the Sparkbrook MP. Our book was on the table in the background of the introductory sequences, and it was said that 'some people' alleged Sparkbrook to be a scene of seething discontent and conflict. Hattersley then interviewed a smiling West Indian and asked him if he was happy. The answer was in the affirmative, and thus we were refuted.

On the other hand, not all of the criticism was unsympathetic, and more than one commentator defended the book's central contention that the influx of immigrants had not of itself caused the lodging-house problem. The *Observer*, for example, pointed out that the supposed 'intolerable strain' which the newcomers had imposed on Birmingham's housing stock had occurred at a time when the total population of the city was in fact falling. The major culprit, as Rex and Moore rightly suggest, had been the council's long defective planning policies.

Sociological responses to the book were less emotional and more searching. A number of rather specific criticisms were voiced. The Sparkbrook project, as I suggested at the outset, was firmly situated in a specific time and place. Not surprisingly, therefore, the issues of typicality were to the fore in subsequent academic discussion. It has been pointed out, for example, that had Rex and Moore studied the Birmingham of the mid 1970s they would have discovered an entirely different situation. By that time, growing unemployment had led to direct competition for jobs between blacks and whites, in both skilled and unskilled sectors alike. Housing, meanwhile, had almost ceased to be a public issue. Extensive new private and council developments on the outskirts of the city had made property accessible to those whites who were unhappy about living in racially mixed areas. This, in turn, left many inner-city dwellings available for rent or purchase by Asians and West Indians. By the end of the decade, therefore, the residential areas of Birmingham had been effectively segregated into an outer ring of good-quality newer housing, occupied almost exclusively by whites, and an inner ring of wards, inhabited by the separate black and Asian communities, comprising old and frequently substandard housing. Overt conflict over housing had, therefore, declined. Racial hostilities, on the other hand, had simply become institutionalized. The status fears of white residents living in areas threatened (as they saw it) by black multi-occupation gave way to outright resistance to purchasing property, or remaining in an area, where 20 per cent or more of the population were coloured.

Coloured immigration seems also to have had different effects in other localities. In Manchester, for example, the less buoyant though more varied local labour market drew in smaller numbers of immigrants to work in a much wider range of occupations. A high proportion were in fact engaged in middle-class employment. Nor was the local housing market as tight as in Birmingham. So, far from contributing to multi-occupation, immigrants actually helped reconstruct the single-occupation family houses that had been subdivided in the 1930s by white landlords catering for working-class English and Irish tenants. Not surprisingly, therefore, racial tension in Manchester during this period was markedly lower than in Birmingham. Research in Moss Side during the 1970s showed white Mancunians having 'a notably lower level of negative attitudes towards black people' than did native Brummies.

Studies in other British cities have also shed some doubts on the universality of the 'suburban ideal'. Rex and Moore themselves acknowledge that their argument rests on the implicit assumption that the various competing classes and ethnic groups are not entirely culturally distinct from one another: 'All participate in a socio-cultural system in which the middle-class way of life enjoys high prestige and in which the move to the suburbs is a built-in aspiration.' 'For the vast majority of the population', therefore, 'a transition to either the private suburban or the council estates has been considered in England a desirable destiny, and one which contrasts favourably with the lot of those who remain behind or succeed them as residents of the inner ring.' 'The city', as they put it, 'does to some extent share a unitary status-value system.'

However, research both in Birmingham and elsewhere has shown that matters may not be that simple. It has been pointed out many times, for example, that the housing behaviour of coloured immigrants is in part a reflection of the values they bring with them from their countries of origin. Badr Dahya, whose research in Birmingham overlapped in time the study by Rex and Moore, suggested that Pakistanis at least did not want to rent council housing because in their culture a landlord had a much higher social standing than a tenant. So, new arrivals from Pakistan bought older and larger houses in the inner city because they preferred to do so, not because they had no alternative. Nor did they experience discrimination in securing mortgages on the scale suggested by Rex and Moore. According to Dahya, many neither wanted nor needed long-term loans, because the particular houses to which they were attracted were already in small demand among whites and so fetched comparatively low prices. Immigrants may well have had a restricted choice of accommodation, but their behaviour is not simply to be understood in terms of the operation of the British housing market, since it is also a function of their own values and aspirations.

A study by Jon Davies and John Taylor, of the Rye Hill twilight zone in Newcastle-upon-Tyne in the mid 1960s, seems to underline Dahya's point. They found that many Indian and Pakistani landlords continued to let rooms after they had paid off their loans. Some had rejected offers of rehousing from the council; many owned more than one lodging-house; several possessed a lodging-house in Rye Hill, but were themselves living in accommodation elsewhere. Davies and Taylor conclude from these findings that Rex and Moore's thesis of colour discrimination fails to explain the behaviour of the immigrants to Newcastle. Far from being 'passive victims', many were dynamic and profitable landlords, who viewed the twilight world of slum clearances, compulsory purchase and redevelopment as a positive business opportunity. The discrimination discovered by the Sparkbrook team was, therefore, only one factor propelling the immigrant towards ownership of lodging-houses. 'To posit discrimination as the *only* cause of the immigrant style of property use would seem both to over-simplify the analysis and also deny the immigrant the capacity to manipulate the environment in which he lives.'

In my view, these sorts of criticism and observation do not seriously challenge the original analysis, since they were fully anticipated by the Sparkbrook researchers. Rex had earlier rejected the exclusively formal approach favoured by Davies and Taylor on the grounds that 'we can never know what significance to attach to replies to questionnaires about housing preference'. It is well known among sociologists, as he later pointed out, 'that certain preferences are not expressed simply because they are unrealistic'. If, for example, immigrants elect to buy inner-city lodging-houses, or rent rooms in them, even when alternative rented accommodation is available either from white landlords or the local authority, that may mean simply that they anticipate discrimination and do not want to make themselves vulnerable to this response. Without further research it is impossible to say conclusively whether Asian entrepreneurs were 'pushed' or 'jumped' into becoming landlords – but the most penetrating research to date, that of Rex and Moore in Sparkbrook, certainly seems to suggest that here, at least, the former is the more likely possibility.

Of course Birmingham is not a microcosm of Britain. But then the authors of *Race, Community, and Conflict* never suggested that it was. They note at the outset that coloured immigrants to many of England's northern cities found large numbers of modest back-to-back cottages for sale at prices they could readily afford. There were no such properties available in Birmingham, where almost the only houses readily accessible were the large, terraced, more expensive town properties formerly inhabited by the middle classes. Rex also observed that there would be 'considerable variations' in the pattern of housing-class conflict according to 'differences in the economic, political and cultural situation in different countries'. His model assumes a working-class movement which has secured some state housing; lack of political power on the part of immigrants and other disadvantaged and disorganized minorities; and, as we have seen, 'an aspiration to relatively detached family life in suburban conditions amongst all groups'. Where these assumptions do not hold, 'other conflict and status patterns may emerge', as for example in many continental European societies where middle classes and working classes alike prefer flatted accommodation near the city centre. The seven types of housing situation and attendant securities of tenure identified in Birmingham in the mid 1960s are specific to that city and time. 'Naturally', it is conceded that 'before they can be thought to have any kind of generalizable quality, they would have to be tested elsewhere.' Other cities, both here and abroad, will have different histories, other forms of housing stock and tenure, and different groups in conflict. Rex and Moore merely suggest, plausibly enough as it seems to me, that their basic model can be elaborated to take account of these differences, since 'what is common to all urban situations is that housing, and especially certain kinds of desirable housing, is a scarce resource and that different groups are differentially placed with regard to the available housing stock'.

In point of fact, therefore, little or no derivative research has been done which casts serious doubts on the picture that is painted of the housing and racial conflicts in Birmingham in the 1960s. However, most of the subsequent sociological debate has been conducted at a theoretical rather than an empirical level and has concentrated on the central concept of 'housing classes'. The problems here are more complex and the outcomes less clearcut. Moreover, discussion of the notion of housing classes quickly becomes unavoidably technical, as is invariably the case in similar disputes about the broader concept of social class from which it is derived. Nevertheless, without unduly oversimplifying matters, it can reasonably be claimed that three basic issues have been raised, and have yet to be resolved by the parties to this particular discussion.

The first of these concerns the *numbers* of housing classes to be distinguished in any urban social system. In fact, at the beginning of *Race, Community, and Conflict* the authors identify only five of the seven classes that are eventually listed, failing to distinguish at this stage between outright owner-occupiers and those buying a house on a mortgage, and between council tenants in long-life accommodation and those in slum stock. Rather confusingly, Rex and Moore have separately argued more recently that other classes could have been added (such as 'workers living in company hostels in which employers control their private and political lives'), and even that any group which is discriminated against in housing (including, for example, one-parent families) may constitute a housing class. Presumably, therefore, the number of classes is almost limitless. Those familiar with class theory will recognize that a parallel criticism is often made in respect of the Weberian claim that it is differential life-chances distributed by the capitalist market that distinguish the various social classes. If classes are defined in terms of the common market situation of individuals, then a potentially huge number of such groupings may be identified, since few individuals wield *identical* power in the labour market. Both the Weberian original and housing class derivative seem prone to an inherent pluralism which leaves class boundaries rather arbitrary and imprecise.

This is closely related to a further problem about the *criteria* for distinguishing the various housing classes. The model supposedly refers to inequalities in access to scarce housing resources, yet the resulting taxonomy identifies seven categories of current housing tenure. The problem here is that people who at the present moment share the same type of accommodation may not share a common capacity to gain access to a more favourable type in the future. My own housing history is a case in point. As a young university lecturer, in my first year or so of employment, I lived alongside skilled and unskilled manual workers in a row of small, terraced, rented properties. With increments and promotion my income has risen over the years. This has enabled me to raise the necessary deposits and loans so that, three houses later, I now find myself in a (suburban!) detached property, on which I am repaying a mortgage. My former neighbours, meanwhile, still rent their original houses, because they are at a relative disadvantage in the labour market, being mostly without paper qualifications and holding jobs lacking a formal career structure. The issues here, then, are rather similar to those that were raised in the discussion of social mobility in Chapter 2. It was pointed out in that context that routine clerical workers, for example, are a highly differentiated workforce rather than a cohesive mass. Today's clerks (Goldthorpe's class III) include both young, highly credentialled graduates gaining office-floor experience en route to managerial positions (class I), and men and women nearing retirement who have entered clerical work from manual jobs (classes VI and VII) late in life, and will stay there. Social class, as John Goldthorpe rightly insists, is about process as much as position. The concept of housing class obviously raises the same sorts of issue. At any one time a specific tenure group may include those who are trapped in a particular sort of accommodation and cannot move; those who choose to hold this form of tenure but could move out if they so wished; and those who, in the fullness of time, certainly will move on as soon as they acquire sufficient 'housing points' or savings. Moreover, the further question is then raised of the extent to which differential access to scarce housing depends upon the distribution of other kinds of scarce resources in society, most obviously the unequal distribution of wealth and wages involved in the system of economic production. To what extent is the competition between housing classes simply a reflection of the more general conflict between social classes in society as a whole?

This question, in its turn, raises one final problem with the concept of housing classes. Critics have argued that, since present accommodation does not necessarily reflect potential power in the system of housing allocation, then the tenure groups identified by Rex and

Moore are not housing *classes* but housing *status groups*: they mirror the distribution of life-styles rather than life-chances. Again, this criticism can be illuminated by reference back to the Weberian original. Weber, in fact, distinguished classes (groups of individuals who share similar life-chances as a result of their common market situation), from status groups, because the latter were defined instead by 'a specific, positive or negative, social estimation of honour', normally expressed in a particular style of life. Ethnic, religious, or caste distinctions, for example, may be said to embody status rather than class differences, if particular privileges (or sanctions) attach to membership of groups so defined. Arguably, therefore, the various types of tenure identified by Rex and Moore are different ways of consuming housing which are positively or negatively evaluated according to the life-styles associated with them. Council tenants in the suburban estate therefore share the same class situation as those paying rent to a private landlord in the zone of transition: neither own property that can be used to generate income. The differences between them are not differences in market power but in style of life – in other words, status differences. It follows, then, that the competition for housing is a status group conflict which may in fact cross-cut social class differences. Weber himself makes precisely this point when he notes that class position (common life-chances) provides no necessary basis for collective action. Whether or not members of a class recognize and act upon class interests as a class is, according to Weber, 'linked to general cultural conditions... and is especially linked to the transparency of the connections between the causes and the consequences of the class situation'. In fact, as he observes, classes tend not to be 'communities' or 'groups', so it is more often the case that the social sources of shared identity and collective action are located in status differences and similarities. For example, West Indian immigrants – home-owners and tenants alike – may unite to express their grievances against the state (as embodied in, let us say, the local police force), if they perceive it to be acting persistently in the interests only of the white majority.

It is obvious that all three of these criticisms stem from what one commentator has called the basic failure 'to explain the relationship between housing classes and social classes'. Rex and Moore would, of course, deny this charge; and, naturally enough, since my own theoretical inclinations are not dissimilar, I find myself tending towards their particular point of view. The fact that those currently occupying a given form of accommodation have different sorts of potential for improving their situation does not necessarily invalidate the concept of housing classes based on current tenure; it merely recognizes the existence of mobility between the different housing tenures. This is analogous to the situation in social class analysis which investigates both the relationship between, let us say, managers and workers, and the movement over time between these two groups.

The fact that some bosses have actually risen from the shop-floor does not deny the relationships of domination and subordination posited by the model of an occupational hierarchy. (Although it might raise some interesting questions about demographic and socio-political class formation among managers.) Similarly, my own ability to move out of rented accommodation and into home-ownership does not of itself negate the assumption that suburban housing is a desirable and scarce resource, nor challenge the fact that, for the majority of people, current housing tenure and power in the housing market tend to coincide at any one time. The relationship between housing-class mobility and housing-class conflicts, like that between social-class mobility and social-class conflicts, is simply an empirical issue which needs to be investigated appropriately. Nevertheless, the charge that Rex and Moore are merely debating status conflicts among groups which have an ambiguous relationship to social classes is potentially very damaging to their claim that housing-class struggles are 'the basic process underlying urban social interaction'. It also raises the broader issue of the connections between the specific theory of housing classes and more general sociological models of social systems as a whole. Since these general models attracted the explicit attention of Rex and Moore, but rarely that of their critics, it is worth considering this matter further.

IV

Almost all critics of the Sparkbrook study address themselves to one or other of its two principal substantive themes; namely, those of housing classes, on the one hand, and race relations on the other. Discussion has tended to concentrate, therefore, on the issues that were identified in the previous section. Does the experience of Birmingham provide a model for the explanation of the ecology of all other urban centres? Are racial conflicts in the city always due to the competition for scarce housing? Can housing-class differences be reduced to relationships of social class more generally? Despite the fact that Rex and Moore answer all of these questions clearly in the negative, subsequent commentators have persistently treated such matters as if they were issues wholly overlooked in the original report, and therefore somehow indicative of theoretical naïveté on the part of the Birmingham team. Often, for example, the research in Spark-brook is assessed as part of the so-called urban managerialist perspective on the city. This label has been applied to a number of Weberian-inspired studies in urban sociology carried out since the mid 1960s, all of which in some way make the broad claim that the managers of the urban system (planners, local government officials, landlords and others) can exert an independent influence on the distribution of scarce urban resources, and so modify (reduce or reinforce) inequalities stemming from the differential rewards of the occupational structure. Critics of this approach invariably claim that, to quote Patrick Dunleavy,

> [its] built-in focus on mediating institutions... generates a possibility of seriously misleading conclusions in which broader structural constraints and determinants of the local or regional context are lost to sight, and excessively individualistic and voluntaristic accounts of urban management are given on a one-off, non-cumulative basis.

I find such charges deeply ironic, since politically the most contentious section of *Race, Community, and Conflict* is the chapter on 'Policy Alternatives', in which the authors make eleven policy suggestions – all but two of which explicitly require action on the part of central government, precisely in order to change the structural context of race relations, housing policy and urban planning. They include, for example, the proposals that the state should raise capital to expand the council-house building programme; should impose on local authorities a nondiscriminatory 'code of housing allocation'; should legislate to liberalize the rules governing immigration into Britain; and give immediate support for research into urban deterioration so that inner-city areas can be properly redeveloped. These hardly suggest that Rex and Moore somehow lost sight of the broader structural constraints on the local urban manager whom they interviewed. Indeed, the Sparkbrook team's intervention into the field of public policy brings us back squarely to the question of the relationship between the theory of housing classes in particular, and more general sociological models of national societies as a whole. In discussing policy alternatives Rex and Moore are deliberately drawing attention to the fact that alternatives do indeed exist. These policy differences tend to reflect conflicts of interests and values between the various parties to the debate. Such conflicts tend to be ignored in functionalist analyses of society, and to be oversimplified by Marxists. Functionalism and Marxism are, therefore, the principal targets of Rex and Moore's sociology of the zone of transition.

This point has been entirely overlooked in the debate about the Sparkbrook study. It is hard to see why this should be so since the researchers themselves are quite explicit about their theoretical intentions. The introductory chapter of *Race, Community, and Conflict* contains a lengthy critique of the functionalist (predominantly conservative) theory which dominated American sociology during the 1940s and 1950s. Functionalists, as is pointed out, tend to assume that any recurrent human behaviour can satisfactorily be explained in terms of the contribution which it makes to the maintenance of the social system as a whole. Social institutions arise because they meet a societal or system need and are therefore in the general interest. Thus, the functional explanation for social inequality assumes that unequal compensation is both necessary and desirable, in order to motivate people to do unequally difficult occupational tasks. In the absence of differential evaluations and rewards human laziness would simply result in social disorganization. (For example, if social security payments approach the level of minimum wages, then the unemployed will lack the necessary incentive to search for jobs.) Social inequality is therefore positively functional and indeed inevitable in any society. Rex and Moore object to this form of sociological explanation on the grounds that 'in emphasizing sociological determinism it allows too litte scope for human agency and appears to affirm that what is, must necessarily be'. By contrast, they argue that 'the determinants of an ongoing social system are to be found in the varied and sometimes conflicting interests of the typical actors in that system'. Clearly, therefore, what is functional (desirable or necessary) from the point of view of one actor is dysfunctional (undesirable or unnecessary) from the point of view of another. Who, for example, determines that the estate agent should earn more, and just so much more, than the nurse? Are the tasks of the former more difficult, and therefore socially more useful or necessary, than those performed by the latter? I doubt whether many nurses would accept this evaluation of the relative worth of the two professions.

However, Rex and Moore are quick also to emphasize that 'the existence of conflicting group interests does not mean that there is a perpetual war of all against all, or of class against class'. They reject the Marxist tendency to interpret all conflict in society as a manifestation of an underlying class struggle. Marxists, as Rex notes, will argue that 'housing classes do nothing more than reflect the class struggle in industry'. Of course, there is some connection between the two: few industrialists live on council estates and few unskilled manual workers have large detached houses in inner suburbia. 'But it is also the case', he continues, 'that among those who share the same relation to the means of production there may be considerable differences in ease of access to housing. This is part of the "superstructure" which manifestly takes on a life of its own.' Black nurses, for example, may find it considerably more difficult to raise a bank-loan than do white nurses. In any case, Marxism embodies its own form of functionalism, since Marxists generally assume that the structures of capitalist society are tailored to suit the specific requirements of capital. Inequality is therefore functional, not for the society as a whole, but for the ruling or economically dominant class in particular.

A decade later, therefore, Moore could justifiably claim that he and Rex 'rejected a functionalist approach to the study of Sparkbrook, recognised that there was some degree of more or less integrated "order" about the city, and that a measure of consensus about, for example, social studies might be found.' 'But', he continues, 'order and consensus were themselves treated as problematic and as the outcome of domination and subordination or of truce in conflict. Order and consensus are not given, they have to be discovered and explained, not used as the basis for explanation. We began therefore from an action frame of reference.' A functionalist would speak of the interest of society (or Birmingham) and adopt as a starting point the values of the majority, or the politically dominant group. A Marxist would start from the assumption that the structure of social relations in the city reflects class formation and class struggle. Rex and Moore, on the other hand, began 'by considering the goals of typical actors representing the various host and immigrant groups'. 'It is', they maintain, 'out of the clash of interests, the conflicts and the truces between these groups that Birmingham society emerges.'

Mention of the 'action frame of reference' indicates that a rather fundamental theoretical point is being made here. It is not difficult to see why. Shortly before the research in Sparkbrook was conceived, Rex published what was in due course to become an acknowledged classic in social theory, a short text on the *Key Problems of Sociological Theory*. Much of this was devoted to a critique of functionalist and Marxist theory. At the same time it offered an exposition and defence of the action frame of reference. Clearly, therefore, the argument of *Race, Community, and Conflict* is an attempt to apply the action perspective to the study of a particular empirical problem.

Sociologists working within the action frame of reference start from the assumption that actors have purposes or ends they wish to achieve; that they manipulate certain means under certain conditions to achieve these ends; and that the conditions are distinguished from the means by the fact that, although they are relevant to the attainment of the end, they are in some part beyond the control of the actor. Of course, not all action is purposive in this sense. Some action is nonrational or affective. In these cases, as Rex puts it,

> we should say that the behaviour was explained if there was evidence that the observed individual desired a particular state of affairs and also accepted certain ritual rules as to the way in which that state of affairs should be attained; or if there was evidence of the individual being in a particular emotional state and accepting certain forms of behaviour as an appropriate means of expression of that state.

Finally, action theorists acknowledge that some human behaviour is best explained in terms of a misinformed, or simply irrational plan of action. The various norms, controls and sanctions which induce an actor to behave in specific ways are then conditions of his or her

action. These include systems of economic allocation, power distribution, ultimate values, religious beliefs and rituals. The difference
between this approach and those of the functionalist or Marxist is that
the ultimate referent of the explanation which it yields is clear and
unambiguous in a way in which the categories 'needs of the social
structure' or 'needs of capital' are not.

Action theorists also postulate that social systems will involve
conflict between, rather than consensus about, the purposes and ends
of human behaviour. Such conflict may lie anywhere between the
extremes of open violence in battle and peaceful negotiation in the
market-place. Societies are therefore plural rather than unitary
phenomena. Groups of people seeking the same or similar ends tend
to come together in pursuit of these; and also, in so far as they might
be adversely affected by them, to oppose the interests of other social
groups. In capitalist societies, for example, these groups are often
defined by common class interests. Such groups may become relatively self-contained social systems for their members. Or, as Rex
puts it, 'the activities of the members take on sociological meaning
and must be explained by reference to the group's interests in the
conflict situation.' Relations between groups are usually marked by an
unequal balance of power so that one group emerges as dominant.
Naturally enough, it will attempt to legitimize its position in various
ways, although some or all of the members of the subordinate group
may reject this claim and endeavour to organize resistance against it.

This perspective, according to Rex,

> would appear to provide a useful framework in terms of which
> many important contemporary social situations might be ana-
> lyzed. The classification of basic conflict situations, the study of
> the emergence and structure of conflict groups, the problem of
> the legitimation of power, the study of the agencies of indoctrina-
> tion and socialization, the problem of the ideological conflicts in
> post-revolutionary situations and in situations of compromise
> and truce, the study of the relations between norms and systems
> of power – all have their place within it.

It is certainly appropriate to the analysis of the zone of transition,
which as we have seen, houses a mixed population (two-thirds
English and one-third immigrant) of varying degrees of permanence
and having conflicting interests. Much of the analysis of *Race,
Community, and Conflict* is a straightforward attempt to determine how
these conflicts are expressed. Rex and Moore demonstrate clearly, for
example, that many of the formal associations in the area, including
tenants', immigrants' and political organizations, are used either
exclusively or in part as a means of organizing to advance special
group interests. Others, such as churches, are inhibited from doing so

(again, to varying degrees) by universalist ideals contained in their charters, or by their national and international affiliations. In some measure the interaction between these various groups is regulated by the police, courts, or (occasional and limited) use of violence. More commonly, however, compromises are painstakingly worked out between the leaders of the various ethnic, class and other groups in the area. This, as Rex and Moore found out, was largely facilitated by the numerous community associations in south-east Birmingham, most notably the Sparkbrook Association, which had not yet succeeded in breaking down the barriers between the various ethnic groups, or integrating them into a nonracial community, but had at least established 'an embryonic concept of Sparkbrook citizenship'.

The important point here is that the Birmingham study starts from the empirically well-founded proposition that social organizations, institutions and structures arise out of the often conflicting interests, needs, aspirations and values of individuals or groups. They are, therefore, most adequately to be explained in these terms. Social outcomes reflect the balance of negotiation, compromise, power and conflict between competing interests. But, contrary to the views of functional sociologists, there are *always* alternative outcomes. Thus, as Rex and Moore convincingly demonstrate, the crowding together of coloured immigrants to Birmingham in the 1960s into multi-occupied lodging-houses does not demonstrate, as many whites at the time believed, that blacks are somehow predisposed towards low domestic standards. This sort of folk-myth can be extremely dangerous, especially in societies with fragile democratic institutions, as the tragic example of Nazi Germany and the myth of Aryan Supremacy clearly demonstrate. Or, rather closer to home, one might predict – as the authors of the Sparkbrook study did in the mid 1960s – that 'the long-term destiny of a city which frustrates the desire [of immigrants] to improve their status by segregationist policies is some sort of urban riot.' One is tempted at this juncture, with the inner-city riots of the early 1980s still fresh in one's mind, to suggest that few of those in authority genuinely want to see sociologists more involved in shaping and informing public policy. All too often, the message from policy-relevant sociological research is not one that the policy-makers themselves care to hear, so they choose simply to ignore it; or, as seems to be the case in the present political climate, they shoot the messenger instead.

8 The rise and fall of the mods

I

By coincidence, Robert Moore was one of the professors interviewed by Alan Rusbridger for 'Who needs sociologists?', the *Guardian* newspaper article which so irritated me that I was prompted to devise this book by way of a reply. Moore, in a spirited denial of Rusbridger's accusations, maintained that British sociology had a 'world reputation' and was 'enormously healthy and widely respected'. Rusbridger remained frankly unconvinced. 'The pressure is on', he observed, 'for more research to be applied, empirical, relevant, policy-based and preferably dove-tailing with another discipline such as medicine or business studies.'

In point of fact, the six studies I have discussed thus far are, to varying degrees, 'applied' and 'policy-based' – or, as Rusbridger would have it, 'relevant'. I have argued, for example, that the seemingly academic concerns of John Goldthorpe and David Lockwood, or Tom Burns and G. M. Stalker, nevertheless have clear implications for social policy in liberal democracies. Goldthorpe's research on occupational mobility suggests that governments will fail to achieve their professed aim of minimizing class influences on social selection, if they persist in assuming that economic advances alone will be sufficient to generate greater social equality, and thus a more open society. Similarly, the *Affluent Worker Study* yields insights into the attitudes of manual workers that make economists' assumptions about industrial behaviour seem simplistic by comparison, as is evident from sociological as against economic analyses of inflationary wage demands. Burns and Stalker's investigation of the management of technological innovation stands in a similar relationship to much of contemporary management science. Obviously, the books by Peter Townsend, Brian Jackson and Dennis Marsden, and John Rex and Robert Moore offer rather more explicit advice to policy-makers in the fields of social welfare, education, and race relations respectively. Indeed, as we have seen, *Race, Community, and Conflict* was the first study in the Survey of Race Relations in Britain – a project specifically devised not only to assemble information but also to advance proposals concerning Commonwealth immigration into this country.

The following three chapters grasp this nettle of so-called relevance still more firmly, since they focus on a trio of sociological books, each of which has a direct application in the design and implementation of public policy. They address the social problems posed by youth subcultures, cultic religious beliefs, and mental illness respectively. The subject of this chapter is Stanley Cohen's detailed case-study of the Mods and Rockers in Britain during the mid 1960s.

II

Folk Devils and Moral Panics was published in 1972. It is probably the most accessible and least obviously academic of the ten studies discussed here. The semi-popular style of presentation belies the rigour of the research. Cohen lists the main sources from which his data are taken in an Appendix to his argument, and these testify to an impressive research programme, the main details of which have been reproduced in Table 8.1. The book may read like a novel but it is, in fact, a thorough and carefully researched analysis of a considerable body of evidence. The accusation I have sometimes heard levelled against it – that it is merely a piece of pop sociology attempting to justify the hooliganism of ungrateful adolescents – could, therefore, scarcely be further from the truth.

Unless one is already familiar with the episodes and characters described by Cohen, his apparent interest in (invariably wet) English Bank Holiday weekends and rather unfashionable South and East Coast holiday resorts, might seem to be little more than a charming sociological eccentricity. However, older readers and followers of postwar subcultural styles will know that these times and places were crucial to the whole Mods and Rockers phenomenon, and to the 'moral panic' which these 'folk devils' prompted. 'Modernism', for the uninitiated, was a form of youth culture which flourished during the 1960s. In its early stages it was associated with small rythmn-and-blues groups, Expresso bars and an Italianate style of 'sharp dressing' which led to the modern, modernist and Mod epithets. Based on London clubs such as the Flamingo and Marquee, it had already reached one of its peaks by 1963. During the mid and later 1960s, however, the culture was both diffused and diluted by commercialism. Much wider associations were quickly built up: with Carnaby Street, Cathy McGowan, Twiggy, boutique fashions, and transistor radios permanently tuned to the pirate radio-station Caroline. By the middle of 1964 there were at least half a dozen specifically Mod magazines, and a television programme reporting the Mod music scene (*Ready, Steady, Go*), which also organized a famous Mod Ball in Wembley. 'This was the time', as Cohen notes, 'when whole streams within schools, sometimes whole schools and even whole areas and housing estates were talked of as having "gone Mod".'

At the same time the Rockers were also evolving as a distinctive subcultural grouping. These were the youngsters who saw the new

Table 8.1 Sources of data for *Folk Devils and Moral Panics*

1. Documentary

(a) Press references to the Mods and Rockers during the research period (Easter 1964 to September 1966), at both national and local level, and tape recordings of most national radio and television broadcasts over the Bank Holiday weekends during these years.

(b) A special collection of press cuttings, compiled for the Margate Corporation by an agency, covering the incidents at Margate over Whitsun 1964. These include 724 separate items covering editorial and columnist comment, interviews with public figures, letters to the press, etc.

(c) Local publications with a restricted circulation, such as parish newsletters, council minutes, annual reports of voluntary associations, etc.

(d) Miscellaneous national documents, including *Hansard* reports of the relevant parliamentary debates in the House of Commons, and House of Lords.

(e) Letters and reports received by the National Council of Civil Liberties alleging malpractices by police or courts during the various incidents.

(f) Re-analysis of interview schedules used in a survey of 44 youths convicted in the Margate magistrates court during Whitsun 1964.

2. Original

(a) Two pilot questionnaires administered to a group of 19 trainee probation officers in December 1964. These covered attitudes to the Mods and Rockers – perceptions of causes, solutions, and so forth.

(b) Interviews and informal discussions in Brighton, Margate and Hastings in 1964 after the first wave of incidents with editors of local newspapers, publicity department officials and a selection of local hoteliers, shop assistants, bus conductors, taxi-drivers and newspaper vendors.

(c) Interviews with, and/or postal questionnaires completed by Members of Parliament for the areas involved, local politicians and those actively involved in action groups set up to work with the Mods and Rockers.

(d) Participation as a volunteer worker for one of these action groups, the Brighton Archways Venture, over three Bank Holiday weekends. (This was a government-funded project, staffed by social workers, designed to provide cheap accommodation and other help for young people visiting Brighton at holiday weekends.)

(e) Sixty-five interviews, obtained on a quota-sample basis, with members of the public standing on Brighton promenade or pier, and watching the Mods and Rockers, on two days over the Whitsun Bank Holiday in 1965. Again these covered perceptions and evaluations of the proceedings: of the type of teenagers believed to be involved, of the police handling of events, of probable causes and solutions, etc.

(f) On-the-spot observations at every Bank Holiday in 1965 and 1966 in either Brighton or Great Yarmouth: of the crowds, police activity, reactions of local residents and visitors, and subsequent court proceedings.

(g) A survey of attitudes to delinquency, carried out in a London borough between summer 1965 and summer 1966, among a sample of 133 'social control agents' including councillors, lawyers, magistrates, social workers, religious leaders, headmasters, etc.

(h) Twenty-five essays written by third- and fourth-form pupils from a school in the East End of London, entitled 'Mods and Rockers', and set by the English teacher as part of normal course work.

Source: Folk Devils and Moral Panics, Appendix.

teenage image personified by the Mods as altogether too respectable. Their own heroes were the early 'ton-up' boys of the motorway. The Rockers, therefore, were associated with black leather jackets, metal studs and motor-bikes. Their favourite haunts were the transport cafés of the motorway, such as The Busy Bee and The Ace at the southern end of the M1, and their musical loyalty was to the crude early rock from which they took their name. To the outsider, the Rockers appeared the less glamorous of the two groups, seeming as they did to be both more working-class and more loutish. They were, as Cohen notes, a less marketable property than their fashionable, club-going, music-oriented Mod counterparts. They were also by far the numerically smaller of the two youth cultures. Already, by the time of Cohen's research, modernism had become such a large and diffuse phenomenon that the so-called Mod was scarcely recognizable as a distinct type at all. By 1965, for example, youth workers in Brighton distinguished at least three groups:

> the scooter boys (dressed in plain but smart trousers and pullovers, plus anoraks, often trimmed with fur; usually uninterested in violence, but involved with the Law in a range of driving offences); the hard Mods (wearing heavy boots, jeans with braces, short hair, the precursors of the skinheads, usually prowling in large groups with the appearance of being jumpy, unsure of themselves, on the paranoic edge, heavily involved in any disturbance); and the smooth Mods (usually older and better off, sharply dressed, moving in small groups and usually looking for a bird).

Of course the Mods and Rockers were not the first of the British postwar adolescent youth cultures. That title must be reserved for the Teddy Boys of the 1950s, worshippers of Elvis Presley and 'Rock Around the Clock', whose drape-suit style was a parody of the Edwardian dandy. However, what made the Mods and Rockers especially noteworthy, and what gives them their standing as one of the cultural markers by which the 1960s in Britain will forever be remembered, was that they 'initially registered in the public consciousness not just as the appearance of new social types, but as actors in a particular episode of collective behaviour... the regular series of disturbances which took place at English seaside resorts between 1964 and 1966.' Thus, as Cohen observes,

> the public image of these folk devils was invariably tied up to a number of highly visual scenarios associated with their appearance: youths chasing across the beach, brandishing deckchairs over their heads, running along the pavements, riding on scooters or bikes down the streets, sleeping on the beaches and so on.

This sort of behaviour attracted the prolonged attention of the mass media, police, courts and politicians, all of whom saw it as a serious threat to social order. It prompted, in other words, a 'moral panic'.

Cohen argues that all societies appear periodically to be subject to such panics:

> a condition, episode, person or group of persons emerges to become defined as a threat to societal values and interests; its nature is presented in a stylized and stereotypical fashion by the mass media; the moral barricades are manned by editors, bishops, politicians and other right-thinking people; socially accredited experts pronounce their diagnoses and solutions; ways of coping are evolved or (more often) resorted to; the condition then disappears, submerges or deteriorates.

In modern Britain, for example, these panics have often accompanied the emergence of various forms of youth culture, sometimes working-class but more recently middle-class or student-based, whose behaviour is seen as deviant or delinquent. The Teddy Boys, Mods and Rockers, Hell's Angels, Skinheads, Hippies and Punks have all prompted such a reaction. Similar panics have been associated with student militancy, football hooliganism, the drugs problem, vandalism, mugging, and most recently the spread of the AIDS virus. During these panics, according to Cohen, the target-groups are identified, not just by their participation in particular events (for example, riots), or in particular disapproved forms of behaviour (such as drug-taking), but as distinguishable social types. Thus, 'in the gallery of types that society erects to show its members which roles should be avoided and which should be emulated, these groups have occupied a constant position as folk-devils: visible reminders of what we should not be.'

Clearly, therefore, Cohen's method is that of the detailed case-study. 'Who on earth', he asks rhetorically, 'is still worried about the Mods and Rockers? Who – some might even ask – *were* the Mods and Rockers?' In one sense, of course, it does not really matter since, as he puts it, 'the processes by which moral panics and folk devils are generated do not date'. Were Cohen writing his book today he might more appropriately use football hooliganism or mugging to illustrate his arguments. Indeed, he concludes his analysis on a pessimistic note, with the prediction that

> more moral panics will be generated and other, as yet nameless, folk devils will be created. This is not because such developments have an inexorable inner logic, but because our society as present structured will continue to generate problems for some of its members – like working-class adolescents – and then condemn whatever solution these groups find.

This conclusion rests on the thesis that any future collective episodes of juvenile deviance will, like those of the past, not only generate moral panics but also rely upon them for their growth. The clear implication here is that, at least in some cases, social control helps to *create* deviance rather than *eliminate* it. How does Cohen come to arrive at such a seemingly paradoxical conclusion?

III

Perhaps the best way to answer this question is simply to describe the events that constitute Cohen's data. Then, in the following section, we can examine the sociological theories of 'labelling' and 'deviance amplification' which he brings to bear on this evidence. By separating (rather artificially) the ethnography and the interpretation in this way I can perhaps convey something of the flavour of the undoubtedly colourful events that are the subject of Cohen's analysis.

His story begins in Clacton, a small East Coast resort with a strictly limited range of facilities and amusements for young people, on a particularly cold and wet Easter Sunday in 1964. On that day, local shopkeepers had become irritated by the lack of business, and the young weekend visitors to the town rather bored. Their annoyance at the weather was fanned by rumours that barmen and café-owners were refusing to serve some of them. A few groups scuffled on the pavements, some stones were thrown and windows broken, while a number of those who had arrived on motor-bikes and scooters started cruising up and down the streets in groups. A couple of beach huts were wrecked and one boy fired a starting pistol in the air. During the course of that Sunday and the following Monday the Mods' and Rockers' factions – 'a division initially based on clothing and life styles, later rigidified, but at that time not fully established' – started separating out. According to Cohen, the overall effect of large numbers of people crowding into the streets, the noise, everyone's general irritation, and the actions of an unprepared and undermanned police force, was to make these two days 'unpleasant, oppressive and sometimes frightening'.

On Monday morning, almost every national newspaper in the country carried front-page reports on the initial events, reinforced during the following days by editorials demanding firm action to forestall repetitions elsewhere. The headlines of the time indicate the contents of these articles: 'Day of Terror by Scooter Groups' (*Daily Telegraph*), 'Youngsters Beat Up Town – 97 Leather Jacket Arrests' (*Daily Express*), 'Wild Ones Invade Seaside – 97 Arrests' (*Daily Mirror.*) Straight reporting of the events was interlaced with theorizing about the motives of those involved: teenagers were described as 'drunk with notoriety', 'hell bent for destruction', 'lacking respect for authority', and so forth. The Home Secretary was reportedly 'being urged' (though it was never specified quite by whom) to hold an inquiry and to take firm counter-measures. A substantial part of Cohen's text is taken up in subjecting this media response to systematic scrutiny, both in respect of the initial incident, and with regard to subsequent similar events elsewhere including: checking the internal consistency of the reports, their factual accuracy and rhetorical content; and interviewing eye-witnesses, participants and local residents.

The first obvious feature of the reporting was that it exaggerated and distorted the events themselves: headlines were sensational and vocabulary melodramatic. Constant repetition of phrases such as 'orgy of destruction', 'beating up the town', and 'screaming mob', conjured up images of besieged towns in which innocent holiday-makers were trying to escape marauding mobs. Thus, local papers in Brighton during Whitsun 1964 referred to 'deserted beaches' and 'elderly holidaymakers' threatened by 'screaming teenagers'. Only by scanning the rest of the paper, or by being present on the spot, could one know that, in fact, during the holiday in question, the beaches were deserted because the weather was particularly bad, and the holiday-makers actually present were there in large part to watch the Mods and Rockers. Cohen documents this sort of over-reporting at length. For example, headlines about Mods and Rockers were frequently misleading, using 'violence' to announce a story which reported that no violence had occurred. One beach hut overturned became 'beach huts were overturned'. The same incident was often reported twice to look like two separate occurrences. Stories which were known to be false were nevertheless widely circulated.

To bring the extent of such exaggeration and distortion home to his readers, Cohen compiled an inventory of characteristics said to accompany the events, including the following key elements: that they involved *gangs*, primarily the *Mods and Rockers* themselves; who *invaded from London* on *motor-bikes and scooters*; were *affluent* and *classless*; *deliberately intent* on *violence and vandalism*; and who inflicted *extensive damage* and *loss of trade* on the local area. It would be tedious to document Cohen's detailed repudiation of these claims in full. By drawing on a variety of types of evidence, most of which are cited in Table 8.1 above, he shows convincingly that they were all without foundation. Not only was there no evidence of any structured gangs in the crowds, but the Mod–Rocker polarization was institutionalized only during the subsequent moral panic about the seaside events, and partly as a consequence of the initial publicity. At Clacton, for example, the longstanding and diffuse rivalry between local and London youths was a much more significant element. Furthermore, throughout the entire period of the research most of the young people coming to the resorts identified with neither group. The bulk of day-trippers were indeed from London, but this was simply the traditional Bank Holiday pattern, and in any case many of the Rockers came from the local villages around the resorts. Only a small minority owned scooters or motor-bikes. The average take-home pay of those charged in the courts was well below the national average and the majority of offenders were working-class. The typical Rocker was an unskilled manual worker and the typical Mod a semi-skilled manual worker. The bulk of the young people present at the resorts came, not to make trouble, but in the hope that there would be some trouble to watch. The total amount of violence was relatively small. Only one-tenth of those arrested at Clacton were charged with offences involving violence. At Brighton, Easter 1965, only seven of the seventy arrests were for assault. The most common offences throughout were 'Wilfully Obstructing the Police in the Execution of Their Duty' and 'Use of Threatening Behaviour whereby a Breach of the Peace was Likely to be Occasioned'. Overall, the cost of damage was ascertained to be little greater than at ordinary Bank Holiday weekends, and the loss of trade (where it occurred) never exceeded what would have been expected due to the accompanying inclement weather alone. Many of the holiday-makers present, when interviewed by Cohen and others, cheerfully admitted that they had in fact been attracted to the resorts specifically by the disturbances themselves: they had 'come to the seaside to see what all this fun is on Bank Holidays'.

Another important element of the media coverage was 'the implicit assumption, present in virtually every report, that what had happened was inevitably going to happen again'. Headlines asked 'Where will they strike next?' and demanded to know 'What can be done about it?' Countless television, radio and newspaper items suggested that one or other camp had threatened revenge 'next time'. Relatively innocent interviews with either a Mod or Rocker – 'Southend and places won't let us in any more. It will get difficult here and so next year we'll probably go to Ramsgate or Hastings' (*Daily Express*, 30 March 1964) – became the basis for predictions of forthcoming disasters. Even when these were not fulfilled, a story was created by reporting a non-event, as for example when a group of Rockers quietly sat through a theatrical performance in an East Coast resort ('Fears When Ton-up Boys Walked in Groundless', *East Anglian Daily Times*, 30 May 1966). In this way, media reports established predictions 'whose truth was guaranteed by the way in which the event, non-event or pseudo-event it referred to was reported'.

These reports also formed the basis for a process of what Cohen calls 'symbolization'. Words themselves ('Clacton', 'Mod', 'scooter') acquired new symbolic powers (as in 'We don't want another Clacton here'). Thus, for example, the word 'Mod' came to symbolize a certain status (delinquent or deviant); objects (clothing, hairstyle, scooters) came to symbolize the word; and, finally, the objects themselves became symbolic of the status. This technique was used in the media to give a clarity and interpretation to events which they often did not warrant. One particularly bizarre example was the headline in the *Dublin Evening Press* (18 May 1964): 'Terror Comes to English Resorts. Mutilated Mod Dead in Park'. The 'mutilated Mod' in question was in fact a man aged 21–5, purportedly wearing a 'mod jacket', found stabbed in Birmingham (well over a hundred miles away), on the Saturday morning before the resort incidents referred to in the first part of the headline actually occurred.

In this way, as Cohen observes, all the information was made available for placing the Mods and Rockers in the gallery of contemporary folk devils:

> the putative deviation had been assigned from which further stereotyping, myth making and labelling could proceed; the expectation was created that this form of deviation would certainly recur; a wholly negative symbolization in regard to the Mods and Rockers and objects associated with them had been created.

This inventory of events and images elicited a public commentary built around certain recurring attitudinal themes and opinions. Editors, politicians, magistrates, police officers, local activists and others articulated a number of (sometimes contradictory) commonsensical theories about the nature of the deviance and the causes of the behaviour in question. Most attributed an enormous social significance to the appearance of the Mods and Rockers, comparing them to 'the marauding army of Vikings going through Europe massacring and plundering, living by slaughter and rapacity' (The *Star*, Sheffield, 18 May 1964); to Britain's wartime enemies of the 1940s; or to the infamous football riot in Peru during which 300 spectators died in a dispute over a disallowed goal. According to the *Police Review* of June 1964, for example, Clacton, Margate and Lima had one element in common – 'restraint normal to civilised society was thrown aside'.

Numerous prophecies of doom followed. Members of Parliament warned that things would get worse until 'steps were taken'. Fantasies were projected about what could have happened, or might still yet happen, and these tended to feature visions of mass civil disobedience and mob rule. The Mods and Rockers became part of a generalized problem (a social trend) in which, to quote Cohen, 'pregnant schoolgirls, C.N.D. marches, beatniks, long hair, contraceptives in slot machines, purple hearts and smashing up telephone kiosks were all inextricably intertwined'. The behaviour of the youngsters at the seaside thus reflected 'the way society itself was going': the decline in religion, coddling by the welfare state, the influence of the do-gooder's approach, and lack of a sense of purpose in the country as a whole. As the *Tribune* (10 April 1964) put it. 'There is something rotten in the state of Britain and the recent hooliganism at Clacton is only one manifestation of it.'

These beliefs and models of explanation then informed the reaction of the organized system of social control. According to Cohen, the agents of social control 'responded in terms of certain images of the deviant group and, in turn, helped to create the images that maintained these folk devils'. The police and the courts, in particular, not only reacted to the moral panic about the Mods and Rockers – their activities helped sustain it. For example, the relevant authorities were 'sensitized' by the reports of the initial incidents, so 'more notice was taken of any type of rule breaking that looked like hooliganism and, moreover... these actions were invariably classified as part of the Mods and Rockers phenomenon'. A sort of mass hysteria built up, so that in the week after Margate (Whitsun, 1964), for example, similar occurrences were reported from a host of scattered localities including Coventry, Bristol, Nottingham and, of all places, Windsor. Most of the incidents of hooliganism were real enough; the point is that public hyper awareness concerning the Mods and Rockers determined the way they were reported and, indeed, the fact that they were reported at all. Similarly, any form of disruption involving teenagers during the few days following a Bank Holiday was invariably described as a 'revenge battle'. Magistrates dealing with routine dance-hall brawls would note that the participants wore 'Mod clothes' and pronounce punishments accordingly. The police began to anticipate trouble, indeed specifically to be on the lookout for Mod-and-Rocker-type incidents, in order to stamp on them quickly. Suspicious-looking youths were kept on the move, refused admission to the resorts, or pinned into one place. 'Potential troublemakers' (such as scooter riders) were harassed (by constantly being stopped to produce their licences) in order to discourage them from remaining in town. Youngsters asleep in their legitimately parked cars would wake in the morning to find themselves surrounded by portable 'No Waiting' signs and police instructing them to move on. Crowds sheltering from the rain in arcades were identified as potential sources of trouble and quickly dispersed into the wet. Individuals who looked like Mods or Rockers were physically separated and broken up into small groups of purportedly homogeneous appearance. Those who objected or refused to 'move along' were immediately arrested as troublemakers. In many (well-documented) cases, 'purely on the basis of symbolization, young people were in fact forced out of town – either by being given "free lifts", or by being turned away from the [railway] station'. According to Cohen, a public drama was enacted, involving ceremonies of public degradation for arrested youths, by making them appear in court without belts to hold up their trousers, by subjecting them to strip-searches in police stations, or force-marching them in a cordon through the streets to the railway station.

The courts then extended the drama and escalated the whole process. In the event of there being large numbers of arrests over a Bank Holiday weekend, this was used as evidence of the need for stiffer penalties; while, conversely, the absence of trouble was taken as proof of their deterrent value. The press dutifully reported the increasingly harsh sentences – but very few of the successful subsequent appeals. Remand in custody was used in punitive and arbitrary fashion against large numbers of those charged. Parents attending the hearings were often rudely addressed and lectured to by the officials in charge. The proceedings thus took on a ritual flavour; invariably they were held at unusual times; advertised several weeks in advance of the Bank Holiday and the anticipated attendant incidents; overlooked by public galleries crowded with spectators, who 'attended in the spirit of a gladiatorial display' and participated enthusiastically in the proceedings by applauding sentences, homilies and pronouncements of guilt. Relatives were sometimes told in advance to bring along enough money for the fines – so the question of guilt or innocence did not usually take up much of the court's time.

Meanwhile, in the society at large, the alleged deviance was itself being widely exploited. Special Mod boutiques, dance-halls and discotheques were opened. At least one of the most prominent of these had a white line painted down the middle of the floor to separate Mods and Rockers. Some of the same seaside shopkeepers who had protested about the loss of trade allegedly caused by the disturbances were nevertheless selling consumer goods advertised by means of the very group images – such as 'The Latest Mod Sunglasses' – which they purported to despise. The *Daily Mail* ran a quiz ('Are You a Mod or Rocker?') and other newspapers and magazines contained regular features on Mod and Rocker styles. In this way, as Cohen notes, commercial interests widened the division between the two groups by exaggerating their consumer differences. 'Mod-hunting', according to one reporter, became 'a respectable, almost crowded subprofession of journalism'. Political radicals hailed the two groups as the *avant-garde* of the anarchist revolution. Conversely, and more commonly, a whole series of moral entrepreneurs made public (and much publicized) requests for more funds to prevent the Mods' and Rockers' 'disease' from spreading, usually for specific organizations to which they themselves happened to be affiliated: the President of the National Association of Chief Educational Welfare Officers called for more officers to be recruited, youth-club leaders requested additional facilities in youth clubs, and so forth. In short, by the mid 1960s, the Mods and Rockers had become folk devils – or, very occasionally, folk heroes – throughout the length and breadth of the British Isles.

IV

Cohen's interpretation of these data is informed by the now established, but at that time highly innovative, transactional or interactionist approach to deviance. In particular, he applies to them the theories of labelling and deviance amplification, both of which were developed during the revolution in criminology associated with interactionism in the mid 1960s. (Other theories also inform the analysis, including specific propositions about crowd behaviour and the social impact of disasters, but I am ignoring these because they are not central to Cohen's explanation of events.)

The labelling perspective is best expressed in the oft-quoted words of Howard S. Becker, one of its leading proponents, who insisted that 'deviance is created by society'. 'I do not mean this in the way that it is ordinarily understood', Becker explained, 'in which the causes of deviance are located in the special situation of the deviant or in "social factors" which prompt his action. I mean, rather, that *social groups create deviance by making the rules whose infraction constitutes deviance* and by applying those rules to particular persons and labelling them as outsiders. From this point of view, deviance is *not* a quality of the act the person commits, but rather a consequence of the application by others of rules and sanctions to an "offender". The deviant is one to whom the label has successfully been applied; deviant behaviour is behaviour that people so label.' This formulation does not prevent researchers from asking orthodox behavioural and motivational questions about deviance – such as 'Why did they do it?', 'What sort of people are they?' and 'How can we stop them doing it again?'. However, it obliges them also to address definitional issues, the three most important of which, according to Cohen, are 'Why does a particular rule, the infraction of which constitutes deviance, exist at all?', 'What are the processes and procedures involved in identifying someone as a deviant and applying the rule to him?' and 'What are the effects and consequences of this application, both for society and the individual?'.

It is these definitional problems that are central to Cohen's study. This is not to say, however, that he considers behavioural questions to be unimportant. Rather crucially, he insists (almost as an aside) that David Downes's earlier subcultural theory of adolescent deviance among working-class youth in Britain offers probably the best structural explanation for the initial development of the subcultural styles themselves, and for the relatively few instrumental crimes (such as assaults and petty-thefts) that were associated with Mods and Rockers events. Downes's *The Delinquent Solution* was first published in 1966 and argues, in common with earlier American subcultural analyses, that delinquent or criminal subcultures provide a solution to the problems faced by their members, who are unable (for a variety of reasons) to achieve internalized goals by socially approved means, and so find in their membership of the subculture some compensation for their failure in conventional society. Thus, for example, the education system might nurture ambitions for success among working-class boys which the strictly limited opportunity structure of the occupational world is unable to fulfil. This 'problem of adjustment' between the worlds of school and work creates 'status frustration' among those affected. Their alternative solution is then the delinquent gang. Such gangs accord status to the oppositional (often 'expressive') values and behaviour which members can more readily display – as well as allowing them to retaliate against the system which has stigmatized them as failures. Delinquent subcultures are thus a fundamentally utilitarian collective solution to the blocked opportunities and recurrent privations of lower-class life. Reflecting on his study some years later, therefore, Cohen insisted (rightly) that '*Folk Devils and Moral Panics*... never suggested that the origins of the behaviour itself could be explained by anything other than a slightly tougher version [via Downes] of original subcultural theory'. Despite this, as he regretfully notes, 'the book was still misinterpreted [together wtih most labelling studies] as implying that there is no need for a structural explanation of the subculture in its own right'.

Clearly, therefore, Cohen is not implying 'that innocent persons are arbitrarily selected to play deviant roles or that harmless conditions are wilfully inflated into social problems'. Nor does he suggest that persons labelled as deviant must acquiesce in this identity. (Numerous studies have shown that some individuals ignore the label, rationalize their illegal activities as somehow morally neutral, or simply pretend to comply with established noncriminal norms.) Rather, the argument of *Folk Devils and Moral Panics* attempts to substantiate the proposition that societal responses to deviance are complex, and may affect the original behaviour in quite unintended ways. In order to illustrate his point, Cohen draws on Edwin Lemert's useful distinction between primary and secondary deviance:

> Primary deviation – which may arise from a variety of causes – refers to behaviour which, although it may be troublesome to the individual, does not produce symbolic reorganization at the level of self-conception. Secondary deviation occurs when the individual employs his deviance, or a role based upon it, as a means of defence, attack or adjustment to the problems created by the societal reaction to it.

Accepting this distinction, one might describe the societal reaction as an 'effective', rather than 'original' cause of the deviance in question. Cohen's study is then pitched strictly at the level of secondary deviance – the level at which deviance 'is subjectively shaped into an active role which becomes the basis for assigning social status'.

Like Lemert, Cohen is aware that the transition from primary to secondary deviance is a complicated process full of contingencies, only one of which is the willingness of individuals to comply with putative deviant labels. Another major determinant of the incorporation of the deviant status into an individual's self-identity is the effect of the societal reaction on putative delinquents themselves. Social control may have the unintended consequence of stabilizing the very identities it is designed to erase. Indeed, the moral panic about the Mods and Rockers, as shaped and encouraged by the mass media, achieved precisely this effect by according to these groups the status of contemporary folk devils. Press reports, as we have seen, painted stereotyped and exaggerated pictures of the groups in question. Most observers of British society in the mid 1960s had no direct knowledge of the Mod/Rocker events and so reacted, instead, to the media presentation. In fact, the various 'moral entrepreneurs' (certain politicians, churchmen, magistrates, and so forth) demonstrably over-reacted, and by so doing set in motion a process of deviance amplification. Cohen developed this idea from the earlier and rather more mechanistic conception of its originator, the deviancy theorist Leslie Wilkins. Amplification occurs when the initial act of deviance (or even normative diversity as, for example, in dress)

> is defined as being worthy of attention and is responded to punitively. The deviant or group of deviants is segregated or isolated and this operates to alienate them from conventional society. They perceive themselves as more deviant, group themselves with others in a similar position, and this leads to more deviance. This, in turn, exposes the group to further punitive sanctions and other forceful action by conformists – and the system starts going round again.

As in the case of labelling, however, there is no assumption that amplification must necessarily occur. Both the societal control system and the deviant group can respond in a variety of ways. Why, therefore, did the various agents of social control (police, courts, Parliament, pressure groups) react so forcefully to the media presentation of the Mods and Rockers events? Why, for example, did they not simply dismiss the newspaper and other reports for what they patently were – a distorted over-reporting of the facts? And, for that matter, why did the press manufacture such an exaggerated inventory of events based on fantasy, misperception and the deliberate creation of sensationalism?

Cohen's answers to these questions are insightful but necessarily more speculative than his analysis of the process of the moral panic itself. The weekend of the original Clacton incidents was particularly dull from a journalistic point of view. The prominence given to events at the resort probably reflected, at least in part, the absence of alternative newsworthy events in Britain and abroad. It is worth noting, in this context, that rowdyism and gang fights were hardly original, even at coastal resorts, and had been relatively commonplace occurrences throughout the 1950s and early 1960s. Clearly, therefore, 'the Mods and Rockers didn't become news because they were new; they were presented as new to justify their creation as news'. Of course, the whole complex Mod and Rockers inventory was not itemized simply because it was 'good news', but once the initial subject had been fixed, its subsequent shape was 'determined by certain recurrent processes of news manufacture'. These cannot be documented in full here, but the most important of them is well known from other studies of the mass communications process, and that is the tendency for events to be selected for reporting in terms of their consonance with pre-existing images. Indeed, the more unclear the item and the more uncertain the journalist is about how to report it, the more likely it is to be interpreted in terms of a general framework that has already been established as 'news'. As a result the inventory for Bank Holiday events became utterly predictable:

> So constant were the images, so stylized was the mode of reporting, so limited was the range of emotions and values played on, that it would have been perfectly simple for anyone who had studied the Mods and Rockers coverage to predict with some accuracy the reports of all later variations on the theme of depraved youth: skinheads, football hooligans, hippies, drug-takers, pop-festivals, the Oz trial.

In an important sense, therefore, the media literally created the disturbances they reported. As we have seen, warnings were issued about every imminent 'little Clacton', about 'riot-raising Rockers who, rumour has it, have it in mind to do a Clacton on Brighton' (*Brighton and Hove Gazette*, 15 May 1964). This sort of emotive groundwork provided all the necessary clues for labelling adolescent holiday-makers and interpreting their behaviour. Elaborate and well-publicized police preparations helped set the stage for the show. The mass media provided, in advance, the shared images and stereotypes with which ambiguous situations could be structured. Thus, for example, 'a stone-throwing incident might not have progressed beyond the milling stage if there were no readily available collective images to give meaning to the activity'. Random events became linked, motives were imputed ('too many pills if you ask me'), and behaviour was grouped with other behaviour thought to be of the same order. Large crowds of adults lined the beaches and promenades to watch the predicted battles, some of the men holding their children above their heads, in order that they might get a better view of the proceedings. Journalists and photographers mingled with the crowds, providing a further stimulus to action, for as Cohen notes,

> If one is in a group of twenty, being stared at by hundreds of adults and pointed at by two or three cameras, the temptation to do something – even if only to shout an obscenity, make a rude gesture or throw a stone – is very great and made greater by the knowledge that one's actions will be recorded for others to see.

Nevertheless, the seemingly pointless behaviour of the teenagers need not have created a full-blown moral panic, because magistrates, editors and politicians could have reacted differently. That they did not choose to do so must be attributed, in Cohen's view, 'to the ways in which the affluence and youth themes were used to conceptualize the social changes of the decade'. These twin themes have dominated most analyses of social change in postwar Britain. We have already seen an important manifestation of the former in the political and popular discussion of embourgeoisement which provided the back-drop for the Affluent Worker project undertaken by Lockwood and his associates in Luton. Britons in the decade after the war, according to the Prime Minister Harold Macmillan, 'never had it so good'. The demographic and economic changes of the 1950s and 1960s also saw the creation of the teenager as an important social phenomenon, a large unmarried generation (aged between 15 and 21), whose average real wage had increased at twice the rate of that for adults. As a reward for full production, the teenager was to be allowed access to the full range of commodities which the market could offer, packaged in a way specifically designed to appeal to the young. Against this background, as Cohen observes, the Mods and Rockers symbolized something far more important than what they actually did:

> They touched the delicate and ambivalent nerves through which postwar social change in Britain was experienced. No one wanted depressions or austerity, but messages about 'never having it so good' were ambivalent in that some people were having it too good and too quickly... Resentment and jealousy were easily directed at the young, if only because of their increased spending power and sexual freedom. When this was combined with a too-open flouting of the work and leisure ethic, with violence and vandalism, and the (as yet) uncertain threats associated with drug-taking, something more than the image of a peaceful Bank Holiday at the sea was being shattered.

The reaction to the Mods and Rockers suggests that, in the midst of the cultural strains of the early 1960s, the wider community's self-appointed agents were attempting to make a statement about moral boundaries – about how much diversity might be tolerated. Arguably, the glossy and seemingly classless Mod image symbolized everything that was resented about the affluent teenager, while its sexual confusion (boys in pastel colours and make-up, girls with cropped hair and flat chests) simply heightened the apparent threat to established age, class and sex barriers. This perception further shaped the societal reaction because it denied to agents of control the possibility of dismissing the seaside incidents as nothing more than (yet another) delinquent brawl among louts from the slums. The participants *appeared* to be reasonably affluent, well-dressed and highly mobile. Without their anoraks and leather jackets they could hardly be distinguished from bank clerks; indeed, some of them actually were bank·clerks, which made their behaviour even more disturbing to the adult world. In-group deviance, as Cohen points out, is profoundly unsettling because 'it threatens the norms of the group and tends to blur its boundaries with the out-group'. Mods seemingly could not be dismissed as stereotypical hooligans from the urban lower classes. Their very ordinariness, their day-time jobs as shop assistants and office boys, suggested growing ingratitude among the young. Adolescents from the slums ('that area' and 'that type of home') might be expected to behave in this way. But the Mods were 'literally and metaphorically too close to home'. They epitomized the postwar economic and cultural changes which were threatening the long-approved style of life in this country. It is this, above all else, that explains the scope of the societal reaction against them. They were punished, not for what they did in the way of violence, damage to property, or inconveniencing others, but rather because of what they stood for; unearned affluence, permissiveness and a challenge to the ethics of sobriety, hard work and deference to established authority.

V

Naturally I find all of this rather convincing. Were it not so I would hardly have chosen Cohen's text to help illustrate my argument about the high quality of much of postwar British sociology. It must be conceded, however, that studies of labelling (under which general heading *Folk Devils and Moral Panics* is usually considered) have attracted a considerable amount of criticism over the years since Becker's classic statement of 1963. The most common complaints are that they ignore the sources of deviant action; can be applied only to a limited range of criminal activities; are too deterministic in their conception of the labelling process; and neglect questions pertaining to power and social structure.

These criticisms are largely unfair. They stem from the fact that the labelling perspective – which is concerned only with the social processes governing the nature, emergence, application and consequences of labels – has itself been associated with studies of deviancy conducted from a variety of (sometimes incompatible) theoretical standpoints. Cohen works within the theoretical tradition of symbolic interactionism. That is, he believes that society is constructed via an exchange of gestures involving symbolic communications and the negotiation of meanings between reflexive actors, who therefore have in common an ability to imagine themselves 'taking the role of the other' in any social interaction. But researchers describing themselves as 'functionalist', 'phenomenologist', 'naturalist', 'ethnomethodologist', 'systemic', and 'dramaturgical' have also been cited as major exponents of labelling arguments. Now, the particular assumptions, propositions and substantive concerns of these various schools of sociology are of no immediate relevance here. The point is, rather, that many of the criticisms of the labelling perspective have been misdirected precisely because they have identified labelling with a particular theoretical stance (for example, systems theory or phenomenology) seeking to address a much wider range of problems and data. Critiques of labelling theory are often critiques of its supposedly interactionist, phenomenological, or other premises and suppositions. In fact, labelling arguments can be accommodated to a range of social theories.

Having thus established its proper intellectual pedigree (or perhaps more accurately its lack of one), it is not difficult to show that most criticisms of the labelling perspective are largely unwarranted, including those mentioned immediately above. So-called labelling theory does not explain the initial motivation towards deviance because it does not set out to do so. The theory offers an explanation of labels, not of behaviour. Thus, as we have seen in the case of Cohen himself, for example, exponents of the labelling perspective usually draw on other sorts of explanation to account for the initial deviance towards which the subsequent societal reaction is directed. Cohen favours a subcultural explanation for the emergence of the Mods and Rockers. Others have offered psychological and environmental alternatives. The important point is that Cohen, in common with almost all other proponents of labelling arguments, is not making the claim that the labels themselves initiate the deviant behaviour. Deviance is not created by societal reaction alone. Nor does the labelling perspective imply, as one critic has erroneously assumed, that the deviant is 'a passive nonentity who is responsible neither for his suffering nor its alleviation'. In the eyes of some critics, studies of labelling depict the deviant as entirely subject to the determinism of societal reaction, having no autonomous capacity to determine his or her own conduct. Again, however, Cohen (like the great majority of other labelling theorists) must be found not guilty on this charge. There is nothing inevitable about labelling or amplification. Both processes, as Cohen points out at some length, are subject to a series of historical contingencies which vary from case to case. These explain why, for example, the Mod/Rocker gatherings of the mid 1960s were the subject of a moral panic that did not develop in respect of similar disturbances perpetrated by working–class adolescents visiting coastal resorts throughout the 1950s. Likewise, it seems unjust to complain that labelling arguments ignore large areas of deviant behaviour, when they clearly do not purport to offer a universal explanation for every form of delinquency. It is true that the processes of labelling may apply, in principle, to all areas of social life – deviant and nondeviant alike. But no labelling theorist known to me makes the claim that societal reactions are the original source of a single type of deviant behaviour, far less the whole panoply of crimes from theft, murder and rape, to blackmail, tax evasion and double-parking. Rather, as with Cohen himself, proponents make the considerably more modest claim that labelling may alter the direction, intensity and incidence of the subsequent experience. For the same reason, studies of labelling do not purport to offer a full-blown theory of the distribution of societal power, or to explain the complex interrelationships among social institutions, organizations, social classes, and other structural phenomena. Labelling theorists cannot agree upon an all-embracing model of social order precisely because their accounts of labelling are rooted within such a wide variety of diverse theoretical projects. In short, labelling arguments do not attempt to explain everything, so it seems unreasonable to criticize them for ignoring concerns that lie far beyond their substantive and conceptual boundaries.

Yet it is not difficult to see why labelling theory in general, and books such as *Folk Devils and Moral Panics* in particular, have attracted widespread and vociferous criticism from almost all quarters. The orthodox criminology of the postwar period, both in Britain and America, treated a crime as an unambiguous event. Each occurrence was clearly defined and therefore could be readily documented and counted. Its correlates were then identified among a wide range of psychogenetic, social and environmental attributes and an appropriate medico-legal remedy prescribed as a cure. This perspective was, to use Cohen's own description, 'canonical': the concepts, definitions and statistics it worked with were seen to be 'authoritative, standard, accepted, given and unquestionable'. The labelling perspective, by comparison, formed part of what might be called a 'sceptical' revolution in criminology and the sociology of deviance during the 1960s. In Britain this scepticism was institutionalized at the establishment of the National Deviancy Conference in 1968. Its members opened up a whole range of definitional questions hitherto largely ignored: 'Deviant to whom?' and 'Deviant from what?'; 'Criminal says who, and why?'. Official statistics ceased to be a resource from which predictions about crimes could be deduced, and became instead a topic for study in their own right, as a social construction embodying numerous untested assumptions about the nature, incidence and causes of crime. Class, ethnic and other systematic biases were detected in the 'construction of criminality'. Deviance was investigated as a career, involving complex processes such as the drift into delinquency, labelling, amplification, stigmatism, role-taking, and the neutralization of guilt or shame – rather than simply an event whose essential characteristics were self-evident and agreed upon by deviants, victims, agents of social control and the wider community alike.

To those on the political Right, the publications that flowed out of the National Deviancy Conference seemed tantamount to the claim that many criminals were in fact victims, more sinned against than sinning. The focus on societal reaction made the audience (police, media, courts), rather than the deviant actor, the crucial variable. Researchers began to ask awkward questions about the agents of social control themselves: 'How are definitions of deviance arrived at?' 'By what procedures is the deviant status ascribed?' 'In whose interests do the judiciary and police operate?' 'How do the crimes of the powerful, the rich, and those in authority escape public attention?' Not surprisingly, the accusation was often made that this new sociology of deviance seemed more intent upon excusing, rather than explaining criminal activity. Labelling theory was particularly vulnerable to this charge since it could be caricatured as offering a crude 'no deviance → slam on label → deviance' model of various undeniably antisocial activities. This perception was probably heightened by the fact that the insights offered by the theory could most obviously be applied to 'expressive' deviance, and for the large part 'victimless' crimes, such as homosexuality, drug addiction, alcoholism, gang membership, and mental illness. Indeed, rather uncharitably, the labelling perspective became known in some quarters as the 'sociology of nuts, sluts and perverts'.

I trust I have shown that, by making clear the modest aspirations and limited substantive terrain of the theory, this accusation can be seen to be unwarranted. Studies of labelling recognize a multiplicity of answers to the problem of explaining deviant behaviour. At worst, therefore, Cohen and his labelling colleagues can be accused only of setting themselves rather modest aetiological objectives. Personally, however, I tend to agree with Ken Plummer, whose robust defence of these studies concludes simply that 'no theory explains everything and the analyst is entitled to set his boundaries'. Identifying the origins of deviant conduct raises one set of issues; but the evidence from studies such as *Folk Devils and Moral Panics* shows clearly that definitional processes may alter the shape of deviant experiences, in ways that introduce additional, and quite distinct, problems for sociological analysis. It is difficult to see how the same theory might explain both sorts of phenomena – why crimes take place as well as how society reacts to them. Sociologists are frequently accused of intellectual arrogance: of 'having an answer for everything', and usually the same, simplistic answer at that. It seems hard that they should have to suffer this charge when, as in the case of Cohen and other labelling theorists, such a self-conscious attempt has been made to spell out both the complexity of the social processes involved and the limited aspirations of the theory itself.

VI

Ironically, however, the most sustained criticism of the labelling perspective has been voiced by those on the political Left, and originated (in Britain at least) from within the National Deviancy Conference, among certain members who favoured a distinctively Marxist approach to the study of crime. From this standpoint, labelling theory was perceived as being strongly supportive of the status quo, because it directed attention towards lower-level agencies of social control – the media, courts and social work departments – rather than the governing elites in whose interests these institutions actually operated. Labelling theorists studied rule-enforcers rather than rule-makers. Their sympathy for the underdog was never translated into a systematic critique of repressive (capitalist) structures. They were, therefore, political liberals rather than true political radicals. In America, for example, Alvin Gouldner accused Howard Becker and his colleagues of 'welfare-state reformism', and of seeking only to engineer limited social changes under the auspices of 'caretaking public bureaucracies'. This accusation brings us back squarely to the question of the 'policy-relevance' of contemporary sociological research so it is worth pursuing a little further.

To at least some Marxists within the National Deviancy Conference, it seemed that labelling had one irreparable defect as a theory of deviance: it failed to offer 'a political economy of crime'. Ian Taylor, Paul Walton, Jock Young and other proponents of this argument spelled out a much grander agenda for a 'fully social theory of deviance' which would situate the insights of subcultural and labelling studies within a structural account of the criminative potential inherent in the capitalist mode of production. These writers were, to use their own words,

concerned with the social arrangements that have obstructed, and the social contradictions that enhance, man's chances of achieving full sociality – a state of freedom from material necessity, and (therefore) of material incentive, a release from the constraints of forced production, an abolition of the forced division of labour, and a set of social arrangements, therefore, in which there would be no politically, economically, and socially-induced need to criminalize deviance.

The study of deviance was, in short, to be linked inextricably with socialist political strategies that allegedly would usher in societies in which crime had been abolished. Advocates of this 'new' or 'critical' approach were convinced that 'a criminology which is not normatively committed to the abolition of inequalities of wealth and power, and in particular of inequalities in property and life-chances, is inevitably bound to fall into correctionalism' and is 'irreducibly bound up with the identification of deviance with pathology'. Indeed, they further insisted that all criminological theories were necessarily tied to political strategies, since they implied policies which advanced specific interpretations of the world and therefore particular interests. In this way one arrives at the familiar Marxist dictum that researchers cannot in principle separate knowledge from ideology – except, of course, for those Marxists attempting to reconstitute criminological theory as a 'dialectic through praxis'. 'The task', according to these critical criminologists, 'is to create a society in which the facts of human diversity, whether personal, organic or social are not subject to the power to criminalize'. All else merely sustains the existing structures of social control and so helps reproduce the power of the dominant bourgeois class.

Much of this new criminology remained entirely programmatic, and amounted to little more than a bad-tempered critique of all hitherto existing theories from the moral high ground of Marxist utopianism. Indeed, to my ear at least, the new criminology sounds remarkably like the old. Both adopt an absolutist stance, whereby definitions and explanations of deviance are assumed to be axiomatic, and the only legitimate interpretation of reality is that agreed upon by a narrow group of professionals standing outside the various subcultures. The so-called critical criminologists are themselves canonical in their approach and simply reproduce the weaknesses of their 1950s predecessors, but in a seemingly radical guise. Alternatively, if we accept their injunction to treat *all* social science as ideology, then the new criminology must be only one more contentious version of reality – politically different from, but epistemologically (or in terms of its standing as 'knowledge') equivalent to, all others already available. Critical criminology, like other sociological theories of deviance, becomes merely an ideology with political objectives. Taylor and his colleagues have, as yet, been unable to resolve this epistemological dilemma. Their theory limits the researcher to a choice between the assertion of absolute wisdom and a collapse into ideological relativism. The possibility that our understanding of deviance might actually be advanced by sociological analyses which relate empirical data systematically to explanatory theories in accordance with the canons of established scientific practice, is simply eliminated. Most sociologists have therefore argued, rightly in my view, that an understanding of the links between crime and the wider political economy will only be achieved if the questions raised by the critical criminologists can be uncoupled from the doctrinal baggage of Marxism.

However, a less dogmatic group of Marxists, located primarily in the Centre for Contemporary Cultural Studies at the University of Birmingham, has also attempted to construct a radical criminology, and in so doing has offered a quite different critique of the older subcultural and labelling traditions. Writers such as Stuart Hall, Paul Willis and Phil Cohen have argued at some length that the various postwar youth cultures are nothing less than attempted symbolic solutions to the problems faced by the working class in modern Britain. The flavour of these studies is still subcultural, but the working-class delinquent is no longer seen as a 'frustrated social climber'. Instead of providing members with an alternative opportunity structure, a means of *adapting* to the strains of the failure to achieve unrealizable goals set by the dominant ideology, the working-class subculture of deviance is seen as a symbolic and heroic *resistance* against the cultural onslaught of advanced capitalism. According to Hall and his colleagues, the working class in postwar Britain has suffered a prolonged crisis of culture and personality, as economic developments have dispersed the locality-based traditional proletarian communities, scattered extended families and eroded the inner-city working-class base of industrial manufacturing jobs in large factories. Against this background of occupational change, growing consumerism, privatism and individualism, the various youth styles are an attempt to appropriate lost space, to recover past solidarity and to express unity with – but at the same time differentiation from – the failed parental generation. As Phil Cohen puts it, these subcultures endeavour 'to express and resolve, albeit magically, the contradictions which remain hidden or unresolved in the parent culture'. Above all else they symbolically retrieve the social cohesion of the traditional working class.

The whole range of postwar youth styles can then be decoded and interpreted as expressions of working-class dissent. Each new development indicates a form of 'resistance through rituals'. From this point of view, the Mods and Rockers become cultural innovators and critics, and the events at Clacton take on a new symbolic resonance. Subculture is nothing less than a political battleground between the classes. Thus, for example, schools become the setting for a daily struggle over control of the indigenous working-class culture. On the one hand, there is compulsory state education based on bourgeois morality and values, discipline and surveillance; on the other, the continuous guerilla warfare of truancy, 'having a laff' and generally 'mucking about'. The school attempts to dominate and undermine proletarian culture while the working-class adolescents strive to protect and celebrate it.

The most obvious problem with these studies, as Stanley Cohen has pointed out, is that the symbolic or magical resistance to subordination is evident only in massive exercises of decoding and deciphering the subcultural styles in question. The assumption is that these phenomena must be saying something to us – if only we could establish exactly what. So, as Cohen notes wryly,

> the whole assembly of cultural artefacts, down to the punks' last safety pin, have been scrutinized, taken apart, contextualized and re-contextualized. The conceptual tools of Marxism, structuralism and semiotics, a Left-Bank pantheon of Genet, Levi-Strauss, Barthes and Althusser have all been wheeled in to aid this hunt for the hidden code.

Thus 'Teddy Boys attacking Cypriot café owners, Mods and Rockers attacking each other, Skinheads beating up Pakistanis and gays, or football hooligans smashing up trains, are all really (though they might not know it) reacting to different things, for example, threats to community homogeneity or traditional stereotypes of masculinity.' Similarly, the facial make-up of the Punks and Doc Marten bovver-boots of the Skinheads are allegedly making an oblique statement about opposition to (or approval of?) some particular past or present social relationships. Of course, the youthful subjects of these studies appear themselves to be largely unaware of the subversive meaning of their activities. When asked about their behaviour, as the Birmingham research itself shows, Skinheads tend to say things like 'When you get some long stick in your hand and you are bashing some Paki's face in, you don't think about it'. Children who disrupt school-lessons by 'larking about' state repeatedly and categorically that they do not know why they do it or why it is so important to them. Apparently, however, this raises no difficulties of interpretation or evidence since subcultural style is a hotch-potch of inconsistencies: things are never quite what they seem. 'Paki-bashing' is to be read as a 'primitive form of political and economic struggle', not because of what the Skinheads themselves say (which is so obviously racist), but because the machine smashers of the early Industrial Revolution would also not have been aware of the real political significance of their actions.

This seems to be a very peculiar sort of proof. The apparently conservative meaning given to the subculture by its own members really hides working-class resistance. The research does not address itself, other than incidentally, to the explicit intentions of the subjects.

Instead, 'the subculture is observed and decoded, its creativity cele-brated and its political limitations acknowledged – and then the critique of the social order constructed'. But, as Cohen observes, 'while this critique stems from a moral absolutism, the subculture itself is treated in the language of cultural relativism. Those same values of racism, sexism, chauvinism, compulsive masculinity and anti-intellectualism, the slightest traces of which are condemned in bourgeois culture, are treated with a deferential care, an exaggerated contextualization, when they appear in the subculture'. Surely, there-fore, he is right to insist that '*somewhere* along the line, symbolic language implies a knowing subject, a subject at least dimly aware of what the symbols are supposed to mean'. Otherwise, how can we be sure that our reading of the style is not imaginary, and that we should not simply take the symbols and behaviour at their face value? How do we *know* that teenagers wearing swastikas are 'ironically distanc-ing' themselves from the explicit message that is usually associated with this symbol? Certainly, nowhere in the Birmingham School studies are we ever told how the subjects of the research actually accomplish this complicated business of irony and distancing, in order to facilitate the necessary recontextualization of their behaviour among its audience. In the end, therefore, Cohen is right to insist that 'there is no basis whatsoever for choosing between this particular sort of interpretation and any others: say, that for many or most of the kids walking around with swastikas on their jackets, the dominant context is simple conformity, blind ignorance or knee-jerk racism'.

It is hard, then, to see how either of these Marxist initiatives advances our understanding of subcultural deviance. Both link their sociological analyses explicitly to a particular political philosophy. Critical criminology openly advocates revolutionary praxis and judges the 'truth' of substantive propositions about subcultural de-viance against the yardstick of socialist values. This is nothing less than overt political bias. The studies undertaken by the Centre for Contemporary Culture Studies are no less partisan and canonical, because they insist that youth subcultures must be read as heroic celebrations of authentic working-class values, and as a form of resistance to bourgeois ideological domination – despite the fact that the subjects of the research cannot and do not recognize themselves in such an account.

So, if studies of labelling do not necessarily imply unwarranted sympathy for the deviant, as is claimed by critics on the political Right, or unjustified support for the 'correctionist' policies of the liberal-democratic status quo, as is claimed by those on the Left, what then are the political implications of arguments such as that advanced by Stanley Cohen? What policy prescriptions should be drawn from these particular sociological analyses?

The answer is, of course, that the policy implications of labelling, as indeed of any other sociological study, depend entirely upon the political objectives one is seeking to achieve. These are a matter for individual conscience rather than sociological prescription. Despite the protestations of those on the Left and Right alike, sociology cannot tell us how we *ought* to live our lives, since this is the task of the prophet or the politician. It can only explain the likely consequences of our actions with respect to the achievement of particular goals which the sociologist *qua* sociologist necessarily takes as given. Cohen is, therefore, quite correct to conclude that different readers can draw different policy implications from his study. Not all of these will be compatible with each other. He notes that

> one might argue, for example, that if the *initial* manifestation of such phenomena as the Mods and Rockers... is difficult or even impossible to prevent, one should attempt secondary prevention: for example, restraining the mass media in order to stop the first stages of amplification. Given a basic consensus... about the need for control or prevention, such an argument is not implausible. Nor is a commonsense view, that certain forms of deviant behaviour are best left alone on pure utilitarian grounds. That is, the cost of mounting any social control operation is just not worth it. Or else a humanitarian liberal view could be argued: many of the punishments were harsh and unjust and should be wholeheartedly condemned.

These and many other policy implications could be deduced from the analysis advanced in *Folk Devils and Moral Panics*. However, the question of policies raises the issue of values, since it is these which govern the setting of political objectives – and sociology does not purport to arbitrate scientifically between competing value stand-points. What the sociologist can do is expose the real (as opposed to the imaginary) consequences of particular policies, as they are revealed by the evidence actually available. Naturally, as a citizen, he or she might well either heartily approve, or strongly disapprove of the policies in question. Either way, this consideration does not, or at least should not intrude upon one's adherence to the rules of evidence governing the presentation of scientific results.

If moral assessments do enter into the analysis, then a charge of bias can properly be made. However, contrary to popular opinion, sociologists do not generally commit this sin. Indeed, arguably, it is those critics who complain that sociology 'lacks policy relevance' who are most prone to inject (or encourage others to inject) particular political premises into their sociological analyses. Such critics general-ly subscribe to the rather naïve view that social engineering on behalf of the status quo is somehow politically and morally neutral. In urging 'policy relevance' on sociology they do not stop to consider the question 'Whose policy, and why?'. What they actually mean is 'policy relevant to achieving the specific objectives of which I personally happen to approve'. Not for the first time, therefore, does it strike this particular observer that many of those who are currently most critical of my profession are themselves guilty of precisely the crime for which they wish to indict postwar British sociology.

9 Sociologists and scientologists

I have argued that, contrary to popular opinion, studies of labelling are not inescapably flawed by political bias. In themselves, they neither justify the behaviour of the deviant, nor recommend alternatives to the policies embodied in the crime control system. Stanley Cohen's *Folk Devils and Moral Panics* is thus a work of sociology – not of ideology – and, as we have seen, is demonstrably less partisan than many of the critiques to which it has been subjected over the years. Cohen has angered the Left and Right in equal measure precisely because, as a good sociologist, he draws a clear distinction between empirical and normative considerations – between explanation, on the one hand, and evaluation on the other. The former alone is the concern of sociology, and it seems to me at least that the majority of postwar British sociologists have respected this distinction by striving towards ideals of objectivity and value freedom in their analyses, despite numerous philosophical and practical hurdles that have been placed in their way during recent years. I therefore reject (and resent) the currently fashionable charge that sociology is merely socialism in academic guise.

Arguably, however, sociology is inherently a subversive activity in quite another sense. Sociologists refuse to accept commonsense explanations as sufficient for understanding social reality:

> The very act of reflecting on the behaviour of people and organizations entails that these activities do not bear their meaning and explanation on their face. The sociologist's pursuit of further or different knowledge after he has already been informed of the 'truth' of the matter by the individuals or organizations concerned, displays the fact that he does not accept the 'self-evident', and that . . . he is prepared to tell some entirely different story.

These, the opening words of Roy Wallis's book *The Road to Total Freedom* (published in 1976), summarize the most obvious difficulty in assessing Wallis's sociological study of the Church of Scientology. When competing definitions of reality are on offer – in this case contrasting sociological and scientological accounts – how is one to adjudicate between them?

This question is raised in a particularly forceful way when the subject of the analysis is a religious cult or sect. Often, in such cases, the belief-systems of the researcher and the faithful are quite divergent or even wholly incompatible. Believers commonly make the claim that they alone can fully understand religious phenomena. This calls into question the very possibility of constructing a sociology of religion. As we shall see, Roy Wallis became embroiled in a lengthy dispute with the Church of Scientology, whose spokesmen condemned his book as a biased, selective account based on an unrepresentative sample of respondents and materials. Above all else, however, Wallis's findings were dismissed by the Church simply because he had failed to 'walk over to the other side and try the view'. In other words, Wallis was not a convert, so his comprehension of Scientology was necessarily constrained by this alone. In fact, as I shall try to show, Wallis was probably in a better position to understand Scientology than were members of that Church themselves. Nevertheless, his study does raise an important issue about the epistemological (or knowledgeable) standing of sociological accounts of the world, as compared to the 'commonsense' accounts offered by actors or other lay observers. I have rather firm views about this matter, although fortunately they seem more or less to coincide with the conclusions reached by Wallis himself, and I will endeavour to make these clear in due course. However, before taking up such a complex issue, one relatively straightforward question must obviously be addressed: what, precisely, *is* Scientology?

II

The founder and lifelong leader of the Scientology movement, Lafayette Ron Hubbard, was a college drop-out who pursued a variety of jobs before being drafted during the Second World War. After retiring from the United States Navy, he became a prolific writer of pulp-magazine adventure, fantasy and science fiction stories. Hubbard also had an interest in the issues of mental health. In a lengthy article, published in the May 1950 issue of the magazine *Astounding Science Fiction*, he sketched out the principles of a new form of psychotherapy and self-help mental training which he called Dianetics. A number of individuals made inquiries about how they might obtain therapy and training in the new techniques, so the Hubbard Dianetic Research Foundation was quickly established to provide these services and to distribute Hubbard's numerous subsequent publications.

Wallis describes the early months and years of Dianetics in great detail. Its theory and practice were rapidly expanded, in part according to original ideas developed by Hubbard and his collaborators, but also by drawing on aspects of the orthodox and fringe psychology already available. A series of short-lived Dianetics Foundations maintained contact with isolated individual followers and the many affiliated groups that sprang up in America and Britain. Courses, tape-recordings, books, pamphlets and speeches by Hubbard and other Foundation staff were made readily available to recruits. Hubbard's first book about the new therapy, *Dianetics: the Modern Science of Mental Health*, was reported by its publishers to have sold 150,000 copies during the first year of issue. However, after a series of organizational failures, acrimonious internal disputes about techniques and a slump in active membership following the initial boom of 1950–1, the Hubbard Association of Scientologists (1952) and then the Founding Church of Scientology (1954) emerged as stable organizational bases from which Hubbard was better able to control the ideas, membership, publications and finances of the movement.

During the mid and late 1950s, Hubbard supervised his new Church from a series of sites in the United States, before moving his headquarters to Saint Hill Manor in East Grinstead, Sussex, in 1959. However, in 1966 the centre of operations was again shifted, this time to a flotilla of yachts (the 'Sea Org') based in the Mediterranean. At the time of Wallis's study in the early 1970s, the Church was governed by an elaborate and extensive bureaucracy ('the Org'), comprising seven divisions, embracing twenty-seven separate departments, all under Hubbard's command. Hubbard's own whereabouts were a closely guarded secret from the mid 1970s until the announcement of his death in 1986. Despite the founder's demise, the Org has continued to issue new programmes, directives and spiritual tasks for the worldwide membership of the Church, estimated in 1988 to be in the region of 6.5 million persons.

Throughout its short history the Church of Scientology has attracted a great deal of media and government attention. In the USA, in the 1950s, a number of Scientologists were arrested for 'teaching medicine without a licence'. In 1958, the US Food and Drug Administration seized large quantities of a substance (Dianazene) marketed by an agency associated with the Church, and reputed to be a preventative against radiation sickness. Over the years, US federal authorities have several times investigated the Church, and confiscated quantities of its literature. The American press has been almost uniformly hostile to Hubbard and has repeatedly claimed that Scientologists abduct and brainwash new recruits. In Britain, press reports denounced Hubbard as a charlatan, and led the Minister of Health to attempt a curb on the movement's growth. For example, between 1968 and 1971, some 145 aliens were refused permission to enter this country in order to study or work at Scientology establishments. In Parliament, the Church was described as socially harmful and authoritarian; as directing itself deliberately towards 'the un-

balanced, the immature, the rootless, and the mentally or emotion-
ally unstable'; and accused, therefore, of 'indoctrinating' children and
other recruits by 'ignorantly practising quasi-psychological techniques
including hypnosis'. It was, allegedly, a 'menace to the personality
and well-being of those so deluded to become its followers'. In
Australia, meanwhile, a public debate in the mass media resulted in an
official inquiry and subsequent ban on Scientology in several of the
major states during the late 1960s and early 1970s. Similar investigations in New Zealand and South Africa stopped short of this, but
placed strict controls on certain of the Church's practices, in particular
the use of the psychological testing device known as the E-meter. The
outcome of a British inquiry was published in 1971, and although this
resulted in a lifting of the ban against foreign Scientologists entering
the country, the lengthy report also contained numerous passages that
were highly critical of the Church's methods and organization.

Wallis's detailed description of that organization suggests that the
corporate activities of the Church are of labyrinthine complexity.
Over the years, Hubbard seems to have launched countless new
organizations and registered large numbers of companies, some of
which only ever existed on paper: the National Academy of American
Psychology, Citizens' Purity League, Citizen's Press Association,
Association for Health Development and Aid, Constitutional Administration Party, Scientology Consultants Inc., Society of Consulting
Ministers, American Society for Disaster Relief, Citizens of Washing-
ton Inc., United Survival Action Clubs, and so on. Alongside these
peripheral and covert enterprises, the Church has openly sponsored a
variety of organizations involved in pressure-group and welfare
activities, including the Citizens' Commission for Human Rights
(seeking to improve conditions in mental hospitals and campaigning
against psychosurgery, involuntary committal and psychopharma-
cology); Narconon (a drug rehabilitation programme employing
Scientology techniques); Applied Scholastics Inc. (a Scientology-based
educational programme for slow learners); and a newspaper, *Freedom*,
which campaigns against both orthodox psychiatry and those critics
who dismiss the alternative methods proposed by Scientology itself.
Such critics have indeed been numerous, and books 'exposing'
Scientology have often been the subject of lengthy and expensive
litigation, as have several cases of allegedly involuntary 'deprogram-
ming' of apostates. At one time, for example, the Church had at least
thirty-six libel writs outstanding against British newspapers.

The Church's convoluted organizational involvements are matched
only by the complexity of its teachings. These are a development of
Hubbard's original writings on Dianetics and rest on a model of the
human mind as a computer. At its simplest, Hubbard's argument is
that the brain promotes the survival of the organism by suppressing
some of the body's painful experiences, and that over the course of

time these repressed memories act as 'blocks' to the efficient operation of the mind. When situations arise resembling those in which the originally painful experience was registered and repressed, the normally 'Analytical Mind' is overcome by a 'Reactive Mind', and this causes the individual to feel some of the pain associated with the formative event. The reactive memory-banks therefore comprise chains of painful experiences called 'engrams', which force the mind to operate under the constraints of severe 'aberrations', thus limiting its capacity and distorting the 'basic personality'. Quite simply, engramic memories are analogous to programming faults and lead the brain to make systematic miscomputations throughout everyday life. Scientologists believe that prenatal engrams constitute between two-thirds and three-quarters of all the engrams acquired by the average 40-year-old person.

In order to restore optimum functioning of the 'basic personality', Dianetic therapy attempts to overcome engram-conditioned 'irrationality', by emptying the bank of engrams from the reactive mind and rendering it 'clear'. In this way, emotional tension, psychosomatic illness and lowered capability are allegedly eliminated, and the analytic mind allowed to operate unimpeded. There are a variety of therapeutic techniques, but they all have the common purpose of releasing engrams (or 'locks'), and transforming these into memories which are subject to the normal control of the analytic mind.

Although some of this terminology seems strange, Dianetics is in essence rather similar to other forms of 'abreaction therapy'; that is, therapy which attempts to restore mental health by getting the patient to re-live actual traumatic experiences. There are, for example, strong similarities with the early work of Freud, who suggested that the root of hysterical symptoms lay in early experiences of psychological trauma. These parallels are explored in some detail by Wallis but need not detain us here. Nor is it possible to document fully the numerous developments in the theory and practice of Dianetics during its early years. These include Hubbard's distinction between 'MEST' and 'theta' (the former is an acronym for the physical universe of Matter–Energy–Space–Time, while the latter stands for the universe of thought); the development of the 'Tone Scale', indicating the amount of 'free theta' available to the analytic mind, and according to which pre-clear individuals and groups can be classified; Hubbard's proliferation of 'logics, corollaries, axioms, and definitions' (for examples see Table 9.1); and his growing commitment to past lives and deaths. We need note only that, as Dianetics expanded, it became theoretically more eclectic and, to the outsider at least, progressively less intelligible.

Scientology merely places the 'technology' of Dianetics in a more spiritual framework. 'Theta' (spirit or soul) is reconceptualized in the plural as 'Thetans', spiritually perfect beings who are the all-powerful

Table 9.1   Examples of Ron Hubbard's 'Definitions, Logics and Axioms'

Axiom 68 – The single arbitrary in any organism is time.

Axiom 69 – Physical universe perceptions and efforts are received by an organism as force waves, convert by facsimile into *theta* and are thus stored.

Definition: Randomity is the mis-alignment through the internal or external efforts by other forms of life or the material universe of the efforts of an organism, and is imposed on the physical organism by counter efforts in the environment.

Source: The Road to Total Freedom, p. 43.

Table 9.2   Examples of Scientologists' Reports of the Processing of Whole-Track Engrams

1. 'Located the incident with the command "Have you ever died?" The E-meter needle dropped. "Was it more than 100 years ago?" Needle dropped . . . Carried on like this and finally located it at 55,000,000,000,000,000,000 years ago . . . "Be in that incident". "What part of that incident can you confront?" and we were away. First picture that came was of the sea, great deal of unreliability but by discussion and continuing the question "What part of that incident can you confront?" various other pictures and sensations uncovered which eventually added up to a section of the incident concerning a giant Manta Ray type of acquatic creature which the preclear had seen while underwater . . . The engram started on a space-ship. The ship had needed an outside repair. On going outside, the preclear had been hit by a meteorite particle which had not punctured the suit. At this point an acute pain under the arm where the meteor had struck, occurred. The Pc clambers back into the space-ship. Later the atomic engines of the ship break down and the Pc has to repair these and apparently receives radio-active burns. He finds that he has to leave the ship and so falls from a ladder into the sea where he encounters the Manta Ray.'

2. '. . . Pc, after a period of 440 years without a body, arrives in error on a planet which is being taken over by "Black Magic" operators who are very low on the ethical scale and using electronics for evil purposes. Having come originally from a "good" planet he battles for a long, long time against the forces of "black magic", which, like a fifth column, are subverting the originally "white magic" populace. It is a losing battle, implant after implant gradually weakening his ability and control by causing hallucinated perceptions. Eventually after a period of spiritual torment and grief he abandons his former high goals and goes over to the "Black Magic" faction, not having entirely given up the idea of outwitting it from within. This occurs some 74,000 years after his first arrival on this planet.
He now goes to another planet by space ship. A deception is accomplished by hypnosis and pleasure implants (rather like opium in effects) whereby he is deceived into a love affair with a robot decked out as a beautiful red-haired girl who receives all his confidences for a period of 50 years [Etc.].'

Source: The Road to Total Freedom, p. 105.

and all-knowing creators of the universe, but who became so absorbed in life's 'games' that they forgot their transcendental origins, and now merely identify themselves with the physical bodies they periodically inhabit. The techniques of Scientology are designed to restore to the Thetans their original capabilities (that is, to help the individual achieve the status of 'Operating Thetan'), by uncovering and eradicating engrams during lengthy question-and-answer (or 'auditing') sessions. For example, one technique involves processing 'whole-track' (past-life) engrams, by recording events possessed as 'facsimiles' or mental images by each Thetan. Table 9.2 reproduces two separate Scientology reports that are typical of those obtained by this method. Wallis reports that literally thousands of auditing techniques have appeared over the years, many of which are no longer in common use, so that 'only a practising Scientologist would be able to say what currently constituted "standard technology"'.

Auditors identify the presence of engrams by recording a client's response to each question on the E-meter. This is a form of skin galvanometer which records increases in salinity resulting from sweat, fatigue, or the pressure with which the client holds the terminals. By its use, Scientologists claim to be able to detect 'body-reads', allegedly reflecting the state of the Thetan. These meters are held to be infallible and are associated with a complex terminology for interpreting their readings, embracing, for example, such concepts as 'theta bop', 'rock slam', and 'floating needle'.

Auditing is intended gradually to eliminate engrams to the point at which the client goes 'clear', and indeed to take him or her beyond this status through a complex hierarchy of progressively elevated spiritual planes, achieved by a mixture of studying Scientology publications, following its courses and intensive auditing. These are all expensive, but justified by the Church on the grounds that clients who ascend the various 'scales of auditing' achieve an enhanced sense of self-actualization, such that successful Scientologists enjoy (to quote Hubbard):

> unbounded creation, outflow, certainty, certainty of awareness, going-awayness, explosion, holding apart, spreading apart, let-ting go, reaching, goals of a causitive nature, widening space, freedom from time, separateness, differentiation, givingness of sensation, vaporizingness, glowingness, lightness, whiteness, desolidifyingness, total awareness, total understanding, total ARC [affinity, reality, communication].

The Success Department of the Church collects and distributes the various 'success stories' which students are encouraged to write. Examples of these are shown in Table 9.3.

Of course, all of this sounds quite unlike conventional religion.

Table 9.3 Examples of Scientology 'success stories'

'What a perfect gradient these Expanded Grades are. I no longer feel afraid of anything. I feel calm and very stable. I can grant more beingness to others. I like myself a lot better too. Ron has given man a terrific thing with the Expanded Grades. It's great to see the things that have been bothering me for years disappearing for good.
    Robin Youngman.

For the first time for a long time I feel free to communicate. It is really great and I know I can do it.
    Shirley Pike.

Right after Clear I hit a keyed out OT state and could change my body size about 1 to 1½ inches in height by actual measurement. Some people swore it was 2 to 3 inches, which it might have been, but it was 1 inch difference the time I measured. The ability was under control and I could do it at will.
    Fred Fairchild OTv1 Clear No 49.

Duplication of data often brings interesting abilities into view. I'm OT1. While studying with intention in the privacy of my bedroom, I heard a noise in the adjoining den. I looked around to "see" what it was, and behold, I looked right through the wall into the next room as though no wall was there. When your intention is very strong you can do what you intend to do. Wow! Do you intend to go CLEAR? And O.T.?
    Herb Stutphin, OT1 Clear No 2313.

Yesterday I was walking down the main street. A woman ahead of me coming in the opposite direction was coughing badly. I put across to her – telepathically – "Are you OK?"
    When she got beside me she beamed and said "Yes, that is a lot better now, thank you". Well? The secret is on the OT Courses – come and get it too.
    Viki Dickey OT.

Today was fantastic. I walked downstairs to get some coffee and the coffee machine was buzzing. So I put my hands out and moved them around the machine putting out beams to bounce back and thereby I could tell by watching the particle flow exactly where the error in the machine was. I found it and corrected the molecular structure of that area in the machine and the buzzing stopped.
    Then I heard my air conditioner rattling so I looked at why it was rattling and it stopped.
    I'm becoming much more at cause. I love it – like Superman!
    Michael Pincus OT.'

Source: The Road to Total Freedom, p. 121.

Nevertheless, Scientology has vigorously defended its standing as a church, despite the fact that its religious practices are, as Wallis puts it, 'quite rudimentary'. The central organizations controlling the movement usually hold some form of Sunday service in a chapel, although this commonly takes the form of a lecture by a 'minister' on some principle of Scientology, or else comprises a group-auditing session. Weddings can be conducted with full legal recognition in some countries, including America, although in Britain a civil ceremony continues to be a prerequisite. Funerals and prayer days are also held. Auditors are required to undergo 'ministerial training' (within the Church itself) before practising professionally or wearing clerical collars. Clearly, however, the theory and practice of the movement is predominantly individualistic in orientation. There is, as Wallis notes, little which has a communal significance that might be recognized and celebrated through public ceremonial. Most of the Church's adherents participate as individuals, by purchasing courses and counselling, although converts who become deeply committed to the movement can readily obtain full-time involvement in its advanced courses, religious ministry, organization and campaigns of social reform.

III

This, then, is Scientology. Of course, I have summarized only a few of its principal features, whereas Wallis gives a comprehensive statement of the Church's beliefs and organization. He also explores, in considerable detail, a much wider range of auditing techniques; the 'Scientological Career' by which new recruits ('casual clients') become committed practitioners ('deployable agents'); and the Church's troubled relations with the medical and psychiatric professions, state and wider society generally. Nevertheless, I do not think that my necessarily compressed and selective account does an injustice either to the teachings of the Church or to the sophistication and scope of Wallis's research.

But *The Road to Total Freedom* is not simply an ethnography of the seemingly exotic behaviour of Scientologists. Wallis addresses himself systematically to a number of sociological issues upon which this particular case-study seems to shed some light. I want to pursue only two of these in the present context. The first poses the question of how cults may transform themselves into sects. The conventional sociological wisdom, as Wallis understood it, was that such a process was not only empirically unlikely but perhaps also *a priori* impossible. Cults, like sects, are religiously 'deviant' by comparison to the normatively sanctioned or 'respectable' church and denominational orthodoxy. However, unlike sects, they are 'pluralistically legitimate' in the sense that membership is perceived to be but one of a variety of paths to truth or salvation. Sects, on the other hand, purport to offer adherents a unique access to such rewards. These two distinctions provide Wallis with the typology of ideological collectivities shown in Table 9.4.

Table 9.4 A typology of ideological collectivities

	Respectable	Deviant
Uniquely legitimate	Church	Sect
Pluralistically legitimate	Denomination	Cult

Source: The Road to Total Freedom, p. 13.

Cults are therefore characterized by what Wallis calls 'epistemo-logical individualism'. They suggest 'no clear locus of final authority beyond the individual member'. As a result, cults tend to be 'loosely structured, tolerant, and non–exclusive'. They make few demands on their adherents; do not maintain a clear distinction between believers and outsiders; have a rapid turnover of membership; and possess fluctuating belief-systems with ill-defined boundaries. They are also doctrinally precarious, since converts can be selective in their accept-ance of teachings, subscribing only to those ideas and practices which seem to lead to the achievement of personal goals. Moreover, the involvement of members tends to be occasional or temporary, and open to threats of schism or secession as local teachers or preachers assert their autonomy. This organizational fragility constantly raises problems of authority and commitment which, if unresolved, will lead to apathy, passivity and indifference among the membership. Cults may well simply dissolve and disappear – indeed, as previous researchers had observed, they regularly did precisely that.

Sects, on the other hand, are distinguished by their 'epistemological authoritarianism'. This gives them features entirely contradictory to those displayed by cults. Crucially, sects have recourse to an 'authori-tative locus for the attribution of heresy', because each lays claim to privileged access to the truth or salvation. They also possess a strictly controlled membership; a self-conception as an elect or elite; hostility towards (or separation from) the state and wider society; and a tendency towards totalitarianism. On the face of it, therefore, cults are unlikely to transform themselves into sects, because 'in order for a cohesive sectarian group to emerge from the diffuse, individualistic origins of a cult, a prior process of expropriation of authority must transpire'. This must be legitimized by a claim to unique revelation, which 'locates some source or sources of authority concerning doctrinal innovation and interpretation beyond the individual mem-bers or practitioner, usually in the person of the revelator himself'. Considerable charismatic skills are required to propound the new gnosis and to centralize authority in this way.

Wallis's argument is that, the difficulties of this transformation notwithstanding, Hubbard successfully implemented a strategy of sectarianization in order to solve the cultic problem of institutional fragility faced by Dianetics in the early 1950s. During those early years, many followers saw Dianetic techniques as offering simply an 'added blessing', one further path to salvation. They were content to select from Hubbard's teachings only those elements which seemed suited to their own particular purposes; to combine these with techniques learned elsewhere; and to develop Dianetic theory and practice by building on the foundations laid by Hubbard himself. Within a matter of months, therefore, the movement was experiencing internal schism and defection. Some of the early converts became sceptical about the possibility of achieving the state of 'clear' by means of Dianetic techniques alone and so began to experiment with other psychoanalytic theories and practices. Many groups having their origins in the various Dianetic foundations subsequently became extremely eclectic, combining Hubbardian theory with (among others) carbon dioxide therapy, New Thought affirmations, Orgone therapy, Gestalt therapy, and Krishnamurti. A few moved into the realms of the occult. In due course the various independent auditors began to claim that their particular approach had produced 'clears'. Some even attracted clients and funding at levels sufficient to challenge Hubbard for leadership of the Dianetic community as a whole.

In order to reassert control over his creation Hubbard therefore announced the revelation of Scientology. This new theory transcended the limitations of the early Dianetics and claimed to offer a unique 'Science of Certainty'. Hubbard denounced as heresy all theoretical and technological innovations not specifically approved by him. An independent organization (the Hubbard Association of Scientologists) and *Journal of Scientology* were established in order to control the new theory and practice, to prevent Hubbard's ideas being submerged under the weight of synthesis or independent innovation, and to attack 'unauthorized' Dianetics practitioners and groups. New procedures for centralized accreditation compelled affiliated groups and individuals to report regularly on their activities if they wished to remain eligible for receipt of Scientology materials. Independent practitioners were threatened with legal action and unaffiliated groups forced to disband. Standardized training procedures were established and centralized in Hubbard's Association. Officers and auditors who failed to comply with the new requirements were regularly dismissed. An elaborate hierarchy of 'sanctification' was erected to help mobilize greater commitment and involvement on the part of the membership. New techniques were generated at a rate that forced clients into close contact with the central organization in order to keep abreast of developments. Gradually, therefore, the flow of information, materials and funds came wholly under the control of Hubbard's expanded central organization.

In this way Hubbard successfully centralized authority within the movement, distinguished its doctrine and practice from competing belief systems, and erected a substantial boundary between members and the world. Little tolerance was shown toward nonconformity by members. Defectors were denounced as 'enemies', 'suppressive persons', or 'fair game', which meant that no Scientologist would be punished by the Church for attempting to deprive such persons of property, or endeavouring to trick, sue, lie to, destroy, or otherwise injure them, by any means available. These policies and practices made the press and other outside agencies increasingly hostile to the movement, but in response the Church simply tightened its central organization and made its internal regime more punitive. Expulsions became more frequent. Autonomous and independent sources of authority outside the bureaucracy were progressively eliminated. An elaborate 'Ethics System' was established to discipline the membership and silence dissenters. In short, Scientology developed all the distinguishing features of a closed sect, organized around a distinct ideology which only the charismatic leader could interpret or extend. One important finding of Wallis's research is therefore obvious: cults are not trivial social phenomena. They *may* develop into sects whose totalitarian structure and activities attract considerable public attention. Contrary to the prevailing wisdom, sects do not emerge only as schismatic movements from existing denominations, or as a result of interdenominational crusades.

The question of public disquiet raises a second and closely related issue, namely, that of recruiting and retaining converts. As Wallis notes, this particular Church 'confronts the conventional world with a deviant reality of massive proportions', since it offers 'a total *Weltanschauung*, a complex meaning system which interprets, explains and directs everyday life by alternative means to conventional, common-sense knowledge'. For example, Scientology proposed a radical alternative to many theories prevailing in orthodox scientific circles, particularly in the area of the psychological and medical sciences. Inevitably, therefore, as the movement grew, its quasi-therapeutic claims brought it to the attention of various state and professional agencies whose authority it implicitly undermined. The US Food and Drug Administration, American Psychological Association, American Medical Association and similar bodies in Britain and Australia all issued hostile reports about the Church, and together with the press and interested politicians began to characterize its teachings as an 'irrational and perverted fraud', perpetrated by an 'evil' organization employing 'authoritarian' techniques of social control, including blackmail, extortion, brainwashing and indiscriminate terror. Needless to say, the Church itself has always denied these charges, maintaining instead that its 'civilizing mission' has been opposed by an international conspiracy embracing health professionals, the mass media and governments alike.

So, who then joined the Church, and why? In answering this

question Wallis addresses himself squarely to the popular debate about secularization as an inevitable concomitant of the development of modern industrial societies. Proponents of the secularization thesis hold that, with the development of science and its evident ability to explain and modify the world we live in, the necessity for religious or magical interpretations of the world diminishes. The declining hold that religion has on people's actions then explains the reduced commitment to religious institutions in most Western societies. However, Scientology is only one of a large number of new religious movements which have appeared and flourished since 1945, despite the relatively secular environments provided by their host societies. Some of these movements can, in fact, be explained as world-rejecting attempts to escape from the impersonality, materialism, bureaucratization and individualism of modern existence. The International Society for Krishna Consciousness (ISKCON), Children of God, Unification Church ('Moonies'), and Jim Jones's 'People's Temple' can plausibly be viewed in this way. Scientology, on the other hand (together with similar movements such as Christian Science, Transcendental Meditation, the Inner Peace Movement and Japanese Soka Gakkai), offers neither an escape from this world nor a promise of transforming it radically. Its practitioners claim, instead, to be more successful than outsiders at achieving the goals already set by the status quo. The movement displays a 'world-affirming' orientation in its bureaucratic structure, scientific rhetoric and focus on individual achievement. Auditing, it is claimed, will lead to 'the freeing of the individual's superhumanly powerful spiritual nature'. His or her current limitations – physical disabilities, psychosomatic illnesses, loneliness, lack of confidence, and the like – will be eliminated, enabling 'clears' to manipulate and so cope more successfully with their existing environments.

This promise is then reflected in the membership itself. Wallis's research suggested that the majority of converts are middle-class:

> The general picture that emerges is of a following of white, young to early middle-aged, adults, mainly married with families, from predominantly Protestant backgrounds and with Protestant or no religious affiliation, white-collar occupations and a high school or college education ... many [of whom] had already ventured into the 'cultic milieu', having acquainted themselves with at least one quasi-philosophical-psychological system.

Three types of motivation can be identified from the accounts given by former and present members. 'Problem-solvers' were attracted by the movement's promise of physical, psychological, or social improvement. These recruits were acutely aware of some personal failure – poor memory, persistent anxiety, chronic mental illness, for example – that was preventing them from achieving personal ambitions or social expectations. Thus, for example, one interviewee, on being asked about his reasons for joining the Church, replied that he 'knew damn well at the time I had to sort myself out. I'd had a nervous breakdown about nine months previous. Found out the medical profession were a load of charlatans and I had to find my own salvation.' 'Truth-seekers', on the other hand, came upon Dianetics or Scientology during the course of a life-long search for truth and the meaning of life. Most had explored other religions and psychologies at some stage during this quest. Wallis quotes at some length the typical story told by one of his respondents, who had investigated comparative philosophy and religions of all kinds throughout most of her life before finally stumbling upon a copy of *Dianetics: Modern Science of Mental Health*. 'I thought if part of this is true, only a little part, it's worth investigating. So I will investigate it. So I wrote and asked where my nearest Centre was.' Finally, Wallis identified considerable numbers of 'career-oriented' individuals, including medical, psychological and psychiatric practitioners, to whom Dianetics offered an additional or alternative therapeutic tool. Indeed, some recruits saw Scientology as offering a new or alternative full-time career to that in which they were already engaged.

In the light of these accounts Wallis concludes that Hubbard's teachings were eminently suited to the contemporary market for religious commodities. Modern industrial societies are indeed secular. Science and technology have greatly restricted the areas of life about which religion can claim to offer authoritative insight. However, industrial and economic rationalization have also brought urbanization and social mobility in their wake, and this has had the effect of rendering personal identity particularly precarious. Status structures have become blurred; multiple criteria now exist for ranking individuals hierarchically; and the gradual disappearance of coherent locality-based communities has undermined established means of situating ourselves and others in social exchanges. In sum, as Wallis puts it, 'social interaction in anonymous urban industrial societies has to be negotiated without the aid of elaborate formulae of civility and identity markers typical of pre-industrial societies'. A substantial proportion of the population is inadequately equipped for such complex negotiations, because they lack appropriate skills of self-confidence, personal attractiveness and interpersonal competence.

Moreover, industrial societies tend to shift the emphasis from ascribed to achieved bases of status placement, so that failure to achieve is defined as a failure of the individual rather than a consequence of socially structured constraints on opportunities. At the same time, however, the unequal distribution of material resources that is characteristic of capitalist societies ensures that, for many, there will be a persisting sense of failure. There are two broad strategies for adapting to these circumstances: on the one hand, individuals might withdraw into psychosis, isolation, illness, or some other role which legitimizes their apparent failure; on the other, they might resort to novel means of securing societal goals, including, for example, crime, training in the presentation of self, or 'seeking esoteric means of securing mobility through the acquisition of hidden knowledge'.

Scientology offers one such means. As Wallis sees it, the average consumer of religious commodities today 'may be less in need of a cosmology than of a solution to anxiety and other sources of psychological concern'. In the competition for clientele in the religious market, Scientology was one of the most successful of the new cultic and sectarian movements, precisely because it was organized along lines more akin to those of the Ford Motor Company than of the established churches:

> It provided assurance of fundamental ability and competence within every consumer, and offered to resolve all the major psychological problems of modern man. It was packaged in a rhetoric of science which had a widespread popular appeal. Its organisation, and the production of the commodity which it purveys were thoroughly rationalised. It developed to a level far in advance of most other contemporary religious movements and institutions the techniques of salesmanship and public relations.

Scientology, in short, represents the logical outcome of the rationalization of Western culture:

> Rationalisation of life in the world has led to the rationalisation of the institution through which salvation is secured. Rational calculation has led to the provision of salvation as a standardized and differentiated commodity available at a set rate per unit (with discounts for cash in advance).

It seems that many modern consumers are only too willing to purchase salvation in this way. At the time of his death, Hubbard's personal assets amounted to more than 26 million dollars, a figure that excludes his numerous, massive and largely untraceable bequests to his family and to the worldwide movement he had mobilized.

IV

Not surprisingly, the most vociferous critics of Wallis's study have been Scientologists themselves, although in at least one notable case an outspoken defender of the Church happened also to be a professional sociologist. Most of this criticism has been directed towards aspects of Wallis's methodology.

Wallis himself describes that methodology as 'eclectic'. By this he means simply that, in order both to generate sufficient information about the Church and to cross-check contentious data against other sources, four different research techniques were employed. Documents provided the principal source of information. Various legal records and supporting testimonies were examined in Britain and the United States. Individuals on both sides of the Atlantic who had earlier been involved with the Church were sought out, and made available to Wallis their sometimes extensive personal collections of Church materials, including publications, notebooks, letters and tape-recordings, as well as communications from the many schismatics and heretics of the early period. The Church itself, on occasions, provided relevant information. However, these materials were supplemented by data gathered during interviews with eighty-three respondents, thirty-five of whom had been involved in the movement during its Dianetics phase and forty-three after its transition to Scientology, together with five individuals who had never been committed to the Church but had relevant information about it from some other point of view. These interviews lasted anything up to ten hours. Respondents were generated by a 'snowballing' technique, starting with the names of potential informants supplied by a former member, and following up the additional contacts that his list generated. Most of Wallis's interviewees were former members of the Church though he states that 'some [were] still committed in various ways to the movement'.

A third strategy, that of sending questionnaires to Church members, proved relatively unsuccessful. Wallis was forced to use as his sampling frame a mailing list of the Hubbard Association of Scientologists International, provided by one of his informants, despite the fact that this was some eight years out of date. Over a period of several months he sent out 150 questionnaires to United Kingdom residents. Not surprisingly, only forty-six of these were completed and returned. Finally, he spent a brief period in participant observation, simply by responding to an advertisement inviting members of the public to attend a Communications Course at Saint Hill Manor. After two days, Wallis found it impossible to continue with the course 'without having to lie directly about . . . acceptance of its content', so withdrew. This brief foray subsequently proved to be intensely troublesome, since representatives of the Church were convinced that Wallis had acted unethically by not revealing his sociological interest, and so (for this and other lesser reasons) became actively hostile to the research almost from the outset. Wallis himself has always maintained that at no point did he make any effort to conceal his identity; that the invitation to East Grinstead 'indicated no constraints upon who would be acceptable to take the course'; that it was clearly open to the public at large and that he could therefore participate 'without revealing any more than that I was an interested outsider'; and that, when the point was reached at which he would actively have had to lie (by, for example, disguising his disagreement with the statements made by instructors), he slipped quietly away.

Leading representatives of the Church were offended by Wallis's behaviour and several times attempted to have his research stopped. In order to forestall threatened legal proceedings Wallis offered to include a commentary commissioned by the movement itself as an appendix to his book. This was agreed, and *The Road to Total Freedom* duly appeared with an appended reply by Dr Jerry Simmons, a sociologist who had formerly taught in the Universities of Illinois and California but who was also a practising Scientologist.

Simmons maintains that Wallis's 'violations of the scientific method are indicative of either a decline in scholastic method or are deliberate and malicious'. Not surprisingly, he denies that the organization of the Church is totalitarian, and insists that its leadership has a 'moral sensibility' towards the well-being of members. Under Hubbard's benign guardianship the cult simply *evolved* into a sect. Indeed, according to Simmons, far from being 'a manipulator or a dark-motivated man', Hubbard 'has been trying for twenty-five years to *give away* any control he has so that he can devote himself to further research and writing'. Simmons's main complaint, however, is that all of Wallis's 'samples' are hopelessly biased: the sample of respondents focuses almost exclusively on 'dissident Clears' or other people who, for one reason or another, have left the movement; while the sample of texts offers an inadequate and misleading picture of the Church's teachings ('a random sampling of, say, a thousand statements written by Hubbard would have been legitimate and would have yielded a quite different picture'). Wallis fails to quote from the files of the 'thousands upon thousands of statements of people who have improved their lives through Scientology'. In Simmons's view, therefore, he has chosen merely to sample a few statements, and to take these out of context in order to confirm his preconceived model of the Church as a totalitarian organization. In short, Wallis 'converts his theories into fact by seeking only data which support them'. He has a mind that is closed to the evidence which supports 'the genuine results of Scientology', but which he cannot see, precisely because he is not a Scientologist. Simmons, by comparison, has had 'seven years of intensive experiences in Scientology', and claims to have found within the movement 'a wealth of valid data, a battery of technology which works, hundreds of new friends, a return of a boyish lightheartedness that I had feared lost forever, and almost more adventure than I can handle'. He concludes, therefore, with an appeal to interested observers to sample for themselves what the Church has to offer: 'Get a copy of *Dianetics: Modern Science of Mental Health* and read it along with this book. See for yourself which is more alive and hopeful *and scientifically objective*.'

Wallis has remained unrepentant in the face of these charges. There are, he insists, no 'sampling errors' in his study because there is no 'sample'. The 'scientific method', as he understands it, is 'no more than an injunction to examine evidence dispassionately and critically'. As such it is not the prerogative of survey researchers. Methods are tools which must be adapted to circumstances. For obvious reasons Wallis could not conduct a social survey of randomly selected practising Scientologists. However, the fact that many of his respondents were no longer members of the Church, and that some were openly hostile to it, suggests (to him at least) only that their information *may* be biased, not that it necessarily must be so. Wallis insists that he has scrupulously cross-checked information secured from informants, 'whether devoted adherents or active opponents', against other sources. Documents were critically scrutinized and handled in the same way. So the fact that the study does not fulfil the criteria of survey research does not, in his view, make it inherently unscientific. Ultimately, however, he is prepared, like Simmons, to leave the matter with readers, who are invited to read Hubbard's work and to compare its 'objectivity' and use of 'the scientific method' with that displayed in the pages of *The Road to Total Freedom*. Of course, for my part I can only urge sceptics among my own readers to try the same exercise and draw their own conclusions about the matter, although as one who has recently completed this task I feel bound to report that I found most Scientology publications to be littered with unsubstantiated assertions, logically contradictory propositions and frankly unintelligible conclusions. I cannot say that I was impressed by the 'scientific and objective' nature of the arguments I encountered.

Other criticisms of Wallis's text have been more circumspect. Wallis himself has since conducted many additional studies of other new religious movements. The early research on Scientology (which formed the substance of his doctoral dissertation) has thus been absorbed into later and more general statements about contemporary sectarianism. His *Elementary Forms of the New Religious Life* (published in 1984) is only the most notable of these. It is difficult, therefore, to extract criticisms directed specifically towards *The Road to Total Freedom* from the wider debates in which Wallis was subsequently involved.

For example, in his later work Wallis extended the typology of new religions originally developed in his doctoral research by isolating a category of 'world-accommodating' movements, to place alongside the world-rejecting and world-affirming types. Innovatory religions with a world-accommodating orientation include the Charismatic Renewal and Neo-Pentecostal Movements, which actually carry few implications for individual conduct in the world, since their principal purpose is to provide stimulation for personal and spiritual experiences. Life, however it is fashioned, should simply be lived in a more religiously inspired manner – and be accompanied by enthusiastic participation in shared religious experiences such as glossolalia (speaking in tongues). This tripartite typology for understanding new religious movements (NRMs) was then criticized by other sociologists of religion who had developed alternative classifications. James Beckford, for example, accepted that Wallis's approach 'offers clarification of the affinities between members' experience of life in rationalized societies and the message of typical NRMs'. However, he also suggests that Wallis's scheme is too crude, since it does not explain how the broad 'orientation to the world' of any particular sect relates to the often quite different outlooks that have been shown to exist among individual members. Beckford's own typology, by comparison, classifies cults and sects according to their 'mode of insertion' into society. That is, movements are distinguished by the 'character, strength, and valency' of the bonds between members, on the one hand, and the 'wider range of relationships generated, sustained and occasionally broken, with people who are not NRM members', on the other. Similarly, other sociologists have designed typologies that highlight variations in the extent and manner of 'moral accountability' among movement members, or in the metaphysics and underlying philosophies of the different belief-systems. Of course, the point about such classification systems is that, in themselves, they are neither correct nor incorrect, but simply more or less useful for whatever subsequent purposes the researcher has in mind. Beckford, for example, is particularly interested in explaining how and why the new religious movements are differentially susceptible to public controversy. From this point of view, it seems appropriate to investigate the social bonds by which members are individually and collectively related to each other, and to groups and institutions in the wider society generally. Beckford's interest in the relationship between sect and society is then quite properly reflected in his classification of new religious movements as distinctive sets of social relationships, a classification that is neither more true nor false than Wallis's own, merely better suited to the task in hand.

Wallis, together with his colleague Steve Bruce, has also challenged the popular thesis, advanced by David Snow and others, that individuals are more likely to be recruited into new religious movements (and indeed social movements generally) if they are linked to them by means of the extra-movement social network of a member. Moreover, individuals (however they are approached) are said to be more likely to join if they are uninvolved in extra-movement networks (lacking dense ties to kin, friends, or colleagues), which can act as countervailing influences. In other words, recruitment via personal networks is more successful than approaching strangers, and more successful among the socially isolated than among those already involved in other social networks. In fact, as Wallis and Bruce rather convincingly demonstrate, there is little support for either of these claims in the strictly limited range of empirical materials cited by their proponents. To the contrary, a good deal of evidence elsewhere suggests that networks are not necessary for success, and that, for example, 'their importance can be far outweighed by other means of contacting potential recruits at particular times'. Dianetics itself secured most of its early following almost entirely through the presentation of Hubbard's ideas in *Astounding Science Fiction*. At various times the Children of God have successfully reached new recruits via the similarly impersonal medium of television.

Lack of space means that we cannot pursue the details of these exchanges here. In any case, they take us far beyond the text of *The Road to Total Freedom*, and address issues that were taken up only in Wallis's later research on other cults and sects. However, the debate about social networks and movement recruitment does offer a pertinent reminder of an issue which was central to Wallis's early work on Scientology, and to which he has returned on several subsequent occasions in discussions with others. Networks may make people 'available' for conversion but, as Wallis and Bruce point out, availability is not a fixed quality. Whether or not one is available for adultery (despite one's spouse and children) will probably depend upon who exactly offers us their company. Similarly, availability for recruitment to a religious movement will depend upon that movement's aims, methods and appeal. In other words, 'recruitment to social movements cannot be understood without exploration of the meaning-endowing activity of the pre-recruit, his active construction of the movement, its aims and importance and his re-construction of his biography, commitments and relationships in this light'. Clearly, there is a general principle of methodology at issue here. Wallis and Bruce insist that, while not everything actors say should be taken at face value (for example, people may be forced to find acceptable 'excuses', where their actions are inconsistent with their beliefs), nevertheless, 'close attention should be paid to what actors say about why they do what they do'. 'Reasons' and 'motives' for joining a religious movement are socially constructed, but notwithstanding their negotiability, they are essential data for the sociologist seeking to explain recruitment. This brings us back squarely to the issues with which we started. How are sociologists to interpret the actor's own 'motivational account' in their attempts to explain his or her actions? And why should we privilege the sociologist's version of events if contradictory stories are told by others?

V

As we have seen, Wallis's interpretation of Scientology was rejected by representatives of the Church, who insisted that he could not possibly *understand* their faith because such insight was open only to those who believed in its teachings. I would argue that this criticism is entirely unconvincing. If, as seems to be the case, the Church is propounding the view that concepts such as 'theta' and 'clear' are ultimately mysterious, then the claim that Wallis cannot understand them is surely self-defeating, since nobody – including sincere believers – can understand the completely mysterious. Indeed, it seems to me that the contrary proposition is more plausible: that Wallis was actually in a better position to understand the movement than were those whom it recruited as members. To take but one example, Scientologists regard the E-meter as infallible, whereas Wallis judges its use to be futile. The important point here is that believers cannot raise the futility of metering as an issue without challenging the entire corpus of Hubbard's teachings about Dianetics. They also lack access to an external vantage point from which the methods of the meter might be questioned or criticized. Consequently, there is simply no alternative to the belief in its findings – unless, of course, one is prepared to abandon *all* of one's Scientological precepts. Wallis, on the other hand, can not only understand the techniques surrounding the use of the meter, and the claims that are made for its findings, but he can also perceive both the inconsistencies in these and the ways in which such inconsistencies are systematically protected from outright refutation. He can, for example, draw illuminating comparisons with similar practices elsewhere. Scientologists themselves can never gain sufficient distance from their own beliefs, or the necessary access to alternative belief-systems, to analyze the use of the E-meter in this way. It is surely they, rather than Wallis, who have closed minds.

Assuming, therefore, that it is not *a priori* impossible to understand religious belief-systems from the standpoint of the nonbeliever, a number of more specific problems surrounding actors' and sociologists' accounts of religious activities then present themselves. These can best be understood by considering briefly the series of papers on language, situated actions and vocabularies of motive written during the 1940s by the famous American sociologist C. Wright Mills. These have since been recognized as classic attempts to further the sociological understanding of motivation. However, they also anticipate some of the subsequent discussion about membership of social movements, including that between Wallis and his critics concerning the status of actors' accounts of their religious activities.

Mills's argument is deceptively simple. He sets himself the task of outlining a sociology of motivation and of distinguishing this clearly from the more usual biological and psychological approaches to the subject. Conventionally, within these other disciplines, motives are conceptualized as 'internal states' or 'drives' pushing individuals towards given actions. From this point of view, the verbal statements that an actor may offer by way of accounting for his or her behaviour are perceived merely to be *ex post facto* justifications (rationalizations), quite separate from the 'real' purposes behind the activity in question. However, Mills argues that the idea of 'internal motives' is simplistic, since precisely what is important about social action is the fact that it is *social*: it involves other actors who, like the initiating agent, interpret and attribute meaning to his or her behaviour. For this reason actors think about *prospective* action in terms of its reasonableness to significant others. Sociologically speaking, therefore, 'a motive is a term in a vocabulary which appears to the actor himself and/or to the observer to be an adequate reason for his conduct'. People query their ability to offer reasonable accounts of their behaviour *before* they act, so that the decision to do something may itself be dependent, wholly or in part, on the perceived availability of socially acceptable motives, a 'vocabulary' which makes a particular course of conduct seem 'reasonable' or 'legitimate'. Of course, these vocabularies are socially and historically located, so that 'plausible explanations' are, as Mills puts it, 'limited to the vocabulary of motives acceptable for given situations by given social circles'. Thus, for example, it is no longer generally acceptable, in contemporary Germany, physically to assault Jews simply on the grounds that they are Jews. At one time, however, a socially acceptable rhetoric in terms of which such assaults could be justified – at least to some Germans – was readily available.

This view of motivation generates a model of social action that is sociologically sophisticated. Mills captures both the dynamic quality of action and the reflective capacity of actors. Motives – acceptable grounds for social action – are continuously imputed to our conduct by ourselves and by others. In attributing motives, both we and they draw on available motivational vocabularies, and assess conduct as reasonable or otherwise in relation to the justification that has been offered. To the extent that motives justify behaviour, they may alter, reinforce, promote, or deter a particular course of action. Indeed, we may begin to act for one motive, and in the course of so doing adopt an auxiliary motive in order to explain the action to others who have called it into question. The latter motive, no less than the former, is a 'cause' of the conduct in question since it facilitates its continuation. Similarly, by attaching certain standardized intentions to given types of conduct, significant others may promote or inhibit the behaviour of their peers. To use the example offered by Mills, we can see how the parent controls the behaviour of the child by ascribing motives to its conduct: actions are called 'good', 'naughty', 'greedy' and so forth, and in this way the child learns what is acceptable and unacceptable behaviour. Motives, then, are the actor's anticipation of the judgement of others; and, at the same time, the means by which peers may influence or attempt to influence the activities of fellow actors.

A huge amount has been written about the sociology of motivation since Mills's time. For example, sociologists of deviance have examined the ways in which delinquents convince themselves that their criminal activities are 'justified', and therefore quite consistent with otherwise conformist values and behaviour. Various 'techniques of neutralization' can be employed to 'excuse' deviance, as in the cases of 'denying the victim' (who got only what he or she somehow deserved), and 'denying responsibility' (where the delinquent excuses himself or herself as a victim of circumstances in which any other reasonable person would have done the same thing). These studies have established not only that people reflect upon their present and anticipated future courses of action, but also that they reconstruct their biographies according to changes either in self-image or in the expectations of others. Clearly, therefore, explanations of conduct are offered *situationally*: that is, the form and content of these explanations will tend to vary, depending upon which significant other is requesting the account, in what context and for what purpose or purposes.

It is not necessary to review this voluminous and complex literature here. The point is simply that Mills's discussion of the role of motives in social action, and status of motivational accounts in sociology, raises two analytically separable – although in practice closely related – issues which, to this day, have remained matters of deep controversy within the discipline. These concern, first of all, the relationship between an actor's expressed motive for pursuing a particular course of action (the *stated* reason), and his or her actual motive for doing so (the *real* reason); and, second, the relationship between the *actor's* explanation for his or her behaviour and that offered by the *sociologist*. More pointedly, we might ask 'Do the actor's stated motives constitute an adequate causal explanation for his or her conduct?' and 'In what sense are sociological explanations of behaviour different from commonsense alternatives?'

These questions are particularly germane where sociological studies of religion are concerned. In *The Road to Total Freedom*, for example, Wallis reports that new recruits to Scientology progressively acquire a vocabulary peculiar to the movement, in terms of which they can articulate their feelings and thoughts, define the behaviour of others and reconstruct their own biographies. They can, for example, describe themselves as feeling 'banky' on a particular day; can locate acquaintances as '1.1 on the Tone Scale'; characterize others as 'showing a high degree of ARC'; or redescribe their past as 'one big reactive mind' to which they do not wish to return. In short, as the recruit moves from being a client to a follower, 'he comes to view his biography in terms of a vocabulary and conceptual scheme provided by Scientology theory and practice, and to see his own goals as only attainable through the achievement of broader goals specified by the movement leadership'. However, followers of Scientology continue, for the most part, to be highly involved in conventional society. Most members of the Church hold occupations outside the movement. They are relatively isolated from each other because, as we have seen, Scientology has developed little in the way of a communal orientation. As Wallis notes, this degree of involvement in a 'conventional' world (of work, family, leisure, and so forth), inhabited by a majority which do not share Scientological beliefs, is a major challenge to the validity or legitimacy of the Church's definition of reality. It requires followers constantly to justify the movement's 'deviant' worldview, both to others and (in consequence) to themselves. Church leaders have devised a variety of mechanisms to cope with this problem. These devices effectively constitute what Wallis calls 'structural and motivational constraints' on the articulation of scepticism or criticism.

For example, ordinary members are encouraged to meet only at formal gatherings organized by the Church hierarchy for the purpose of disseminating the downward flow of information, rather than for the fostering of debate or discussion among its followers. Indeed, the Church's Code of Ethics forbids collective discussion and criticism as a 'general crime', alongside other 'high crimes' such as 'dependency on other mental or philosophical procedures than Scientology', 'continued membership of a divergent group' and 'inciting to subordination'. The elaborate hierarchy of sanctification also serves as a barrier to criticism, since those on the lower rungs of the ladder are constantly offered the promise that any lingering doubts will be dispelled by information that is not yet available to them, but will become so when a more elevated status is achieved. The many hundreds of neologisms invented by Hubbard ('randomity', 'itsa', 'opterm', 'expanded gita'), and the apparently mysterious quality of much of his writing (including axioms which state that 'The static, having postulated as-is-ness, then practises alter-is-ness, and so achieves the apparency of is-ness and so obtains reality'), also serve to convince members that there is always more to learn before they will be in a position to criticize the beliefs and practices of the movement. Almost all Church publications are prefaced by an 'Important Note' which states that 'The only reason a person gives up a study or becomes confused or unable to learn is that he or she has gone past a word or phrase that was not understood'. One fails to understand Hubbard, not because he is talking nonsense, but because one has missed some earlier word in the text. Similarly, auditing failures are 'explained away' as a consequence of 'withholds' (failure to disclose something which should have been reported), or of auditors employing 'out-Tech' (a practice not approved, or conducted in a manner not approved by Hubbard himself).

These constraints ensure that, as Wallis puts it, 'the individual learns to doubt his own judgement; to locate some meaning in the un-doubted mystification of much of Hubbard's writing; or to acquiesce to some half-comprehended and yet half-incomprehensible statement in the hope that all will be made clear to him at some later point'. However, they also raise major difficulties for sociologists seeking to interview members about their motives for joining the Church, or reasons for remaining loyal to it. Quite simply, motivational accounts elicited in this way may well simply reflect the ideology and social organization of the movement, since they are likely to be couched in terms of a vocabulary and 'reconstructed' biography that members have acquired since their conversion to the faith.

Wallis himself does not discuss this problem – at least not in *The Road to Total Freedom* – but it is one which has greatly exercised other sociologists of religion. In a study of Jehovah's Witnesses, for example, Beckford found that members' accounts of their conversion were closely related to the ideology and organization of the Watch-tower Society itself. For instance, interviewees universally denied that they had experienced some sort of sudden revelation, or come to the movement because a crucial turning-point had been reached in their lives. Rather, they stressed that their membership had been accom-plished gradually, as a result of repeated exposure to Watchtower teachings and personnel over many months or years. Conversion was simply a steady progression of subtle changes in outlook and action. As Beckford notes, this way of constructing 'motivational accounts' among Witnesses simply reflects the Watchtower Society's perception of its special place in history, and its exclusive Covenant with God as the unique respository of His will. Given this ideology, 'it is inconceivable that the God who has contracted into a special and exclusive relationship with the Watchtower Society could also legiti-mize unilateral arrangements with a privileged individual', and the accounts given by members merely acknowledge this. New recruits learn that, in describing their conversion, 'in view of the slow and progressive way in which God has supposedly revealed the secrets of His plans for the World, it is fitting for their personal spiritual development to follow a similar pattern'.

Beckford concludes from this observation that 'actors' talk about conversion ceases to be an objective resource for the sociologist and becomes, instead, an interesting topic in its own right. To study conversion is then to study the variety of conditions under which it makes sense to talk about being converted.' Consequently, he takes issue with 'those attempts to explain religious conversion which do not acknowledge the fact that actors' accounts of experiences cannot be objective reports in a neutral observation language but are artfully accomplished constructions. They ... embody the socially transmit-ted rules for constituting certain experiences as religious conversions.' Not surprisingly, therefore, he is critical of Wallis's use of actors' accounts of their own motives for joining, supporting, or leaving Scientology, since he believes this to be 'insensitive to the special requirements of research into actors' changing sense of self-identity, meaning, etc.' In Beckford's view, accounts do not provide reliable evidence as to motives, and cannot therefore serve as unproblematic resources for the sociologist who is trying to understand social action.

Wallis and Bruce subsequently addressed themselves at some length to this particular issue. In a series of exchanges with a number of critics they attempted to 'rescue motives' for sociological study generally and, therefore, to defend Wallis's earlier explanation of why particular individuals were recruited by, and stayed loyal to, the Church of Scientology. As we have seen, this explanation rests (at least in part) on the accounts offered by members and former members in sociological interviews with Wallis himself, accounts which Beckford seems to suggest we should simply disregard because 'they are not fixed, once-and-for-all descriptions of phenomena as they occurred in the past'. It is soon apparent from these exchanges, however, that Wallis and Bruce fully appreciate the fact that respondents' accounts cannot be treated as if they offered 'objective' reports on a 'fixed' reality. Rather, their own view of this matter (and it is one which I endorse most strongly), is that good sociology 'steers a middle course between routinely discounting actors' accounts of their action . . . and an . . . approach which insists that such accounts are all we can really know'.

As was suggested previously, the problem with the former (what one might call 'structurally determinist') approach is that it rests on the unrealistic assumption that shared objective characteristics somehow generate shared definitions and common action – so that, for example, similarly isolated individuals are equally available for recruitment to social movements. In fact, as Wallis's own research and that of many others has repeatedly shown, not all isolated individuals join such movements. Clearly, therefore, without investigating actors' 'definitions of the situation', we cannot actually say why *some* isolated individuals were recruited while others were not, or why they were recruited to one *particular* social movement rather than another. The danger inherent in the latter approach, on the other hand, is that it threatens to trivialize sociology by translating all questions about social behaviour ('Why do people join religious movements?') into questions of discourse analysis ('How do people talk about joining religious movements?'). Presumably, since we cannot get at the 'real' reasons behind conduct, we must simply give up the attempt. It is possible only to study the anatomy of accounts – how they are structured, offered, and so forth. Obviously, if the motivational stories told by actors are denied any explanatory status whatsoever, then most of what currently passes for social science is rendered obsolete. However, as Wallis and Bruce point out, there is a logical objection to Beckford's claim that we can learn nothing about the reasons or intentions behind some previous course of conduct from an actor's present account of it; namely, that this claim implicitly asserts what is explicitly being denied. That is, 'the tacit claim that the underlying reality is not being presented in accounts crucially depends on being able to compare the account with the prior reality', since 'some insight into "real" motives must underlie any claim that the motivational story being advanced by the actor is not what it seems'.

The onus would seem to be on Beckford, and the many other methodological radicals (or ethnomethodologists) who share his point of view, to reveal the specific procedures by which they are granted unique access to this epistemologically privileged view of actors' 'real' motives. As yet they have been unable to do so. It seems appropriate, therefore, to conclude this chapter with a short summary of Wallis and Bruce's own procedures for 'rescuing motives'. These seem, to me at least, to constitute an entirely reasonable approach to the study of motivational accounts and also to be a sound basis for the claim that sociological explanations are not merely commonsense ('what everyone already knows'), translated into a specialized and private jargon.

They start from the premise that accounts are hypothetical. Actors can be deceived about their own motives. Sometimes, for example, a person may not wish to acknowledge (even to him or herself) what he or she really believes. Alternatively, when presented with evidence that seems to contradict a motivational tale, people may change their minds about their 'real' motives or attempt to redescribe the conduct to which these intentions pertain: 'In short, actors' accounts, like sociologists' accounts, are efforts to conceptualize and explain behaviour and beliefs, and both are equally hypothetical.' Of course, it may well be the case that there are considerable discrepancies between the two versions of reality: they offer 'competing hypotheses resolvable only by reference to the evidence'. Under these circumstances, the sociologist may reject the actor's account, if, for example, there is a disjuncture between the alleged motives and the reality of his or her action. Where church leaders claim to have the welfare of converts at heart, but nevertheless forbid communication between members of the same family, regularly administer corporal punishment for trivial infringements of church rules and supress all attempts at questioning their own commands, then one can reasonably set the actor's account aside in favour of an alternative advanced by the sociologist. Thus, the claim made by leading Scientologists that their Church is fully considerate of members' wishes is simply less plausible than Wallis's conclusion that this is a totalitarian organization, in view of the evidence provided by the behaviour of the Church leaders themselves.

Often, however, both accounts are seemingly consistent with the data at hand. Resolution of the conflict between them therefore requires the specification and discovery of types of evidence which will be compatible with the one but not the other. Sometimes this is possible, but occasionally such materials are not available, and may in fact never become available. Thus, to take the example given by Wallis and Bruce, 'whether Joseph Smith of the Mormons was a charlatan or really did believe himself to have received plates of gold containing the text of the *Book of Mormon* from the angel Moroni, may simply be unresolvable in practice even though both believer and sociologist know perfectly well what would constitute relevant evidence'. In situations such as this, where believers attribute causal efficacy to a supernatural agency (such as 'God' or 'theta') which the sociologist cannot recognize, the researcher does not treat the two claims as competing (thus implying that the actor is wrong); but, instead, 'treats the claims as related by an equivalence rule (for "God did so-and-so" read "actor believes God did so-and-so")'. In other words, the sociologist does not exclude the possibility of God's agency, but recognizes that the only way we might observe this is in what people believe. Such beliefs can then be included *within* socio- logical explanations without either affirming or denying their validity.

It is clearly the case, therefore, that both actor and sociologist are in the same business of providing explanations; that is, advancing hypotheses which, where they conflict, are resolvable in principle if not always in practice by recourse to further evidence. Nevertheless, according to Wallis and Bruce, there are three important differences between sociological and commonsensical explanations of social conduct. First, sociologists routinely undertake observation, compari- son and reflection on a *systematic* basis as a matter of course, whereas actors only occasionally do so. Actors are, quite properly, concerned more with living than explaining. Sociologists, on the other hand, are bound by the established canons of scientific procedure, as these pertain to logical consistency, empirical proof, the limits of gener- alization, and so forth. Second, and as a consequence of this, actors' explanations 'typically arrive at a point of satisfaction earlier'. Under normal circumstances, they are not required to press beyond the attribution of 'appropriate' motives, in order to explore 'the condi- tions under which beliefs and motives of this type are formulated'. Thus, for example, leading Scientologists hypothesize that members are 'free' to leave the movement at any time, and take the fact that so few choose to do so as a reflection of their continued 'commitment' to the Church's ideals and teachings. However, by going on to explore empirically the limits set by the relevant social and nonsocial condi- tions of action, the sociologist may well come to appreciate the extent to which members feel themselves constrained to continue in the faith, simply, for example, to avoid making the embarrassing admission (to themselves as well as others) that the decision to invest large sums of money in Scientology courses was a serious error of judgement. Few of us will happily admit to having bought a pig in a poke – far less to having done so on a regular basis, over several years and on each occasion from the same source. Finally, actors are preoccupied with the personal rather than the general, whereas 'sociologists seek, through systematic comparison, to explore typical patterns, to formulate general accounts, and thus to achieve some explanatory economy'. Similarly, where actors do make generalizations, they are usually content to do so without regard for the typicality of the cases before them. Sociologists, if they are to retain their credibility, must demonstrate that particular instances are representative in all appropriate respects.

Of course, as Wallis and Bruce recognize, these differences do not suggest a sharp distinction between sociological and commonsense accounts of the world. Rather, they point to the conclusion that sociology is a more systematic and rigorous form of commonsense, requiring constant reference to social and historical context. This means that more often than not sociologists will reject the conventional wisdom of the person in the street. For example, popular belief may have it that the unemployed are work-shy scroungers whose failure to escape the dole reflects incorrigible laziness. However, systematic sociological study has confirmed time and again that the great majority of those without jobs are genuinely seeking employment, and are far from content with their dependency on state welfare payments. The 'social and historical contexts' (for example, labour markets) in which they find themselves often seriously constrain their ability to find work. In one sense, therefore, as was noted at the outset, the sociological enterprise is indeed inescapably subversive. Its principal objective is to de-mystify the world in which we all live. Governments, on the other hand, like certain sectarian religious movements, tend to deal in ideologies and invariably seek to mystify reality for their own particular political purposes. That, indeed, is the very stuff of politics. Understandably, therefore, governments tend to frown upon sociological studies – unless, of course, the results of these studies can be used to endorse official policies and objectives. To the extent that sociologists reject the many demands that they pursue 'applied' or 'relevant' research, as defined by the government of the day, they are clearly resisting an attempt at substituting ideology for science; I do not see why I or my sociological colleagues should be in the least bit apologetic about this.

10 *On the social origins of clinical depression*

I

The vexed question of the relationship between sociological and other accounts of social behaviour is also raised by the last of the three most obviously policy-relevant studies which I have included among my selected texts. George Brown and Tirril Harris's *Social Origins of Depression* summarizes the results of a lengthy sociological study of psychiatric disorder in women. The authors attempt to identify stressful life-events (such as separation from one's spouse, a change of residence, or even witnessing a serious accident) which are causally linked to mental disorder. However, from their earlier work on schizophrenia, they are aware of the possible contamination of causal analyses that can arise from the tendency among patients to search retrospectively for potential provoking agents which might help explain their psychiatric disorders. In other words, some respondents make an *ex post facto* 'effort after meaning' which *might* lead them to reinterpret their biography, perhaps even as a result of unintended prompting during the course of the sociological interview itself. They assign a meaning after the onset of depression to an event that happened beforehand which they would not necessarily have considered noteworthy prior to the illness. Such reworking of the past can seriously compromise any causal analysis. An observed association between mental disorder and severe life-events might, at least in some part, be simply an artefact of the research design. The unit of study (stressful life-event) and its putative consequences (clinical depression) appear to be causally related precisely because they have been confounded during the process of measurement.

I argued in the previous chapter that Roy Wallis faced a similar problem in handling respondents' statements about their loyalties to Scientology. These accounts are subject to what Wallis calls 'extensive structural and motivational constraints' progressively imposed by membership of the Church: members tend to reconstruct their biographies according to a logic and ideology that are learned after conversion. However, while recognizing the practical difficulties for causal analysis raised by the social construction of motivational rhetoric, Wallis nevertheless insists that good sociology starts from the actor's own account, and then steers a middle course between routinely discounting it (the structural–determinist view), or accepting that this account is all that can ever be known about the behaviour in question (the ethnomethodological position). In Wallis's view, it is usually possible to arbitrate between sociology, commonsense and the actor's own explanation for a particular course of conduct (if indeed there are contradictions between these), by implementing the established rules of scientific procedure governing logical consistency, empirical proof and the limits of generalization. In short, sociology is more systematic than commonsense, and sociological explanations are as a rule more rigorous than those offered by actors themselves.

As we shall see, Brown and Harris not only endorsed this general view of the relationship between sociological and other accounts of social behaviour, but also devised an innovative research technique for circumventing the problems raised by respondents' post-onset re-interpretations of meaning. This required the researchers to assess the severity of the various life-events in each individual's biography irrespective of how the interviewee herself felt about them. In other words, Brown and Harris ignored (at least at the outset) respondents' reports as to how threatening any particular event was, and substituted their own. As I hope to demonstrate below, the rationale for this seemingly eccentric approach is actually quite sound, and the results are markedly more convincing than one might expect.

Because Brown and Harris base their conclusions on social survey materials, their discussion tends to be couched in the technical language of aetiology (causation), with particular reference to the problems of identifying 'interaction effects', 'spurious links' and 'contamination' due to confounding variables. (The medical framework that underpins epidemiology tends also to encourage the sometimes confusing use of specialist terminology throughout the book.) However, the researchers' survey-based approach to the problem of depression merely offers a somewhat more numerical and formal treatment of the same explanatory and analytical issues that are raised in Wallis's study of Scientology, and illustrates yet again the lengths to which most sociologists will go in order to prevent bias of any kind from entering into their analysis.

II

Brown and Harris are, in fact, so sensitive to the methodological problems surrounding the study of mental illness that they devote the first third of their report (fully a hundred pages of text) exclusively to the discussion of research strategy and techniques. It would be tedious – and in any case entirely impractical – to attempt a summary of all the salient issues here. However, it is necessary to consider explicitly the principal aspects of research design, because so much of the subsequent controversy hinges about these technical and conceptual issues.

The study is based on a sample of women aged between 18 and 65 living in the Inner London Borough of Camberwell. Two groups were interviewed. One of these consisted of 114 psychiatric patients undergoing treatment as residents or out-patients at local hospitals during the early 1970s. The other, comprising two separate samples totalling 458 respondents, was a comparison group selected at random from the general population (with interviews being conducted during 1969–71 and 1974–5). There is a two-fold rationale for including this comparison group. First, and most obviously, it provides additional untreated cases for study. More importantly, however, the researchers wished specifically to test the hypothesis that 'clinical depression is an understandable response to adversity', so it was necessary to esablish empirically whether or not stressful life-events occurred more commonly before the onset of illness, by comparing depressed women with those who displayed no such symptoms. Both groups were given systematic clinical interviews by one of the two sociologists, irrespective of whether patients were also seen by any of the research psychiatrists associated with the study. Furthermore, for the first fifty patients the other interviewer also contacted a close relative, collecting additional information about events, difficulties, the timing of onset of psychiatric symptoms, and other relevant data. This was then used as a check on the reliability of the accounts provided by respondents, particularly with regard to the precise timing of onset and changes in the course of the disorder, about which the researchers obtained extremely high levels of agreement between relatives and patients.

Camberwell was chosen as the site of the project principally because of the researchers' contacts with local hospitals having well-established psychiatric services, but also because social class was to be considered explicitly as a variable for investigation, and the borough was sufficiently heterogeneous in the class composition of its residents. The research concentrates on women, not only because women form the majority (usually about two-thirds) of the depressed patients seen by psychiatrists, but also in order to avoid the risks of bias associated with a high refusal rate among those sampled. Interviews required several hours of each respondent's time, and the research team reasoned (quite plausibly) that women would be more likely to agree to participate in the study, simply because they were more often at home during the day. In fact, thirty-five male patients were also interviewed, as were thirty-four women contacted independently via two sets of local general practitioners who had been asked to pass to the team the names of any female patients who had consulted them about a recent onset of depression. A random sample of 154 women aged 18 to 65 living on North Uist in the Outer Hebrides (representing some 40 per cent of eligible women on the island) were also interviewed in 1975. However, these three special groups figure only intermittently in the analysis and add little to the findings reported for the main sample, so nothing more will be said about them in this context.

In the event, the interviewers established that as many as 17 per cent of the 458 women they saw in Camberwell were psychiatrically disturbed at some time during the year prior to interview, the majority of these being clinically depressed. A further 19 per cent were considered to be borderline cases. Women included in either of these categories had their designation as an 'onset case' or 'borderline case' independently corroborated by a psychiatrist. It was, of course, necessary to exclude these individuals from the comparison group, in order to prevent misleading diminution of any differences between it and the group of patients, and this reduced its effective size from 458 to 382. ('Borderline cases' were included among the remaining 'normals'.) However, the researchers then turned this (wholly anticipated) development in the research to their advantage, by using the depressed women whom they excluded from the comparison group as an independent check on certain characteristics found among the patients. For example, they were able to identify social factors of aetiological importance in explaining depression which also influenced who then received psychiatric care, by comparing the life-events and circumstances of the patients with those of women among the general population who were clinically depressed but had not sought medical attention.

Most of the women sampled from among the general population of Camberwell were asked about their lives during the twelve months immediately preceding the interview. However, if the researchers identified the onset of a depressive episode during the first three months of this year, a thirteen-week period was always covered before the onset. Among some cases, therefore, this extended the time-span covered by the interview to fifteen months. All 114 patients were seen within six weeks of hospital admission (for in-patients) or attendance (for out-patients). In most cases the researchers dealt with the year prior to interview, but again this period was extended backwards by anything up to thirteen weeks, where onset occurred during the first three months of the relevant year.

The interviews themselves were preceded by months of painstaking preparation, and informed by previous experience gained over many years during the earlier studies of schizophrenia, particularly with regard to the measurement of life-events. The Present State Examination (PSE), which asks about symptoms in the last month, was modified to cover the twelve months before interview or admission and was used to measure the amount, severity and nature of psychiatric disorder among the sample – the 'dependent variable' of the study. Life-events (the putative 'independent variable') were identified by questioning the women about a comprehensive list of events which could be dated more or less precisely and were likely to be followed by strong negative or positive emotions. The list, which contained thirty-eight types of occurrence falling into eight broad categories, embraces a wide range of events involving *'change* in an activity, role, person or idea' (see Table 10.1.) The interview schedule was structured by this list, but was also sufficiently flexible to allow the specially trained interviewers to probe in depth the precise circumstances surrounding any event, by consulting a lengthy reference book which provided guidance about what to inquire after and include. (Only three interviewers were used in the first Camberwell survey, and four in the second, and all received several months of training.) Moreover, the researchers also gathered information about *ongoing* difficulties (as opposed to life-events occurring at discrete points of time) associated with work, housing, health, children, marriage, social obligations, friends, leisure, money, neighbourhood and general disappointments. These questions ensured that potentially stressful circumstances which were relatively constant, but did not generate a particular crisis during the preceding year, were nevertheless recorded – as, for example, in the case of a woman living for three years in two small damp rooms with her husband and two children. Other such 'ongoing difficulties' included a son's drug-taking, receiving unpleasant letters from a parent about living with a man, and being forced to move from a house to a furnished room because of non-payment of rent. Once identified, these sorts of difficulties involved interviewers in collecting a good deal of supplementary factual material – about the exact state of repair of a house, frequency

Table 10.1 The categories of significant life-events

1   Changes in a role for the subject, such as changing a job, and losing or gaining an opposite-sex friend for the unmarried.
2   Changes in a role for close relatives or household members, such as a husband staying off work because of a strike.
3   Major changes in health, including admissions to hospital and developing an illness expected to be serious; and
4   Similar changes in close relatives or household members.
5   Residence changes and any marked change in the amount of contact with close relatives and household members.
6   Forecasts of change, such as being told about being rehoused.
7   Valued goal fulfillments or disappointments, such as being offered a house to rent at a reasonable price.
8   Other dramatic events involving (a) the subject, e.g. witnessing a serious accident or being stopped by the police when driving; or (b) a close relative or household member, e.g. learning that a brother had been arrested.

Source: Social Origins of Depression, p. 67.

of contact with social services, precise degree of handicap associated with a chronic illness, and so forth. Finally, the interview covered in a similarly exhaustive fashion the feelings and attitudes surrounding each event, in order to establish 'what it *meant* for the woman – in the sense of the thoughts and feelings she had before, at the time, and after the event'. For example, respondents were asked about the extent to which they had anticipated each event, about worries beforehand, whether or not they discussed their worries with others, if this made them angry, tense, ashamed, and so forth.

The interview schedule for life-events and ongoing difficulties is included as an appendix to the report, and one can hardly fail to be impressed by its comprehensive coverage of the practical, emotional and cognitive developments that might possibly be associated with these circumstances. However, I have always been especially struck by the thoughtful subsequent *coding* of this material, and in particular the various strategies that the researchers employed in order to prevent contamination between variables during the measurement process.

One such problem is raised by the very definition of depression. Psychiatrists have clustered a wide variety of symptoms under this label, although they generally accept that the depressed person usually experiences certain changes of mood (involving crying, restlessness, tiredness, sadness and loss of interest), together with other cognitive, somatic, or behavioural symptoms (including disturbance to sleep, loss of appetite, irritability, feelings of guilt, and social withdrawal). It is conventional, in diagnostic terms, to distinguish certain subcategories of the disorder: manic-depressive psychosis, endogenous depression, reactive-depressive psychosis, and so forth. One particular distinction, that between neurotic and psychotic depression, has been a subject of considerable debate among psychiatrists. The former is generally indicated by feeling worse in the evening, by finding difficulty in making decisions, and by crying and worrying a great deal. Symptoms of the latter include feeling worse in the morning, weight loss, constipation, delusions, hallucinations, agitation, and early-morning waking. Psychotic depression is held to arise autonomously (or endogenously) – perhaps as a result of genetic transmission. Neurotic depressions, on the other hand, are a response to external circumstances or difficulties. Psychiatrists cannot agree as to whether these represent separate conditions, or merely two extremes of a continuum of symptoms, with most cases of depression falling somewhere between. Moreover, like other subcategories of disorder, the distinction between psychotic and neurotic tends to confuse the act of classification with the subsequent search for causes and consequences. The categories are themselves aetiological, since they incorporate an assumption about causality within their definitions, rather than searching for causes independently. As Brown and Harris wryly observe, 'if one of the criteria for classifying someone as "psychotic-ally" rather than "neurotically" depressed is the absence of a precipi-tating event, then it is bound to follow that research based on this criterion will pinpoint a connection between events and neurotic rather than psychotic depression.'

In order to avoid such circularity in their aetiological reasoning, the Camberwell researchers therefore accepted the diagnostic classifica-tion of neurotic and psychotic *symptom patterns*, but (unlike psychia-trists) refused to accept that this distinction implied anything about the presence or absence of certain types of precipitating events. In other words, they followed clinical judgements about what was to count as a case of depression, but excluded from the diagnostic categories any variables which could be considered of possible aetiological signi-ficance. The research team subsequently developed a five-fold scale, ranging from 1 (marked) to 5 (mild), which they used to rank the overall severity of symptoms displayed at different points in time during the illness. (Some examples of overall severity ratings are shown in Table 10.2.) In due course, they were able to demonstrate that overall severity was only modestly associated with the psychotic/ neurotic distinction (the former tends to be characterized by a greater sense of hopelessness or resignation); and, more importantly, that the various social causes which provoked onset of depressive disorder were in fact correlated equally well with *both* of its supposed types. In short, as Brown and Harris put it, their analysis suggests that 'the psychiatric tradition has been misleading in its claim that there are, in any sense, two clearly distinct forms of depression and that the psychotic type is in general not "reactive"'.

The other major source of contamination in the causal analysis has already been mentioned. Psychiatrists generally accept that there is a causal link between stressful life-events and depression. However, not only does the conventional classification of types of depression actually presuppose such a link, but it is also possible that patients themselves make retrospective efforts to identify a particular difficulty to 'give' to the psychiatrist, both in order to be co-operative, and to facilitate self-understanding of their (otherwise mysterious) illness. The possibility cannot be ruled out that patients may have recon-structed their past in the light of their present mood. It is perhaps this 'effort after meaning' – rather than a causal link – which explains the association between life-events and depression. As was indicated above, the Camberwell team devised a highly original solution to this problem, by developing what they term 'contextual' (as opposed to 'self-report') scales of life-events and ongoing difficulties.

Contextual scales excluded all considerations of how the woman herself felt about particular events and circumstances. Interviewers recorded the occurrence of events and difficulties guided only by the interview schedule and reference manual discussed above. However,

Table 10.2   Examples of overall severity ratings

point 1
This involved an attempted suicide or gross retardation, e.g. staying in bed all day. Subject had been depressed and anxious for a few weeks, staying in bed more than two hours longer than usual, losing interest in her appearance, her housework and her knitting, with substantial loss of sleep and appetite. Just before admission she said life was not worth living and wanted to stab herself. A few days later she wounded herself quite seriously on the neck with a knife. She tried to hide the wound from her daughter and husband, becoming agitated and saying she did not want them to be blamed for it, or sent to prison. She was found the next day with the gas on, reading a book on methods of suicide.

point 2
She was terribly depressed and upset. She cried on and off nearly every day. She said life was not worth living, several times. She was very tensed up and her usual lack of energy became worse. She also became very slow. Her appetite substantially decreased. She lost interest in her clothing and her children and lost affection for them.

point 3
She looked miserable and depressed. She lacked energy – and would drop off to sleep. She was slower at doing things and did less around the house. She was quieter and sometimes did not answer. She lost interest in Bingo and betting. She worried about her job – she had been getting very forgetful at work and had complaints about this. She would wake up at night and would have difficulty getting off to sleep again. She was irritable and lost interest in her appearance. Her appetite decreased. She would worry about the psychiatric treatment of her daughter.

point 4
She was miserable, felt lost, and did not know what to do. She could not swallow or eat, had weight loss, slept badly, and had the shakes.

point 5
She was restless, fidgety, had constipation and always thought people were looking at her.

Source: Social Origins of Depression, pp. 306–8.

as Brown and Harris observe, this approach has one obvious weakness in that it treats as identical a wide range of events that are in fact different. The birth of a child, or death of a close relative, does *not* mean the same thing for all women. A happily married middle-class woman, with a house in her own name, an au pair, doting grand-mother and a substantial income from the stock market, is unlikely to experience childbirth as a threat in the same way as a working-class woman, separated from her violent husband, dependent on income from her own employment, and living in rented accommodation 400 miles away from her only relatives. The contextual scales therefore recognize this variation by assessing each event strictly in relation to its surrounding circumstances. Interviewers collected extensive biographical information about every event and difficulty. They subsequently recounted these details to the other members of the research team, without mentioning the woman's reactions to the event, or indeed whether or not she was psychiatrically disturbed. Each team-member then rated the different dimensions of the event, independently and without discussion, by 'using their judgement of how much threat such an event would involve for most people in biographical circumstances like those of the respondent'. For example, the event was judged in terms of its expectedness, the amount of support that was available to the subject, and so forth. From the point of view of understanding the aetiology of depression, it later emerged that the most important of these scales was the contextual measure of 'threat', which rated the threat or unpleasantness of each event – as judged by the research team rather than the respondent – in terms of its short-term and long-term implications. Severity of threat was assessed as 'marked', 'moderate', 'some', or 'little or none'. In this way, both the definition of a life-event itself, and the measured qualities of this unit of analysis (in terms of, for example, its effect in generating tension or changing routines) were accomplished without reference to any emotional upheavals that followed it.

Brown and Harris describe in considerable detail the precise procedures for rating events, explaining how they used a series of 'anchoring examples' to facilitate the assessment of severity, 'taking into account only biographically relevant circumstances surrounding the event' and how they thought 'most people would react given this configuration of circumstances'. Briefly, they achieved a high rate of inter-rater agreement about events, including for example 92 per cent agreement about the occurrence of long-term markedly and moderately threatening events. (These form about half of the events recorded among patients, around one quarter of those identified in the community sample, and contain all the events that were subsequently to be identified as important in provoking onset of depression.)

The researchers also instructed interviewers to collect detailed information, not only about events or difficulties and the precise circumstances surrounding them, but also about what these developments meant for the woman involved. As we have seen, the respondent's own thoughts and feelings were excluded from the process of contextual rating, which was carried out without considering her personal reaction to each event. However, as a separate exercise, these reactions were then rated by the research team, again according to a complex but standardized procedure, in order to yield 'self-reported' (as opposed to contextual) scales of measurement.

In this way the researchers constructed four scales of threat: contextual long-term, contextual short-term, self-reported long-term and self-reported short term; and each was rated on a four-point scale of severity. Since it was the first of these which was to prove particularly useful in constructing a causal model of depression, it is worth reporting that Brown and Harris document a good deal of agreement between the contextual and self-reported measures of threat among both patients and the general population alike. (The figures yield agreement coefficients of no less than 84 per cent and 95 per cent respectively.) However, as the authors themselves point out, the close correlation that pertains between the contextual and self-reported measures of threat is actually irrelevant. To observe the degree of correspondence is to misunderstand the methodology, since 'it is not that open-ended measures of life-events are necessarily invalid – simply that it is at present not permissible to rule out the possibility that they are'. Patients *may* exaggerate the threat of events in their retrospective effort after meaning. The Camberwell methodology allows us to rule out the possibility that such biographical reconstructions have contaminated the causal analysis. The fact that the overall results of the project are hardly changed if calculation is based on self-report alone does not detract from the sophistication or necessity of the contextual approach.

The detailed consideration (here reported only in its essentials) given by Brown and his colleagues to issues of methodology generally, and coding in particular, is easily explained. In their review of previous work on psychiatric disorder they demonstrate fairly conclusively that neither clinical studies nor epidemiological approaches successfully resolve the issues surrounding causality. The former are always open to the accusation that, in an attempt to make the experience of mental illness meaningful to the individual, the psychoanalyst simply imposes a *post hoc* interpretation on events during the process of therapy. Alternative ideas about aetiology are then equally plausible until some form of empirical testing is devised which can arbitrate between them. Survey approaches, on the other hand, despite their promise of arriving at suitable generalizations, have nevertheless failed to provide a convincing causal framework or model to which clinical interpretations can meaningfully be related. In the view of Brown and Harris, at least, previous epidemiological studies have not linked broad social categories (such as social class) to intervening processes (such as social roles) or immediate causes (stressful life-events), and thence to disorder (in this case clinical depression), in a meaningful and testable way. So, how does *Social Origins of Depression* transcend these limitations, and how persuasive is the causal explanation devised by its authors?

III

The Camberwell surveys demonstrated a clear association between depression, on the one hand, and both life-events and ongoing difficulties on the other. In the former case, it was 'severe' events (that is, events having a 'marked long-term' or 'moderate long-term' threat focused either on the woman herself or jointly with someone else) that had a higher rate among patients than normal women. 'Major' ongoing difficulties (where degree of contextual severity was again rated by the team, independently of the woman's own evaluations of her circumstances), seemed to play a similar aetiological role.

In broad terms, severe events were more than four times as common among patients than among normal women, with major difficulties more than three times more common. Each of these two types of 'provoking agent' had an independent effect in producing depression. Of the patients 61 per cent and of onset cases 83 per cent experienced an event or difficulty of causal importance, as compared with 49 per cent and 57 per cent respectively when severe events were considered, suggesting that the influence of events was about twice that of difficulties. However, the researchers could find no 'additivity' of events and difficulties, since there was nothing in their data to show that exposure to both provoking agents – or multiples of either – significantly increased the risk of depression. For example, 21 per cent of the women in Camberwell who had one or other but not both provoking agents developed depression during the year, compared with 27 per cent of those experiencing a severe event together with a major difficulty – a difference well below the level of statistical significance. Similarly, additivity of events had only a modest effect on outcomes, with the results confirming that only among those experiencing three or more severe events was there evidence that multiple exposure slightly increased the risk of breakdown. Moreover, it was only multiple *unrelated* severe events that had this effect, since related events did not seem to add to the likelihood of onset.

Of course, as the authors themselves concede, the notion of a 'long-term threat' is rather abstract. Do the severe events that seem to bring about depression have anything specific in common? The interview materials suggest strongly that 'loss and disappointment are the central features of most events bringing about clinical depression'. About three-quarters of all severe events occurring to patients and cases involved significant and unambiguous loss, such as a separation or threat of it, a life-threatening illness to someone close, a major material loss or disappointment, an enforced change of residence, severing of a close relationship, or crisis involving some element of loss (such as being made redundant in a job held for a long time). Conversely, if the proportion of persons is considered, 79 per cent of patients and 88 per cent of cases who had a severe event had at least one involving a loss of the kind just mentioned.

A rather different aetiological issue arises in the case of those interviewees whose depression stemmed from a major difficulty rather than a severe event; namely, the puzzle of 'why in the absence of a severe crisis a woman whose difficulty has already lasted so long should become depressed at that particular time'? The answer seems to lie in the tendency for depressed women with a major difficulty and no severe event to have a *minor* event just before onset. At least half of the women in this category experienced a seemingly trivial incident, but one which provoked a fundamental reappraisal of circumstances, and in due course a depressive disorder. In this way, minor incidents acted as catalysts 'leading to a new assessment of the hopelessness of life', and so played an important role in translating the experience of a major ongoing difficulty into clinical depression.

In total, therefore, only twenty-eight patients were without either a severe event or a major difficulty prior to onset. Brown and Harris investigated each of these exceptions in turn, and upon close inspection discovered that in fact most actually had experienced difficulties or events sufficient to provoke illness, but that the methodological rules operated by the researchers had 'misclassified' their circumstances as not severe or long-lasting enough to count as provoking agents. This is also true of the four onset cases in the community who seemed likewise to have experienced neither a severe event nor a major difficulty. Paradoxically, the discovery of these misclassifications actually strengthens rather than weakens the study, since it suggests that the researchers' estimates about the size and importance of the aetiological effect of the social environment are, if anything, rather conservative.

Having identified the two major categories of provoking agents, Brown and Harris then related these to other social variables, notably that of social class. The surveys revealed clearly enough that depression was much more common among working-class women than among middle-class women. Of the former 23 per cent were classified as onset cases as compared with only 6 per cent of the latter. However, it was no easy matter to uncover either the meaning of this association, or the nature of the causality involved. Most obviously there was a methodological problem created by the fact that both major difficulties and severe events were themselves more common among the working than the middle class. The association between class and depression might therefore have been 'spurious' – that is, artefactually generated by the causal link between both variables and the provoking agents.

Indeed, at first sight this seemed to be the case. Although there was no class difference in the risk of developing depression among women without children, nor any variation in the rate of severe events across the different phases of the women's life-stages, the data did show marked class differences in the experience of severe events among women with children. One in three working-class women with children experienced a severe event as compared with one in five middle-class women with children. Further study showed that this class differential was restricted exclusively to the category of 'household events', which formed about one-third of total severe events, the others being socio-sexual, health, or miscellaneous crises of various kinds. Household life-events typically experienced by working-class women included husband losing his job; son in trouble with the police; husband sent to prison; leaving a job because of family responsibilities; arrangement to be rehoused falling through; threat of eviction by landlord; being forced to have an unwanted abortion because of poor housing conditions; and court appearance for non-payment of rent (husband unemployed). Household events for middle-class women were rather different in nature: lover leaving to go abroad; builders working on the family house leaving without completing the job; husband discovered to be having an affair; husband discovering woman's own affair; a son having to go to a special school because he was 'backward'. In other words, the household life-events experienced by working-class and middle-class women typically reflected their socio-economic circumstances, with the former having more numerous and more severe events than the latter. Ongoing difficulties reflected this same general pattern, with the most unpleasant being experienced by the working-class women, more frequently, and for longer periods of time. For example, 61 per cent of working-class women were rated as having at least one marked difficulty, as compared with only 38 per cent of those from the middle class. However, unlike events, the frequency of difficulties did not differ with life-stage, although not unexpectedly 'health difficulties' as well as 'household difficulties' showed significant differences between the classes.

In summary, the Camberwell data revealed that the risk of depression was related to class only among women with children, but also that it was also women with children who showed a class difference in the rate of severe events and major difficulties. Is the relationship between class and depression therefore spurious? Do class differences in the occurrence of the provoking agents explain class differences in the incidence of depressive onset? The answer, perhaps surprisingly, is that they do not. If the analysis is limited only to women with children and who have had a severe event or major difficulty, 31 per cent of working-class women are found to have developed depression, as against only 8 per cent of those from the middle class. (The data are shown in Table 10.3.) In other words, working-class women with children at home are four times more likely to experience an onset, even when the comparison is restricted to those having been exposed

Table 10.3   Percent of women developing a psychiatric disorder (i.e. onset caseness) in the year, by whether they have children at home, social class, and whether they had a provoking agent (always before any onset)

	Severe event/ major difficulty	No severe event/ major difficulty	Total
	%	%	%
Women with child at home:			
working-class	31 (21/67)	1 (1/68)	16 (22/135)
middle-class	8 (3/36)	1 (1/80)	3 (4/116)
Women without children at home:			
working-class	10 (3/30)	2 (1/44)	5 (4/74)
middle-class	19 (6/31)	1 (1/63)	7 (7/94)
All women			
working-class	25 (24/97)	2 (2/112)	12 (26/209)
middle-class	13 (9/67)	1 (2/143)	5 (11/210)
Total	20 (33/164)	2 (4/255)	9 (37/419)

Note: Figures in brackets are raw numbers – actual and eligible – for each cell.
Source: Social Origins of Depression, p. 168, Table 6.

to a suitable provoking agent. In statistical terms, the researchers still found a significant class difference in the likelihood of developing depression, having standardized for class differences in life-events and difficulties. They admit that 'this clear-cut and largely negative result provided a fulcrum around which our investigation turned'. It indicated, to them at least, that 'further factors must intervene to modify the impact of severe events and major difficulties and that these had to be discovered if class differences in depression were to be explained'.

Further analysis of the data suggested that four such factors could be identified. Each of these factors reflects the social ties of a woman – the quality and depth of her personal relationships – and acts to protect against, or create a socially generated vulnerability to clinical depression. (For this reason Brown and Harris refer to them as 'vulnerability factors'.) They are: loss of a mother before the age of 11; having three or more children under 14 living in the house; lack of employment outside the home; and lack of an intimate relationship with someone in whom the respondent can confide. Broadly speaking, the figures show that risk of depression increases progressively with exposure to these vulnerability factors, but *only in the presence of a provoking agent.*

For example, although 47 per cent of women who had lost a mother developed depression, as compared with only 17 per cent of the remaining women, none of those who had lost a mother but was without a severe event or major difficulty did so. Like each of the other vulnerability factors, this one seems largely incapable of producing depression of itself, although it significantly increases the risk of onset when either a severe event or major difficulty is present. Across the sample as a whole, 11 per cent of women with a provoking agent but no vulnerability factor developed depression, as compared with only 1 per cent of those having a vulnerability factor but no provoking agent. Provoking agent and vulnerability factor are not therefore interchangeable in terms of the aetiology of depression. According to Brown and Harris, at least, they behave differently and seem to reflect distinct causal processes.

Now, as with events and difficulties, vulnerability factors are differentially distributed by class. Working-class couples are more likely to have 'segregated marital roles', that is, separate duties, responsibilities, leisure interests, and social relationships. The risk of early death is greater among the working class, so children more commonly are left without one or other parent during their youth, and working-class families are also more likely to have greater numbers of children born in quick succession. Consequently, working-class women are less likely than middle-class women to have a husband or boyfriend as a confidant; are more likely to have lost a mother in their youth; and more commonly will have three or more children under 14 at home (though they are not more likely to be without formal employment). Of course, as we have already seen, since it is working-class women with children who have the highest rate of severe events and major difficulties, it is precisely this group who has the greatest chance of experiencing *both* a provoking agent and a vulnerability factor. And, as the researchers confidently conclude, 'this is enough to explain the entire class difference in risk of depression among women with children'. For example, among women in the general Camberwell population exposed to a provoking agent, not having a husband or boyfriend as a confidant, with either three or more children under 14 in the home or having experienced early loss of a mother, 83 per cent of those from the working class developed depressive symptoms, compared wtih only 50 per cent of their middle-class counterparts. The results for the hospital patients also conform to this general pattern – with two notable exceptions. While patients are comparable to onset cases in terms of their 'measured intimacy', they have not suffered early loss of a mother with nearly the same frequency, and indeed do not differ from normal women in the proportion having three or more children under 14 living at home. In fact, this seeming inconsistency is relatively easily explained. A young and densely spaced family does increase the chances of a depressive disorder occurring in the presence of provoking agents. However, once a disorder has developed, contact with a psychiatrist is made less likely precisely because of the responsibilities associated with bringing up several young children. This variable therefore works in one way to increase the risk of depression and in the opposite way to influence contact with a psychiatrist. Furthermore, since early loss of mother is also correlated with the presence of three or more young children in the home, and the latter factor decreases the chances of a woman consulting a psychiatrist, then early loss of mother will itself be associated with reduced chances of seeing one.

Finally, in reporting the details of their analysis, Brown and Harris identified a number of 'symptom-formation factors' which influenced the form and severity of the depressive disorder. It appears from their data that, although exposure to more than one severe event only moderately increases the risk of developing depression, a major loss or disappointment can markedly increase the depth of a depression once onset has already occurred. As the authors put it,

> it it as though new loss and disappointment increase the depth of a woman's hopelessness and this leads to a worsening of her depression: that a woman depressed after the emigration of her son to Australia might not have got worse if her father had not died ten weeks after the start of her depression.

In general terms then, by investigating the frequency of 'change-points' at which 'an increase or decrease in the number of symptoms led to a noticeable change in a woman's psychiatric state', the researchers were able to establish that severe events could produce, as it were, further 'onsets' within an established depression. Experience of a previous depressive episode also increased the severity of depression, as did loss of a mother before 11, which turned out to be the only symptom-formation factor also (as we have seen) capable of acting as a vulnerability factor.

On the basis of these results they proposed the model of depression shown in Figure 10.1. Three broad groups of factors are identified as producing and shaping depressions – provoking agents, vulnerability factors, and symptom-formation factors – each of which 'relate[s] in differing ways to a central experience of hopelessness which develops out of the appraisal of particular circumstances, usually involving loss'. Women who suffer such a loss are deprived of a source of value or reward in their lives. According to Brown and Harris, loss is important to the genesis of depression because 'it leads to an inability to hold good thoughts about ourselves, our lives, and those close to us'. Loss of faith in one's ability to attain significant and valued goals is also important. Of course, loss of an important source of positive

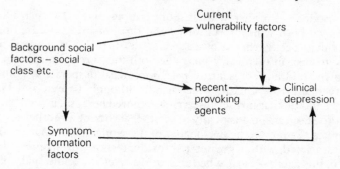

Figure 10.1 A causal model of clinical depression
Source: Social Origins of Depression, p. 48.

value may provoke an immediate sense of hopelessness about the provoking incident, as well as a wide variety of feelings ranging from distress to anger – but it does not always lead to thoughts about the hopelessness of one's life in general. It is this *generalization* of hopelessness that is believed by the researchers to be at the core of clinical depressions. Their own study, as well as those conducted by others, suggests that a person's self-esteem is crucial in determining whether generalized hopelessness develops. This is because

> response to loss and disappointment is mediated by a sense of one's ability to control the world and thus to repair damage, a confidence that in the end alternative sources of value will become available. If self-esteem and feelings of mastery are low *before* a major loss and disappointment a woman is less likely to be able to imagine herself emerging from her privation.

This explains the unitary effect of the seemingly odd assortment of vulnerability factors. Low self-esteem is the common factor behind them and, indeed, it was a term often used in interviews by the women themselves.

Of course, it is not difficult to see how, as the authors put it, 'the relevance for the women of the three vulnerability factors occurring in the present would probably lie in generating a sense of failure and dissatisfaction in meeting their own aspirations about themselves, particularly those concerning being a good mother and wife.' However, the role of loss of mother before 11 among the vulnerability factors is rather harder to discern, at least in its relevance for generating chronic low self-esteem. Strictly speaking, it is not a 'situational' element in the way that the others are and seems to add the additional factor of 'childhood experiences' into the model. This particular experience might, however, be related to an adult depressive episode in a number of ways. For example, given that such a loss is correlated both with low intimacy and three or more children under 14, it may be that her mother's early death makes a woman more likely to rush into an early marriage with the 'wrong' man, and that her own children represent, in part, somewhat desperate attempts to rectify this error. On the other hand, although Brown and Harris freely concede that further research is required here, their own data do seem to suggest, provisionally at least, that loss of a mother actually generates changes in the personality of the woman, since such a loss is still associated with a greater risk of depression for women with a provoking agent – even when one or other of the additional vulnerability factors is also present. That is, two-thirds of women with low intimacy or three or more children under 14 became depressed if they had also lost a mother before age 11, as compared with only one-quarter of women who had not suffered such a loss. Perhaps, as the authors propose, 'loss of mother before eleven may have an enduring influence on a woman's sense of self-esteem, giving her an ongoing sense of insecurity and feelings of incompetence in controlling the good things of the world'. However, as they themselves recognize, this speculation does rest on the assumptions that the mother is the largest source of support to a child, and the main means of controlling his or her world until about age 11, after which point the child is more likely to exert control directly and independently. Research elsewhere does tend to support these assumptions, although the evidence about the damaging effects of maternal deprivation is by no means as unambiguous as Brown and Harris seem to want their readers to believe. This, for me at least, is one of the few instances where the Camberwell team's exemplary caution in drawing inferences from the data perhaps gives way to the understandable temptation to draw on a convenient argument, not wholly justified by the evidence available, simply because it rather neatly explains an otherwise puzzling finding.

IV

It has to be conceded that some of my sociological colleagues have not been wholly convinced by these arguments. However, what is interesting about the controversy surrounding *Social Origins of Depression*, in the present context at least, is that, yet again, it gives the lie to the myth perpetrated by its critics that British sociology is fundamentally innumerate and lacks respect for statistics.

Some of the technical issues debated during the subsequent exchanges were in fact relatively straightforward. Keith Hope, while recognizing 'the stringency of its sampling procedure and the care which went into the assembling of the data', expressed concern that the study nevertheless left a number of important sampling questions unanswered. The authors had sampled Camberwell 'households'. How did they define these? (More than one household can share the same address.) What was the sampling frame? What was done if a household contained more than one woman? Did the team explore the possibility that women in large households may have a greater chance of a severe event or major difficulty than women living in small households, precisely because of the housing difficulties which they themselves found were related to the incidence of depression, so that the former may have been 'over-sampled' or 'under-sampled' in various ways? For example, did a woman in a household with several men have a greater chance of appearing in the sample than a woman living in a household with several other women, and did the differential composition of households by class affect the probability of different kinds of women being selected for study? These sorts of detailed sampling issues *might* be important given that a large propor-tion of respondents (no less than 52 per cent of the first Camberwell survey) lived in privately rented (and therefore shared?) accommoda-tion. Moreover, and not surprisingly given that he was a member of the Oxford research team investigating social mobility in England and Wales, Hope was also concerned about the definition of class em-ployed by Brown and his colleagues. He notes that the Camberwell team assigned a class standing to women living alone in virtue of their own jobs. Clearly, since it is generally acknowledged that the distribution of jobs among single or separated women differs from that of fathers and husbands, 'there may be built in to the analysis a contamination among class, events, and intimacy'. Hope also suspects that the rating of life-events may be class-biased to some degree: middle-class women usually run little risk of being evicted or having their husbands sent to prison; working-class women do not necess-arily expect such events to happen, but may be better equipped to deal with them than the researchers supposed. Thus, in assessing these and other class-related events and difficulties the team unintentionally introduced their own class bias into the ratings.

Brown and his co-workers accepted some of these criticisms, but rejected others. As was indicated earlier, *Social Origins of Depression* represents the distillation of more than two decades of studying stressful life-events, first in relation to schizophrenia and only then with regard to depression. Much of this work first appeared in the medical and other academic journals. Indeed, Hope's critique was not in fact levelled at the book itself, but at an earlier article, published in the journal *Sociology*, in which the Camberwell team outlined their aetiological model and reported preliminary findings for the patients and the first of the two community samples. In some cases, therefore, Hope's reservations were addressed simply by incorporating the necessary clarification within the text of the later monograph. For example, in their book Brown and Harris provide clear information about the definition of households (by communal eating arrangements), and the source of the community samples (local authority records of housing). They also make it clear that, in the 15 per cent of selected households where more than one eligible woman was present, individual respondents were selected at random. However, they do accept that small biases may have crept into the selection, so that women in both multiple-household addresses and larger-than-average households will be slightly under-represented – although they also insist that a comparison of the relevant parameters with those provided for Camberwell by the National Census suggests that these effects are likely to be small.

In their initial reply to Hope (a short article in a subsequent volume of *Sociology*), the Camberwell team also argued that the basis of their occupational classification was unlikely to be a significant source of bias, since fully 85 per cent of women were rated occupationally according to their husbands' jobs. Moreover, since many women living alone had the same class standing whether their own or their previous husband's occupations were used as the basis for this assessment, in fact only 8 per cent of class ratings were based on a woman's own occupation in contrast to that of father's or husband's. Later, in their book, they were able to confirm that, in practice, 'taking account of a woman's current or past occupation added practically nothing to the size of the association between social class and prevalence of psychiatric disorder obtained by the use of husband's occupation alone'. They also reported that the results of the analysis were not significantly changed, irrespective of whether one measured social class according to the Registrar General's six-fold classification of occupations (which claims to rank occupations according to their 'general standing within the community'), the Hope-Goldthorpe Scale (a measure of the 'social desirability' of occupations), or the team's own Bedford Scale (an amended version of the Registrar General's classification, which also took account both of education and an index of prosperity based on ownership of a car and a telephone). In the event, the team settled on a simple distinction between middle class and working class, based on the Hope-Goldthorpe occupational rankings.

The question of possible class bias in the rating of life-events is perhaps more difficult to assess. Both the original articles and the subsequent book provide a good deal of information about how ratings on the various scales were accomplished. As we have observed, the technique of contextual rating is designed to prevent contamination of the causal analysis through the respondent's retrospective 'effort after meaning', but also seeks to avoid superficiality by taking into account the unique features of events and difficulties in each person's biography. Ultimately, therefore, as Brown and Harris recognize, the rating exercise 'does indeed involve an interpretative judgement on the part of the rater', so 'we clearly cannot rule out the possibility of some bias'. However, they remain convinced that their methodology strikes the proper balance between incorporating the circumstances surrounding an event into a severity rating, and treating these circumstances as extraneous vulnerability factors. A number of findings from their data suggest that this conviction may be sound. For example, with regard to the view that the severity of working-class events may have been over-rated, additional analysis reveals that 'controlling for severity of events does not eliminate the class difference in disturbance rates'; that 'there is no greater discrepancy between the reported (subjective) severity of threat and contextual (objective) rating for working-class than for middle-class women's scores'; and, finally, that 'when the number of vulnerability factors is controlled, the chances of breakdown following an event or difficulty are comparable for women in the two class groups'. These results all suggest that the ratings of severity are broadly comparable between classes.

Hope's objections were directed principally towards the techniques by which Brown and Harris generated their data. However, a number of critics have contested the analysis, notably the causal model proposed by the Camberwell team, and in particular the distinction it draws between provoking agents and vulnerability factors. In defending themselves against these charges, Brown and his colleagues were involved in a series of exchanges that became increasingly mathematical over the years, centring largely on the relative merits of different statistical techniques for identifying and disaggregating causal effects.

For example, the psychiatrist Paul Bebbington argued that the causal inferences drawn by Brown and Harris *might* be correct, but that the published analysis was neither convincing nor conclusive. The Camberwell model holds that there is an association between vulnerability factors and depression only in the presence of life-events, and that the association between life-events and illness is increased in the presence of a vulnerability factor, both propositions being justified by reference to the observed degree of association between the relevant variables. However, one obvious problem here is that its authors tend to measure the *degree* of the associations by applying the chi-square statistic, a test which is conventionally used as an index of the *significance* of an association rather than a measure of association itself. In fact, since the value of chi-square is dependent both upon the degree of association and the sample size, it could only be used legitimately as a correlation coefficient, comparing two samples, if the samples were of equal size. In the Camberwell study, as we have seen, the sample sizes vary and, as is clear from the numbers shown in the published tables, they are never identical for any of the relevant comparisons.

Of course, the application of an inappropriate measure of association does not alter the numbers actually occurring in the cells, so the original argument might nevertheless still be sound. A more serious charge, therefore, is the claim that Brown and Harris do not rule out alternative – and no less plausible – explanations of the research findings. Their procedure of partitioning 2 x 2 x 2 tables fails to test all the possible relationships that might pertain between key variables. As we have seen, the authors argue that vulnerability to depression among women at home with a youngest child under 6 years old is greater in the working class; that vulnerability is greater among women who lack access to a confiding relationship; and that absence of such relationships among women with a young child is more common in the working class. They conclude from this partitioning of the relevant tables that, for women with a young child, the class difference in vulnerability is largely explained by the class difference in poor marital relationships. Moreover, since this group of women account for almost all overall social class differences in rates of disorder, these too can be explained by the problem of poor marital relationships. In fact, as Bebbington points out, this argument would be conclusive only if an appropriate four-dimensional contingency table had been constructed: that is, vulnerability by class by quality of marital relationship by life-stage. This same proviso applies to the other vulnerability factors – loss of mother before the age of 11, presence of three or more children under age 14 in the home, and employment status. Of course in some cases, the numbers involved in these four-way partitions would be tiny for certain cells in the tables, which is presumably why the authors did not adopt this approach. Nevertheless, in the absence of an analysis which tests all possible relationships between the relevant factors, testing only the most obvious of these in a selective series of two-way or even three-way crosstabulations may result in more complex associations being overlooked.

Bebbington also suggests that the statistical technique of log-linear modelling offers a more appopriate approach to the analysis of causal models based on the complex interactions of multidimensional contingency tables. This technique allows all possible predictions to be tested by setting up the different hypotheses in terms of the marginal probabilities of the contingency table. In each case one can compare the expected cell frequencies resulting from a given model with those actually observed for the real world. By moving through a hierarchy of models embracing independence, two-way association, three-way association, and so on between variables, and testing at each stage the goodness of fit between the cell frequencies obtained from the model and those actually observed, it is possible to determine whether significant improvements are gained by allowing for more complex associations ('interaction') between the variables involved. That is, one can test directly whether the relationship between two variables is significantly different across the levels of some third variable, and in this way specify the simplest model that best fits – or predicts – the observed values.

Other critics have in fact re-analyzed the Camberwell data using this technique, and claim that the findings show life-events and vulnerability factors do not interact in the fashion suggested by Brown and Harris, but rather that they have independent effects upon illness. It is simply not necessary to introduce the complex interaction postulated by the original 'vulnerability model' in order to obtain a satisfactory fit between the log-linear model and the obtained frequencies. An alternative model of 'independent provocation' explains the findings quite satisfactorily. The distinction between provoking agents and vulnerability factors is therefore false.

Unfortunately, the matter is a good deal more complex than this. It is simply not the case that the Camberwell team's more crude partitioning approach yields an incorrect model of the relationship between the aetiological factors, whereas the more sophisticated log-linear technique generates a model that is demonstrably more sound. For example, recent research by David McKee and Runar Vilhjalmsson has shown that alternative forms of multivariate analysis support competing interpretations of the data, because they rest on different assumptions about the functional form of the relationship between the dependent and independent variables. Linear probability equations assume that the probability of an outcome is a linear function of the independent variables, whereas logit specifications assume functions which generate sigmoid (S–shaped) curves, linear only in the middle range because they are curved towards the upper and lower limits (see Fig. 10.2). In practice, the estimated results for these specifications are usually comparable, except in those cases where the dependent variable is highly skewed. The Camberwell data, unfortunately, take precisely this form. For example, as was observed above, only 17 per cent of the women sampled were psychiatrically disturbed at some time during the year prior to interview. The rest were classified as normal. The problem here is that, at the extremes of a curve – where the slope is approaching zero – a unit change in the independent variable yields an increasingly smaller change in the dependent variable, so that when the dependent variable is highly skewed this mathematical property of sigmoid models makes it harder to reject the null hypothesis of 'no effect' having occurred. Contrari- wise, if marginal estimates are calculated on the assumption that probabilities of an outcome are a linear function of the independent variables, then estimated effects are likely to be more significant with a highly skewed dependent variable. Because the slope is constant (as shown in Fig. 10.2), there should be no reduction in the magnitude of effects, even though outcome proportions are extreme.

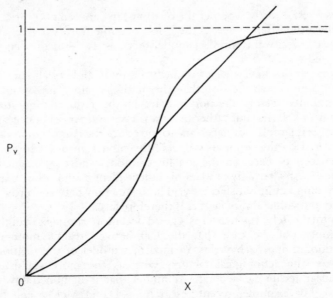

Figure 10.2 Comparison of linear probability and logit functional forms
Source: Adapted from McKee and Vilhjalmsson, 'Life Stress, Vulnerability, and Depression', Fig. 1.

The important point to grasp here is that the presence or absence of 'interaction' may depend on whether we are studying additivity in terms of linear probability differences or probability ratios. An example taken from the Camberwell data makes this clear. In the absence of life-events, the differential probability of being depressed because of an absence of social support is 2 per cent (there is a 3 per cent risk among those with a confidant as against 1 per cent risk for those without). In the presence of life-events the differential probability rises to 22 per cent (32 per cent risk among those without a confidant as compared to 10 per cent among those having one). These two percentages – 2 per cent as against 22 per cent – differ significantly, so Brown and Harris take this to be evidence that social support modifies the effect of life-events on depression, a conclusion which implies a linear probability specification between the variables. The difference between the percentages is simply so large that a modifying effect must be present. However, the *relative* risk of being depressed or not in the absence or presence of support is almost identical between the two groups, being about 3 : 1 in each case. In the absence of life-events, 3 per cent to 1 per cent; 32 per cent to 10 per cent in their presence. A log-linear analysis based on the calculation of probability ratios would therefore suggest that, in terms of relative risk, there is no significant modifying effect present.

The mathematics of this argument may be unclear to the layperson, but the effects of choosing one rather than the other probability equation as the basis for the analysis should be obvious to all. When a statistical model is estimated which assumes that the relationship between stressful life-events and depressions conforms to a linear function then the Camberwell team's vulnerability model is confirmed. That is, lacking an intimate relationship with husband or boyfriend, having three or more young children at home, and early loss of mother all significantly intensify the effect of provoking agents on the risk of depression, but have not independent effect of their own. On the other hand, if the relationship between the dependent and independent variables is assumed to have a sigmoid (and therefore logarithmic or logistic) function, it transpires that the so-called vulnerability factors each have a direct or main effect on depressive risk. Rather than modifying the effect of provoking agents they act like additional provoking agents themselves. For this reason, McKee and Vilhjalmsson conclude that 'there is no compelling reason to view these factors as being anything other than additional ongoing life strains; they clearly do not fall into a conceptually distinct category'. Their re-analysis of the Camberwell data supports an alternative 'strain model', in which lacking intimacy, losing one's mother and having three or more young children at home 'would all constitute ongoing life strains which independently increase the likelihood of depression'.

It appears to be the case, therefore, that depending upon the statistical methods employed, Brown and Harris's vulnerability model can be confirmed or refuted by reference to the Camberwell data. On balance, however, it seems probable that in the long run the model is more likely to be proved correct than incorrect by subsequent studies. McKee and Vilhjalmsson are obliged to concede that, while each specification makes different mathematical assumptions about the functional form of the relationship between the dependent and independent variables, 'the choice between specifications is largely a matter of judgement and not one which can be made on empirical grounds', since 'these assumptions pertain to unobservable population parameters for the dependent variable; that is, the true *probability* of someone being depressed'. In reply, Brown has argued that the whole question of whether the appropriate functional form of relationship between independent and dependent variables is linear or logistic is largely meaningless, since neither 'stress' nor 'depression' can be measured according to a true ratio scale of the type required to settle this issue conclusively using multiplicative modelling techniques. Neither variable provides for equal intervals between its ordered categories and neither possesses a non-arbitrary zero point. He insists, therefore, that no amount of mathematical sophistication can disguise this shortcoming. Moreover, he and Harris have identified eight subsequent studies, all of which replicate the Camberwell findings concerning the role of intimacy as a vulnerability factor. (Only one derivative project has failed to do so.) The Camberwell team themselves have recently carried out a separate study of working-class women in Islington, using improved measures of 'vulnerability' to identify parental lack of care in childhood or adolescence, low self-esteem and negative interaction in marriage (for married women) or lack of a close relationship outside the home (for single mothers). Their findings confirm the thesis that provoking agents and vulnerability factors are not simply additive in their effects. As in the earlier study, having one provoking agent increases the risk of depression over no provoking experience, but having two or more provoking agents in no way increases the risk over having one. Once again, the risk of depression for a woman who has a vulnerability factor but no provoking agent is extremely low (two chances in 170 – or 1 per cent), while the presence of a provoking agent increases the risk to 20 per cent (8/41) for those with one vulnerability factor, 35 per cent (12/34) for those with two vulnerability factors, and 60 per cent (6/10) for those with three. Furthermore, if depressive onset were a simple function of added 'stress' then the form of additivity between two or more provoking agents should be of the same order as. the form of additivity between one provoking agent and a vulnerability factor. It is not. Two provoking agents have a risk of just 8 per cent (3/36), whereas among women having one provoking agent and one vulnerability factor, the risk of depressive onset is more than 20 per cent.

V

These findings tend to suggest that vulnerability factors and provoking agents are not comparable phenomena. It seems, therefore, that while the authors of *Social Origins of Depression* might be faulted for not using multiple methods, or for failing to conduct a wholly exhaustive analysis, subsequent research has tended, on balance, to support rather than undermine their original model.

My own reservations about the argument are infinitely more modest than these mathematically sophisticated objections. For example, I have always been somewhat troubled by the rather low numbers in some of the tables, particularly those which are used to support certain key propositions of the causal model. Table 10.3 offers a suitable illustration of my point. It will be remembered that the authors are here examining the relationship between provoking agents, social class and depression. Their claim is that these data support the central proposition that, even when the analysis is restricted to those having a provoking agent, working-class women with children at home have a four times greater chance of developing depression than do their middle-class counterparts. However, a glance at Table 10.3 shows that in the crucial cell at the top left-hand corner, the middle-class percentage (8) is derived from only three cases of depressive onset among thirty-six eligible interviewees. Several other important tables have similarly low numbers in the relevant cells. These are especially worrying if they involve social class as a variable (and most do) because of the necessarily crude working class/middle class distinction employed by the Camberwell team.

But these are relatively minor quibbles. They do little to detract from the methodological sophistication of the Camberwell study. The policy relevance of this research should also be obvious – even to the most ardent of sociology's many critics. There seems little doubt that a wide range of debilitating medical conditions have their origins (at least in part) in social or psychosocial factors. A sociologist is undoubtedly better qualified than a physician to pose the question as to how far psychiatric or physical disorder is the result of living in a particular form of society. But his or her answer is unlikely to appeal to simple-minded critics of the discipline, precisely because the manifest complexity of social processes invariably renders a simple explanation inadequate, so that even the most sophisticated (and expensive) sociological research is unlikely to offer instant solutions to the many important problems addressed by the discipline.

Of course, this disclaimer will not appease critics who demand that sociologists be ignored (or even suppressed), because their research 'lacks policy relevance'. In my experience, however, such critics generally subscribe to a hopelessly naïve view of social engineering. They have in mind a model of the sociologist as institutional plumber; if society fails to function properly then one calls in the sociologist to fix things. He or she should be able rapidly to track down the source of the problem and suggest how an appropriate repair might be effected. Of course, plumbers themselves can work in precisely this fashion because water behaves in ways that are entirely predictable from the laws of physics. If one punctures a water-pipe with a nail while hanging some kitchen shelves, then a leak will inevitably result. No amount of persuasion or abuse will make the water molecules flow past the hole rather than through it. (I have verified this, rather unfortunately, from recent personal experience.) Human behaviour is, however, noticeably less predictable than that of the chemical elements. Solutions to what are seen to be 'social problems' are correspondingly less certain. Yet sociologists are commonly expected to provide instant explanations, more or less on demand, for every form of supposed societal breakdown, from sporadic outbreaks of football violence to a secular increase in the rate of divorce. Politicians, educationalists, reformers and journalists expect simply to be able to call up the institutional plumber, have him or her locate the source of the problem (usually with minimal expense) and identify a sure solution.

Like most sociologists, I can provide numerous illustrations of this attitude from personal experience. The most recent of these concerns the so-called Hungerford Massacre, during which an armed man killed or wounded several of the inhabitants of a small market-town in southern England, without warning and, apparently, without reason. On the morning following these events I was contacted by the producer of a magazine programme on a local radio station, who wanted to know not only 'why the Hungerford gunman did it', but also 'why other people commit similar mass murders elsewhere'. The radio producer's assumption – and it is one that seems also to underline the frequently voiced claim that sociology 'lacks policy relevance' – is that almost all forms of social behaviour have a simple explanation. The subcultural behaviour of Mods and Rockers (and the reaction of others to this), a commitment to the somewhat bizarre teachings of L. Ron Hubbard, and the social distribution of clinical depression among women, are all to be explained by – the societal equivalent of the nail puncturing the water-pipe. It is the job of the sociologist to identify the nails so that others can stop the leaks.

This model breaks down, of course, when confronted by the complexity of social action. Among other things, for example, we know that the same behavioural outcomes can be prompted by a variety of motives and values; that identical ends are often pursued by quite different means; that several individuals acting together can produce a consequence unintended by all; that people sometimes feel constrained to act in ways which they would otherwise wish to avoid; and, last but not least, that individuals, groups and even formal organizations quite regularly pursue incompatible objectives which they happily justify by reference to contradictory principles and values. By carefully documenting all of this, sociologists have confirmed what other intelligent observers of society long ago realized from more casual inspection: namely, that the complexity and unpredictability of human behaviour makes sociology a more ambitious and difficult enterprise than any natural science. The physical world is simply not that contrary. Quite rightly, therefore, it has sometimes been said – and not by sociologists – that the problems of studying nuclear physics are child's play compared to the problems of studying child's play. Protons, electrons, magnetism, electrical currents and such like all behave in a regular, indeed law-like and therefore utterly predictable fashion. Moreover, nuclear physicists do not have to address the problems of motivation, since to know *how* an atom will react when exposed to a magnetic field is also to know *why* it so reacts. To the best of our knowledge, atoms do not possess individual will and cannot therefore decide consciously whether to be attracted or repelled by magnetism. Identical atoms will always behave in identical ways. Compare the much more difficult task of the sociologist, attempting to explain why only certain adolescents are attracted to youth subcultures; or why sectarian religious communities are differentially successful in retaining the loyalties of converts; or why some working-class women are more at risk from depression than their middle-class counterparts.

The claim that sociology 'lacks policy relevance' and cannot be 'applied' is therefore naïve. The fact is that for good epistemological and methodological reasons sociologists rarely offer simple explanations for the complicated patterns of human interaction. The Camberwell study of the origins of clinical depression is a good illustration of the often dazzling complexity of social causation. But this study also suggests that, current popular opinion to the contrary, sociologists are equal to the explanatory tasks before them – given the necessary research resources. However, as I have already argued at some length in the preceding chapters, it is all too often the case that those in authority choose not to hear the sociological answers.

11 Families and social networks – a conclusion

I

I write this final chapter almost exactly one year to the day since Alan Rusbridger's 'Who needs sociologists?' ruined my breakfast and so annoyed me that I was prompted to write this book by way of a reply. On the face of it, of course, the scale of my response is out of all proportion to the original offence. A brief, superficially researched and hastily written article located on page 21 of a newspaper with a relatively small circulation scarcely merits a 100,000 word volume in reply. At a more profound level, however, Rusbridger's perfunctory piece epitomizes the sustained barrage of criticism to which I and my colleagues have been subjected during the past decade. Sociology has acted as a magnet to every current of anti-intellectualism within the British Establishment. In that respect, at least, Rusbridger's assessment was entirely accurate: the subject has been singled out for peculiarly harsh treatment by unsympathetic governments and an uncomprehending media. Some sociology departments have been closed, while those that remain have experienced serious job losses; research funding has been harder to come by, and more often tied specifically to projects devised by others, at the behest either of the government or Civil Service; accusations of incompetence, irrelevance, left-wing and anti-capitalist bias have been rife. Too many friends and colleagues have been forced to retreat to the more liberal climates of North America and Australasia. Others have lost heart and withdrawn with their pensions into early retirement, leaving younger colleagues to fend off the bailiffs. And still the innuendo persists. Last night, for example, I watched a popular television advertisement in which a distraught adolescent telephoned his grandmother to report that he had 'failed all his exams' – or, more accurately, failed all except pottery and sociology, but then they hardly counted. That, in a nutshell, is what I am objecting to: the popular perception that, in the Britain of the 1980s, sociology simply does not count.

Looking back over the previous chapters I see that I have already replied to these accusations at some length. By using the rhetorical device of selecting my favourite ten empirical studies of postwar Britain, I have tried to show that good sociology is neither incompetent nor biased, but offers instead an understanding of ourselves and our society which, properly used, could both inform and enlighten public policy. Much of British sociology is empirical: it may not be rooted in elaborate statistics but, as I hope I have demonstrated satisfactorily, understanding is more important than mere numbers alone. It is also policy-related to an extent that belies popular accusations of irrelevance. The elites in our society may disapprove of the policy implications – but that, as I have argued throughout, is an entirely different matter. Sociology, because it refuses to take social processes at face value, is inherently sceptical. Governments deal in ideologies and pursue partisan objectives, for these are the very stuff of politics. And that is why sociologists are everywhere mocked – or sometimes worse – by those in authority. Indeed, it is an enlightening experience to travel to the state-socialist societies of Eastern Europe and observe how sociology is routinely suppressed by the communist parties holding power, but because of the subject's allegedly *right-wing* and *anti-socialist* bias. These governments also accuse sociologists of being subversive and incompetent – although in this case because their studies point to the gap between the rhetoric of Marxist-Leninism and the inefficiency of command economies and injustices of left-wing authoritarianism. Of course, it would be foolish to deny that some British sociology is indeed biased and incompetent, but then that is true of any natural or social science – including (as I have argued) contemporary economics, a subject about whose limitations governments have nevertheless remained curiously silent.

My volume is therefore somewhat odd in its construction. Readers have been taken on a Cook's Tour of topics, places, methods and theories: from symbolic interactionism among the Mods and Rockers in Clacton to causal modelling of life-events among depressive women in Camberwell, by way of informal interviews in the homes of Huddersfield, a survey of manual employees in Luton, and an application of the action frame of reference to the study of race relations in Birmingham. Some of my concerns have been undeniably worldly – such as the attempt to convince readers that Peter Townsend's study of poverty is a serious indictment of the social policies of successive postwar governments in this country. Others were rather more academic in orientation, notably my ventures into the realms of odds ratios and log-linear modelling, which served, I hope, to illustrate the statistical sophistication of colleagues whose intellectual problems actually demanded this particular skill. At least one of the texts selected for discussion, Roy Wallis's report on the Church of Scientology, could be described as, almost literally, out of this world. Arguments having a more general application – including my observations about value-freedom, policy-relevance and the nature of sociological theory – have been fully expressed as I have gone along.

I do not intend, therefore, merely to repeat myself in lieu of a proper conclusion. I want, instead, to discuss, if only briefly, one further substantive example of the strengths of postwar British sociology. This final text perfectly illustrates an elementary point which, above all else, seems to me to provide a strong *raison d'être* for my own professional activities and those of my colleagues. It shows, quite simply, that sociologists can point to important connections between aspects of social life which on the face of it would seem to be quite unrelated. In other words, they can bring to the study of society a profound understanding of the *interconnectedness* of social phenomena, and one which cannot be found in any other science. The text in question is Elizabeth Bott's *Family and Social Network*, which offers numerous insights into the possible relationships between social networks, conjugal roles and people's beliefs about society. These could only have been unearthed by a socioligist.

II

In some ways the choice of Bott's monograph as the last of my texts is rather perverse. For one thing it was actually the first of the ten books to be written. The research upon which it is based was conducted during the early 1950s and the book itself was published as long ago as 1957. Moreover, Bott was something of a disciplinary migrant, who came to the study of family life in postwar Britain only after having conducted anthropological fieldwork in North America. In 1964 she also became a practising psychoanalyst. The Preface to the second edition of *Family and Social Network* (published in 1971) was therefore written, not by a sociologist, but by the distinguished Professor of Social Anthropology at the University of Manchester. Nevertheless, it is not unreasonable to cite her book as an example of sociology at its best, since Bott refers throughout to 'the sociological field work' on which it is based and the 'sociological analysis' which it reports. So, while it is true to say that Bott's work has also been highly influential in other fields, it has conventionally been received as a classic of modern sociology, and this is clearly how the author herself viewed the outcome of her studies.

The intellectual origins of her project were, by comparison, rather uncomplicated. Shortly after the end of the Second World War, the Family Welfare Association asked for and obtained the assistance of the Tavistock Institute of Human Relations, in order to establish a Family Discussion Bureau undertaking casework with 'troubled' families and married couples. As a parallel project, the Institute and Association sponsored a study of 'normal' families, with a brief to examine 'social relationships and ideology (in the non-political sense)... the unconscious aspects of the relationship between husband and wife... the interplay of their personalities, and of the emotional tasks of the marriage'. Bott's volume is a partial report which describes the sociological aspects of the subsequent findings. A medical psychoanalyst, nonmedical psychoanalyst and social psychologist were also involved in the study, although the psychological and psychoanalytical materials were published separately.

Those involved in the project never envisaged themselves as doing anything other than merely exploratory work. Their general aim was simply 'to understand the social and psychological organization of some urban families'. This objective, as Bott later observed, 'was so general that it could hardly be called a problem'. Specific techniques and concrete issues were developed 'as we went along' and 'only after a considerable time'. In due course, for example, 'some families' came to mean only twenty couples. Not surprisingly, therefore, Bott insists that her book cannot claim to be a systematic survey of family life. No attempt is made to derive empirical generalizations about life in modern Britain. Rather, the book arrives at 'interpretations and hypotheses... that may be tested on other families', in the hope that these 'may lead to further and more systematic comparisons'. Her achievement, as she rather modestly describes it, 'consists not so much in finding complete answers as in finding interesting questions to ask'. In fact, the questions were to prove so interesting that they kept large numbers of sociologists and anthropologists fully occupied during the 1960s and 1970s, and continue to reverberate through these disciplines even today.

It is for this reason that I have chosen to conclude my volume with a discussion of Bott's text. I have, as it were, saved the best till last. For if I were forced to select but one among my favourite sociological studies, then this would have to be my choice. Some of Bott's speculations have now passed into conventional wisdom; many have been extended by subsequent researchers; but few have been shown to be wholly misconceived. Her purposes may have been purely exploratory, but to my mind at least, her achievement constitutes probably the most original piece of sociological research to have emerged during the postwar era.

III

Finding the families to interview proved to be a surprisingly difficult task. The researchers simply did not anticipate the problems they would face in contacting sufficient numbers of suitable and willing subjects. They wanted to study 'ordinary' families. This ruled out couples who had at any time contacted an outside agency for assistance with familial problems. (Two of the families eventually selected had actually sought such help in the past.) It was decided to concentrate on families with children under 10 because 'this phase is considered to be one of the most crucial in familial development'. (All the families therefore had children, one to four in number, the mode being two.) All were to be English and of mostly Protestant background. However, because the team wanted to compare the effects of different social environments on the internal organization of families, they allowed social class to vary. (The occupations of the husbands therefore differed considerably, as can be seen from Table 11.1, while their annual incomes ranged from £330 to £1,800, before tax, at 1952 values.) All were to be resident in London. They were not to constitute an organized group (although, in the event, there were three pairs of friends among the families actually chosen). Finally, couples had to be willing to participate in a lengthy series of interviews, each lasting two or more hours. (Eight home interviews proved to be the minimum given by a single family, with nineteen as the maximum, in each case supplemented by two or three clinical interviews as well.) Eventually, however, with the help of a variety of intermediaries, including general practitioners, schools, clergymen, friends and colleagues, twenty couples were selected from the twenty-five who offered themselves for study.

Questions were asked on five main topics (A copy of the interviewing schedule is included as an appendix to Bott's book.) First, a social history of each partner was collected, including detailed genealogies of the husband and wife, together with a history of the marriage up to the time of the interviews. Second, information was collected about the internal organization of the family, including the overall social division of labour. Typical days and weeks were documented; responsibility for the various work-tasks was identified; decision-making processes were described. For each task, the interviewers tried to establish who did what, who was responsible for seeing it done, how disagreements about it were settled, and whether or not these arrangements had altered in any way during the course of the marriage. Couples were also asked about how they thought their situation differed from those of their parents, other relatives and friends. A third series of questions dealt with informal relationships outside the family, including contact with relatives, friends and neighbours. Information was gathered about the sex, age and occupation of social contacts, nature of friending relationships and frequency of visits, and exchanges with neighbours; about whether each relationship was maintained largely by one or other marital partner; and about respondents' perceptions of the frequency and quality of social interactions between friends, neighbours and relatives. The penultimate section of the interview schedule dealt with formal social relationships, such as contacts with schools, health and welfare services, clubs and neighbourhood associations. In each case the researchers explored the frequency and methods of contacts, feelings about the relationship, and perceptions of its consequences for the

Table 11.1 Relationship between conjugal segregation, type of network and occupation

Families in descending order of conjugal segregation	Type of network	Occupation of husband	Type of occupation (rated by research staff)
Newbolt	close-knit	finisher in large boot and shoe firm	semi-skilled manual
Mudge	medium-knit	police constable	semi-skilled manual
Dodgson	transitional	owner-operator of small tobacco and sweet shop	semi-skilled manual
Barkway	transitional	accounts clerk in department store	clerical
Redfern	transitional	draughtsman in firm of architects	semi-professional
Baldock	medium-knit	self-employed in radio repairs	skilled manual
Apsley	medium-knit	general commercial manager in light engineering firm	professional
Wraith	transitional	WEA lecturer	professional
Appleby	medium-knit	painter and decorator	skilled manual
Fawcett	medium-knit	clerk in insurance firm	clerical
Butler	transitional	plumber	skilled manual
Thornton	medium-knit	manager of health food shop	semi-professional
Hartley	medium-knit	sundry supplies buyer for medium-sized industrial firm	semi-professional
Salmon	medium-knit	Establishments officer in public health department of local authority	semi-professional
Jarrold	medium-knit	repairer of optical instruments in large firm	skilled manual
Bruce	loose-knit	temporary clerk in Gas Board	clerical
Denton	loose-knit	accounts executive in advertising agency	professional
Bullock	loose-knit	statistician in welfare agency	professional
Woodman	loose-knit	pottery designer, working as occupational therapist in hospital	semi-professional
Daniels	loose-knit	deputy manager of fire department in insurance firm	semi-professional

Source: Family and Social Network, Tables 2 and 3.

family. Finally, couples were asked for their views on money, social class, family life, and about a range of general political, social and religious issues.

It is clear from Bott's description of the home interviews that these were fairly free-flowing discussions. The interviewer simply used the various topics as catalysts to provoke discussion between the marital partners, adapting the order and form of questioning to the circumstances, and allowing discussion to wander away from the assigned topic. Interviews were conducted either by Bott herself or by J. H. Robb (the social psychologist on the team). Couples also attended for clinical interviews with one of the psychoanalysts. These covered the subjects of health, personal development, relationships with parents, sexual development, and the impact of children on the family, but little use is made of this material in Bott's own report.

The central finding of her book can be stated fairly concisely. The data showed that there was considerable variation in the 'conjugal roles' of husbands and wives, notably in the amount of time they devoted to shared activities and interchangeable tasks, as compared to independent activities and complementary tasks. For example, in some families there was a marked social division of labour between the partners, so that the husband had his particular tasks and responsibilities while those of the wife remained quite separate. He gave her a set amount of housekeeping money each week and she had no knowledge of how much he kept for himself or how he spent it. Nor did the couple share their leisure time and recreation. He went to outside events with his friends while she stayed at home or visited relatives and neighbours. The husband had his social contacts and the wife had hers. Neither partner considered that they were unusual in this respect. In other families, however, the husband and wife spent much of their time together, shared many activities and interests, and had a much less rigid division of household tasks and duties. They maintained that husband and wife should be equals, sharing as many family responsibilities and spare-time pursuits as possible, and actually put this ideal into practice. Husbands regularly did the cooking and laundry; wives routinely tended to the garden and some household repairs; while much of the couple's leisure time was passed in the joint pursuit of similar interests in music, literature, politics, and entertaining friends. Here again the partners thought that their behaviour was typical of their social circle. Bott refers to the former sort of family as being organized around 'segregated conjugal role-relationships'. The latter are described as having a 'joint conjugal role-relationship'. In between these two extremes there were many degrees of variation.

The research also showed that these variations in roles were not directly associated with the more obvious sociological categories, such as household income, occupation, or social class. It can be seen from Table 11.1, for example, that the husbands having the most segregated role-relationships with their wives tended to be in manual occupations, while those having joint role-relationships with their wives were quite commonly professionals, but there were several clearly working-class families that had relatively little segregation; and, conversely, several professional families where segregation was quite marked. As Bott herself puts it, having a working-class occupation seems to be a necessary, but not a sufficient cause of only the most marked degree of conjugal role-segregation. Nor was the degree of segregation of conjugal roles a function of family life-cycle, since all of the families were more or less in the same (childbearing) phase. Attempts to relate role-segregation to the type of local area in which families lived proved equally unsuccessful: it was not simply the case that couples with the most segregated roles lived in homogeneous areas of low population turnover while those with predominantly joint relationships lived in heterogeneous areas having a high turnover of residents.

But the degree of role-segregation was not entirely idiosyncratic. Rather, the data suggested that the structure of conjugal roles was in fact related to the form of the family's informal social network, in other words the pattern of social relationships with and between relatives, neighbours and friends.

Bott found that all the families were involved in social networks rather than organized groups. In the latter case, the component individuals would form a cohesive whole, sharing common aims, interests and a distinctive subculture. Networks, on the other hand, comprise members not all of whom have social relationships with one another. However, although all the families belonged to networks rather than groups, there was a considerable degree of variation in the connectedness of the networks themselves. Some networks were 'close-knit' in the sense that many members knew and met each other. Others were 'loose-knit' and embraced few such relationships. Figure 11.1 gives a schematic representation of the difference between these two types. Again, there are relative degrees of connectedness with a good deal of variation between the extremes. It transpired from the data that those families having a high degree of segregation in the role-relationship of the marital partners had a close-knit network. That is, many of their friends, neighbours and relatives were themselves acquaintances, and met independently of the family of study. Contrariwise, families having a relatively joint conjugal role-relationship had a loose-knit network of friends, neighbours and relatives, few of whom actually knew one another.

On the basis of these findings, Bott therefore proposes the formal hypothesis that 'the degree of segregation in the role-relationship of husband and wife varies directly with the connectedness of the family's social network'. Her explanation for this seemingly odd association, again derived from the research findings, is that persons in close-knit networks are involved with friends who all interact regularly with one another. They tend, therefore, to reach a consensus on norms, and to exert informal pressure on one another both to conform

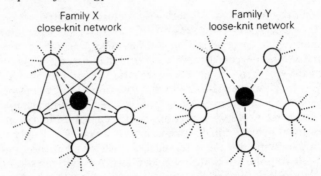

Figure 11.1 Schematic comparison of the networks of two families

The black circles represent the family; the white circles represent the units of the family's network. The broken lines represent the relationships of the family with external units; the solid lines represent the relationships of the members of the network with one another. The dotted lines leading off from the white circles indicate that each member of a family's network maintains relationships with other people who are not included in the family's network. The representation is, of course, highly schematic; a real family would have many more than five external units in its network.

Source: Bott, 'Urban Families: Conjugal Roles and Social Networks', Fig. 1.

to these norms, and to retain membership of, and active participation in, the network. If a husband and wife bring prior membership in such networks to their marriage, and if the conditions are such as to allow these relationships to continue, then the marriage itself is simply superimposed on the pre-existing pattern, so that the spouses tend to be drawn back into separate activities with people outside the new nuclear family. The marital partners continue to derive emotional satisfaction from these external relationships, and make correspondingly fewer demands on the spouse, so that this external assistance facilitates a rigid segregation of conjugal roles. On the other hand, if the partners coming to a marriage have had prior involvement in loose-knit networks or if the conditions are such that their networks become loose-knit after marriage, then they must seek in each other both the emotional satisfaction and help with the various familial tasks that couples in close-knit networks can obtain from outsiders.

Table 11.1 confirms that, at least among those families participating in Bott's study, the degree of conjugal segregation is therefore more closely associated with type of network than with type of occupation. The Newbolts are in fact the only family having a highly segregated conjugal role-relationship associated with a close-knit network. At the other extreme there are five families having a joint conjugal role-relationship associated with a loose-knit network. According to Bott (who gives lengthy accounts of each family, which for reasons of brevity it is not possible to reproduce here), the intermediate types generally follow the postulated pattern. Families having a fairly marked degree of role-segregation, approaching that of the Newbolts, tended to have relatively close-knit networks. Those with more loose-knit networks had more joint conjugal relationships. As Table 11.1 shows, some families were in transition from one type of network to another, a process usually connected with a residential move. Here, too, the association between network connectedness and role-segregation was moving in the predicted direction.

But what factors affected connectedness itself? Obviously, because of the small number of families involved in the study, it was necessary to go beyond the field data in an attempt to identify the forces that shaped the density of a family's social network. Drawing on her general knowledge of urban industrialized society and on sociological research conducted by others elsewhere, Bott suggests that connectedness will depend upon 'a whole complex of forces' generated by the occupational and economic order. These forces 'do not always work in the same direction and may affect different families in different ways'. Moreover, connectedness cannot be predicted from a knowledge of situational factors alone, since it also depends on 'the family's personal response to the situations with which they are confronted', and in turn 'their conscious and unconscious needs and attitudes'.

Bott's arguments about the determinants of network connectedness are therefore necessarily speculative – but again highly insightful. She suggests that families may choose to introduce friends and neighbours to each other, or they simply may not, so that the personalities of the husbands and wives will be one important factor affecting such choices. However, because of the division of labour in the research project, nothing more is said about the psychological make-up of the couples in the study at this stage. Rather, she moves on to an explanation of how these sorts of choice are limited, and 'shaped by a number of forces over which the family does not have direct control'. In an urban industrialized society, these factors will include economic ties among members of the network, type of neighbourhood, opportunities to make relationships outside the existing network, and geographical and social mobility. For example, connectedness of social networks will be increased if relatives can help each other to get jobs, if they hold property rights in common enterprises, or expect to inherit property from one another. Similarly, if a network is localized so that most of its members live in the same immediate area, then they will be more accessible to each other and correspondingly more likely to interact socially. These localized networks are more common, according to Bott, where the inhabitants of an area feel that they are socially similar and share the same social standing. Networks are also more likely to be close-knit if the husband's occupation does not generate many opportunities to form new relationships with persons unknown to the other members of his social circle. If, for example, he is engaged in a job in which his colleagues are also his neighbours, then his network will tend to be localized, and its degree of connectedness correspondingly high. Finally, of course, a family's network will become more loose-knit if either they or their social contacts move away geographically or socially from the other members.

All of these factors tend to promote close-knit networks among manual workers and more loose-knit networks among those in professional occupations. Entry to the professions is governed by examination, so relatives cannot give one another much help in this respect. Homogeneous communities of manual workers, many of whose residents tend to work in a local dominant manufacturing or extractive industry (for example, steel works or coal-mining) are fairly common – or at least were so at the time of Bott's research in the early 1950s. Comparable neighbourhoods of people belonging to the same profession – so that the local area comprised mainly doctors or chartered accountants – would be most unusual. Similarly, professional training leads to the formation of relationships with people who do not know one's family, school friends or neighbours, and professional careers often require geographical mobility in the pursuit of promotion. Both factors militate against the formation of close-knit social networks. However, Bott is insistent that social class is related to network connectedness only in complex ways, so that there is no simple correlation of manual occupations with close-knit networks and nonmanual occupations with more loose-knit forms. As she puts it, 'families with close-knit networks are likely to be working class, but not all working-class families will have close-knit networks'. Only in the working class is one likely to find a combination of factors all working together to produce a high degree of connectedness: a concentration of people in the same or similar jobs resident in the same neighbourhood; low population turnover and continuity of relationships; jobs and homes in the same local area; opportunities for friends and relatives to help one another obtain employment; little demand for geographical mobility and little opportunity for social mobility. But not all husbands in manual occupations have close-knit family networks. It may be, for example, that working-class families live in heterogeneous areas with a mixed occupational structure. It is only some types of manual employment that are localized. Job opportunities may lead working-class families to move from one area to another. Husbands may work and live in different places.

In short, connectedness is determined by a whole complex of forces, and is not the result of social class alone. It cannot even be predicted from a knowledge of all the relevant situational factors, since it depends also upon personality factors that are quite specific to couples themselves. Nevertheless, the research does suggest strongly that segregation of conjugal roles is related more directly to the connectedness of networks than to class. For the most part, factors associated with class affect the segregation of conjugal roles only indirectly, through having an effect on the connectedness of a family's social network.

IV

Bott's subsequent arguments follow directly from this fundamental insight into the relationships between conjugal roles, network connectedness and social class. For example, her data also showed that people disagreed profoundly in their views on class, so much so 'that we sometimes wondered if they were talking about the same society'. However, she is not especially surprised by this, since the earlier findings suggest so strongly that the effective social environment of a family is its network of friends, neighbours and relatives, rather than the 'total society' or even the 'local community':

> Although a finisher in Bermondsey and an account executive in Chelsea are both members of the larger British society, they live in different worlds; they have different jobs, different friends, different neighbours, and different family trees. Each bases his ideas of class on his own experience, so that it is hardly surprising that each has a different conception of the class structure as a whole.

The raw materials of an individual's class ideology are thus located in primary social experiences – at work, among colleagues, in schools, and in relationships with friends and neighbours – rather than in his or her position in an abstract socioeconomic category.

For this reason, Bott found that 'them and us' power-based models of society were used by the people in her sample who identified strongly with the working class and expressed no desire to be socially mobile – the plumber, tobacconist, and radio repairer. Classes were seen as conflicting groups of 'bosses' and 'workers'. The latter advanced by organizing themselves collectively to resist the demands of the former. By contrast, those who claimed middle-class identities tended to conceptualize the class structure in prestige terms, comprising upper, middle and lower classes of people sharing distinct subcultures, manners, accents, tastes, incomes and occupations. According to these respondents, betterment could be achieved through individual movement facilitated either by education or by personal friendship with people in a higher class. The commercial manager, WEA lecturer, sundry supplies buyer, draughtsman, statistician and one of the clerks talked in these terms. Prestige models were also used by the other clerks, the optical instrument repairer, and the painter and decorator, although these interviewees extended the number of classes to anything between four and eight. Bott argues that these were all people who felt some incompatibility in their class position: they were working-class by occupation but regarded themselves as having more in common intellectually and culturally with professionals. Had they used a three-category prestige model, they would have had to place themselves in the bottom class, something which they were unwilling to do 'because it would have meant acknowledgement of absolute rather than relative inferiority'. A multi-category model, on the other hand, offered the possibility of situating themselves in a class at least second from the bottom of the hierarchy. Finally, the more 'intellectual' of Bott's respondents used mixed power and prestige models, embracing the various dimensions of economic power, status, skill and subculture.

On the basis of these findings, Bott offers the hypothesis that 'when an individual talks about class he is trying to say something, in a symbolic form, about his experiences of power and prestige in his actual membership groups and social relationships both past and present'. So, when people are asked to compare themselves with others in a wider (let us say national) context, they manufacture a picture of their general social position out of the raw material of their immediate social experiences. For example, the plumber's two-category power-based model of the class structure arose out of his membership in a closely integrated working-class neighbourhood during his childhood; his experience of unemployment; his relationships with colleagues and superiors at work and with his neighbours and friends in his local area; together with some indirect information he had gathered over the years about the 'idle rich' in modern Britain. Thus, his principal class reference groups were derived from the mixed housing estate where he and his wife lived and comprised 'workers' like himself whom he contrasted with the resident 'adminstrators', 'black-coated workers' and 'technicians' (affiliated to 'the bosses'). Similarly, the optical instrument repairer's eight-category prestige model reflected his own and his wife's diverse and varied life-experiences: mainly working-class occupational backgrounds but with extended families that were in many instances occupationally mobile; a scholarship to a public school frustrated by the medical examination; previous marriage to an Army lieutenant, and succession of office jobs on the part of Mrs Jarrold; the variety of training courses undertaken by her husband; active membership in a number of voluntary and political associations; and a large number of friends, scattered all over the South of England, whose occupations ranged from those of minor professional to skilled manual worker. These experiences, and the aspirations that this couple held for their three children, were reflected in their self-placement as 'poorer middle class': a class of 'nice people', including suburbanites, lesser civil servants, office and clerical workers, who valued their friendship with the intelligentsia and higher professionals. Other respondents constructed classes, assigned norms and values to them and made evaluations of their society on this basis, by an exactly parallel process. In short, as Bott puts it, 'the individual constructs his notions of social position and class from his own various and unconnected experiences of prestige and power and his imperfect knowledge of other people's... He is not just a passive recipient assimilating the norms of concrete, external, organised classes'.

Some thirty years later, and with the advantage of hindsight, these observations now seem rather commonplace. Indeed, even at the time, many of Bott's peers praised her study for 'having the merit of being obvious once one has thought of it'. But that is precisely the point: no one had thought of it. It required a sustained sociological investigation to identify and explain the links between apparently unconnected aspects of conjugal role-relationships, the structure of social networks and the variation in norms and ideology. The fact that these connections are now part of the accepted wisdom is testimony to the incisiveness of Bott's original analysis. Here, surely, is an example of what C. Wright Mills called 'the sociological imagination' at its most powerful and illuminating.

Of course, some of Bott's more specific propositions have failed to stand the test of time. Subsequent research tends to suggest that the relationship between network connectedness and role-segregation is less regular than she suspected, but that there is a strong relationship between marital role-segregation and membership of specifically mono-sex networks, an aspect of extra-familial contacts which Bott tends to overlook. Residence in a rural rather than an urban area adds a further complication. Farming families, for example, seem commonly to combine a close-knit social network with highly segregated role-relationships. It is also clear that, in conducting research into conjugal roles, one must distinguish clearly between 'role', in the sense of what is normatively expected, and 'role performance' – or what actually happens. Bott herself specifically denies using the term in reference to 'all behaviour that goes on between people'. Rather, a conjugal role-relationship is defined by her as 'those aspects of a relationship that consist of reciprocal role expectations of each person concerning the other'. However, she also maintains that 'in the case of familial relationships the line between formal institutionalised expectations and individual expectations is often difficult to draw', so that 'in effect the term role-relationship means those reciprocal role expectations that were thought by husband and wife to be typical in their social circle'. Recent studies of the household division of labour and the patterning of leisure between husbands and wives have shown that matters may not be that simple. Professed ideals of marital equality may co-exist with highly segregated, husband-dominated, in short, unequal conjugal role-relationships. Similarly, husbands may perform a substantial number of domestic chores, while still believing that it is 'her job' with which they are lending a helping hand.

Given the exploratory nature of Bott's study, it would have been surprising had later investigators not gone on to explore more systematically the relationships between conjugal roles, migration, social mobility, class, opportunities for friends and relatives to help one another, and the numerous other variables which Bott herself provisionally identified as related to network connectedness. But nowhere in this now extensive literature have I encountered a critical reappraisal proposing that these several aspects of social life are wholly unrelated. Nobody has seriously suggested that conjugal role-segregation is quite disconnected from the structure of social networks. Indeed, we now know a great deal more than hitherto about the complex ways in which these phenomena are intertwined, precisely because – and only because – contemporary sociology has further explicated these relationships. We are, therefore, just that little bit better equipped to understand the unintended consequences of our institutional structures and subtle constraints upon our individual actions. For this reason, although it is by no means obvious at first sight, Bott's study has strong policy implications. As she notes, 'many clinical workers, doctors, and family research workers take it for granted that joint organisation is the natural and normal form for familial behaviour to take. Advice based on this assumption must be rather bewildering to families in close-knit networks'. This knowledge, in turn, renders fractionally more secure our recent – and precarious – achievement of mutual tolerance between, and respect for, fellow human beings. That alone is sufficient to justify the sociological enterprise. And it is why British sociology deserves to be praised rather than scorned for its achievement.

Further reading

2 Social class and social mobility

Social Mobility and Class Structure in Modern Britain was published by Oxford University Press in 1980 and, in a revised second edition, in 1987. The principal conclusions are summarized in John H. Goldthorpe, 'Employment, Class and Mobility: a Critique of Liberal and Marxist Theories of Long Term Change', in Hans Haferkamp and Neil J. Smelser (eds), *Theories of Long Term Social Change* (University of California Press, 1988). The classic statement of the liberal position is Clark Kerr *et al.*, *Industrialism and Industrial Man* (Harvard University Press, 1960), reiterated in Kerr's *The Future of Industrial Societies* (Harvard University Press, 1983), although the implications for class stratification are more obvious in P. M. Blau and O. D. Duncan, *The American Occupational Structure* (Wiley, 1976). This position has recently been forcefully restated in Peter L. Berger, *The Capitalist Revolution: Fifty Propositions About Prosperity, Equality and Liberty* (Gower, 1987). A concise summary of the liberal critique of Goldthorpe's treatment of absolute and relative mobility is Peter Saunders, *Social Class and Stratification* (Routledge & Kegan Paul, 1990). Recent descriptions of the class structure in advanced capitalism from a Marxist point of view include Erik Olin Wright, *Classes* (Verso, 1985), and Rosemary Crompton and Gareth Jones, *White-Collar Proletariat* (Macmillan, 1984). An earlier treatment of the theme of proletarianization will be found in Harry Braverman, *Labour and Monopoly Capital* (Monthly Review Press, 1974). The best textbook on social mobility is Anthony Heath, *Social Mobility* (Fontana, 1981). On social class more generally see Peter Calvert, *The Concept of Class* (Hutchinson, 1982). The debate about Goldthorpe's approach and conclusions took place largely in the pages of the journal *Sociology*, and includes articles by Roger Penn, Rosemary Crompton, Anthony Heath and Nicky Britten, Michelle Stanworth, Robert Erikson, Angela Dale *et al.*, Hakon Leiulfsrud and Alison Woodward, and of course John Goldthorpe himself, in vols 14–21 (1980–7). An alternative account of social mobility in Britain, based on data from the Scottish Mobility Project and largely critical of Goldthorpe, will be found in Geoff Payne, *Mobility and Change in Modern Society* (Macmillan, 1987). Max Weber's 'Science as a Vocation' is reprinted in H. H. Gerth and C. Wright Mills (eds), *From Max Weber* (Routledge & Kegan Paul, 1970).

3 Education and culture

The first edition of *Education and the Working Class*, published by Routledge & Kegan Paul in 1962, disguises the locale of the study. A subsequent, slightly revised Penguin edition of 1966 identified the setting as Huddersfield and made a number of other minor amendments to the text. Marsden's autobio-graphical essay, effectively a short life history of the eighty-ninth successful grammar-school child in the sample, appears in Ronald Goldman (ed.), *Breakthrough* (Routledge & Kegan Paul, 1968). A much longer and very powerful treatment of the same themes is given in David Storey's excellent semi-autobiographical novel *Saville* (Johnathan Cape, 1976). Contemporary critiques of Jackson and Marsden's argument, from the political Right, can be found in Harry Davies, *Culture and the Grammar School* (Routledge & Kegan Paul, 1965), and Robin Davis, *The Grammar School* (Penguin, 1967). More recent appraisals are included in Frank Musgrove, *School and the Social Order* (Wiley, 1979), and A. H. Halsey *et al.*, *Origins and Destinations* (Oxford University Press, 1980). The latter includes extensive data on social origins and educational destinations taken from the Oxford Mobility Study of the 1970s. A comprehensive overview of the sociology of education is P. W. Musgrave, *The Sociology of Education* (Methuen, 1979), but a much clearer picture of how developments in the subject relate to changes in the social and educational contexts can be gained from Jerome Karabel and A. H. Halsey, 'Educational Research: A Review and an Interpretation', in their *Power and Ideology in Education* (Oxford University Press, 1977). The central text of the 'new sociology of education' is Michael F. D. Young (ed.), *Knowledge and Control* (Collier-Macmillan, 1971). On the considerable achievements of the comprehensive system which replaced selective education, both in raising levels of educational attainment overall and in eliminating class and gender-based differences within these, see Andrew McPherson and J. Douglas Willms, 'Equalisation and Improvement: Some Effects of Comprehensive Reorganisation in Scotland', *Sociology*, vol. 21 (1987). Of course, in many other parts of Britain, there remains an enormous gap between the rhetoric and the reality of the comprehensive schools. On this point see, for example, Stephen J. Ball, *Beachside Comprehensive: a Case-Study of Secondary Schooling* (Cambridge University Press, 1981). The best book about how the New Right assessment of, and therefore current government policy towards, education serves to reintroduce and worsen inequalities in attainment, and also fails to meet the educational needs of the late-twentieth century, is probably Phillip Brown's *Schooling Ordinary Kids: Inequality, Unemployment, and the New Vocationalism* (Tavistock, 1987). A more polemical critique will be found in Brian Simon, *Bending the Rules: the Baker 'Reform' of Education* (Lawrence & Wishart, 1988). The classic formulation of the thesis about the 'organic' working-class community and the cultural loss associated with mass indus-trialism is Richard Hoggart, *The Uses of Literacy* (Chatto & Windus, 1957). The 'organic tradition' of writing on the British working class is criticized in John H. Goldthorpe, 'Intellectuals and the Working Class in Modern Britain', in David Rose (ed.), *Social Stratification and Economic Change* (Hutchinson, 1988). The best statement about the relationships between 'private troubles' and 'public issues' is still C. Wright Mills, *The Sociological Imagination* (Oxford University Press, 1959).

4   Poverty in an affluent society

Poverty in the United Kingdom was published by Penguin in 1979. An earlier version of the central argument about poverty as relative deprivation is given in Townsend's contribution to a volume entitled *Poverty, Inequality and Class Structure*, edited by Dorothy Wedderburn, and published by Cambridge University Press in 1974. Critical responses include David Piachaud, 'Peter Townsend and the Holy Grail', *New Society*, 10 September 1981 (with a Reply by Townsend in the issue for the following week), and Paul Ashton, 'Poverty and its Beholders', *New Society*, 18 October 1984. Left-wing criticisms of the concept of poverty are well represented in John Westergaard and Henrietta Resler, *Class in a Capitalist Society* (Penguin, 1976), while the arguments of the Right are summarized in Keith Joseph and Jonathan Sumption, *Equality* (John Murray, 1979). Townsend's exchange with Amartya Sen will be found in the *Oxford Economic Papers*, vols 35 and 37 (1983 and 1985), commencing with Sen's article 'Poor, Relatively Speaking'. Meghnad Desai's defence of Townsend's interpretation of his data, 'Drawing the Line: On Defining the Poverty Threshold', can be found in Peter Golding (ed.), *Excluding the Poor* (Child Poverty Action Group, 1986). The figures which I cite for the growth of poverty in the 1980s are taken from Carey Oppenheim, *Poverty – the Facts* (Child Poverty Action Group, 2nd edn, 1988). There are many good overviews of the literature on poverty as a whole, and of the history of policies designed to combat it, including Susanne MacGregor, *The Politics of Poverty* (Longman, 1981), Pete Alcock, *Poverty and State Support* (Longman, 1987), and Richard Berthoud *et al.*, *Poverty and the Development of Anti-Poverty Policy in the United Kingdom* (Heinemann, 1981). T. H. Marshall's essay on 'Citizenship and Social Class' is reprinted in his *Class, Citizenship and Social Development* (Greenwood Press, 1973). A sympathetic critique, which places Marshall's arguments in a comparative context, is given in Michael Mann, 'Ruling Class Strategies and Citizenship', *Sociology*, vol. 21 (1987). W. B. Gallie's article 'Essentially Contested Concepts' is in the *Proceedings of the Aristotelian Society*, vol. 56 (1965). Finally, those who feel intimidated by the sheer bulk of Townsend's magnum opus might alternatively consult Ken Coates and Richard Silburn, *Poverty: The Forgotten Englishmen* (Penguin, 1970), or Joanna Mack and Stewart Lansley, *Poor Britain* (Allen & Unwin, 1984). Both are relatively short and highly readable research reports which also say something, in passing, about Townsend's work. The latter is particularly interesting since it defines poverty as the lack of certain 'essentials' which were selected by members of the general public. In that sense it attempts to discover what standard of living is considered acceptable by the society as a whole – an approach which has certain obvious similarities with Townsend's own.

5 Managing the new technology

Tavistock Publications issued *The Management of Innovation* twice, first in 1961, and in a second edition (incorporating a lengthy new Preface) in 1966. Those who are unfamiliar with sociology will find the essentials of the argument spelled out simply and briefly in Burns's articles on 'Industry in a New Age', *New Society*, 31 January 1963, and 'On the Plurality of Social Systems', in J. R. Lawrence (ed.), *Operational Research and the Social Sciences* (Tavistock, 1966). Brief criticisms can be found in Gathorne V. Butler, *Organisation and Management* (Prentice-Hall, 1986), and Lee Bolman and

Terrence E. Deal, *Modern Approaches to Understanding and Managing Organisa-tions* (Jossey-Bass, 1984). An empirical study of 110 US factories, which provides convincing evidence to support the Burns and Stalker thesis about the importance of 'organic' organization for efficient research performance, is reported in Frank Hull, 'Inventions from R & D: Organisational Designs for Efficient Research Performance', *Sociology*, vol. 22 (1988). There are numer-ous – mostly unrelievedly boring – texts available on organisational theory as a whole. Three notable exceptions are D. S. Pugh *et al.*, *Writers on Organisations* (3rd ed, Penguin, 1983), R. M. Jackson, *The Political Economy of Bureaucracy* (Philip Allan, 1982), and Graeme Salaman, *Class and the Corporation* (Fontana, 1981). The best-known critique of mainstream organizational analysis, from a 'social action' perspective, is David Silverman, *The Theory of Organisations* (Heinemann, 1970). The neo-Marxist approach is well represented in Stewart Clegg and David Dunkerley, *Organisation, Class and Control* (Routledge & Kegan Paul, 1980). For a reply on behalf of the mainstream see Lex Donaldson, *In Defence of Organisation Theory* (Cambridge University Press, 1985). Rosemary Stewart's text on *The Reality of Organisations* was first published by Macmillan in 1970, and again (in a revised edition), in 1985. The recent management texts referred to towards the end of the chapter include Richard Tanner Pascale and Anthony G. Athos, *The Art of Japanese Manage-ment* (Simon & Schuster, 1981); Terrence Deal and Allen Kennedy, *Corporate Cultures* (Penguin, 1988); Walter Goldsmith and David Clutterbuck, *The Winning Streak* (Weidenfeld & Nicolson, 1984); William G. Ouchi, *Theory Z* (Addison-Wesley, 1981); Thomas J. Peters and Robert H. Waterman, *In Search of Excellence* (Harper & Row, 1982); and Frank Gibney, *Miracle by Design* (Times Books, 1982).

6 Workers and their Wages

The three volumes of the *Affluent Worker Study* were published by Cambridge University Press during 1968 and 1969. Jennifer Platt has written a detailed account of the project, on which I have leaned heavily, and this can be found in Colin Bell and Helen Roberts (eds), *Social Researching* (Routledge & Kegan Paul, 1984). Her article also gives bibliographical details of the main publica-tions associated with the project, including David Lockwood's classic article on 'Sources of Variation in Working-Class Images of Society', which was first published in the *Sociological Review*, vol. 14 (1966). The many subsequent studies of working-class 'social consciousness' to which Lockwood's study gave rise, and to which I refer in the text, are reviewed in Gordon Marshall, 'Some Remarks on the Study of Working-Class Consciousness', in David Rose (ed.), *Social Stratification and Economic Change* (Hutchinson, 1988). For a trenchant critique of these studies, see R. E. Pahl and C. D. Wallace, 'Neither Angels in Marble nor Rebels in Red: Privatization and Working-Class Consciousness', in the same edited collection. The secondary literature on the Luton project is simply voluminous. In my discussion I mention Leslie Benson, *Proletarians and Parties* (Methuen, 1978), especially Chapter 5; Mar-garet Grieco, 'The Shaping of a Work Force: A Critique of the *Affluent Worker Study*', *International Journal of Sociology and Social Policy*, vol. 1 (1981); and John Westergaard, 'The Rediscovery of the Cash Nexus', in R. Miliband and

J. Saville (eds), *The Socialist Register* (Merlin, 1980). Useful discussions will also be found in Gavin Mackenzie, 'The "Affluent Worker" Study: An Evaluation and Critique', in Frank Parkin (ed.), *The Social Analysis of Class Structure* (Tavistock, 1974), and C. T. Whelan, 'Orientations to Work: Some Theoretical and Methodological Problems', *British Journal of Industrial Relations*, vol. 14 (1976). Among the derivative studies, strong support for almost all of the claims made by the Affluent Worker team is presented in Richard A. DeAngelis's excellent and much overlooked study of French workers, *Blue-Collar Workers and Politics* (Croom Helm, 1982). Contradictory findings are reported in Malcolm H. MacKinnon, 'Work Instrumentalism Reconsidered', *British Journal of Sociology*, vol. 31 (1980), and Paul James Kemeny, 'The Affluent Worker Project: Some Criticisms and a Derivative Study', *Sociological Review*, vol. 20 (1972). 'The Current Inflation: Towards a Sociological Account', is included in Fred Hirsch and John H. Goldthorpe (eds), *The Political Economy of Inflation* (Martin Robertson, 1978). This collection also contains several interesting alternative explanations of inflation by economists, political scientists, historians and other sociologists. The sociological view of inflation is further developed in Michael Gilbert, 'A Sociological Model of Inflation', *Sociology*, vol. 15 (1981). Goldthorpe's particular interpretation was later criticized in Michael R. Smith, 'Accounting for Inflation in Britain', *British Journal of Sociology*, vol. 23 (1982).

7 Race and housing in the inner city

Race, Community, and Conflict: A Study of Sparkbrook, was first published in 1967 by Oxford University Press for the Institute of Race Relations, under the senior authorship of John Rex and Robert Moore, and with the assistance of Alan Shuttleworth and Jennifer Williams. The crux of the argument is spelled out, rather more systematically according to some commentators, in Rex's article on 'The Sociology of a Zone of Transition', in R. E. Pahl (ed.), *Readings in Urban Sociology* (Pergamon, 1968). I have also found his *Race, Colonialism and the City* (Routledge & Kegan Paul, 1973) to be useful in setting the Sparkbrook research in its intellectual and historical context. Chapter 3 of this text also contains Rex's replies to some of the early critics of the Birmingham study. Moore's reflections on 'Becoming a Sociologist in Sparkbrook' give an interesting 'warts-and-all' account of the research methods, and can be found in Colin Bell and Howard Newby (eds), *Doing Sociological Research* (Allen & Unwin, 1977). Critical commentaries on the project include Roy Haddon, 'A Minority in a Welfare State Society', *New Atlantis*, vol. 2 (1970); Jon Gower Davies and John Taylor, 'Race, Community and No Conflict', *New Society*, 9 July 1970; Badr Dahya, 'The Nature of Pakistani Ethnicity in Industrial Cities in Britain', in Abner Cohen (ed.), *Urban Ethnicity* (Tavistock, 1974); J. R. Lambert and C. Filkin, 'Race Relations Research: Some Issues of Approach and Application', *Race*, vol. 12 (1971); and Mary Couper and Timothy Brindley, 'Housing Classes and Housing Values', *Sociological Review*, vol. 23 (1975). Robin Ward's article on 'Race Relations in Britain', *British Journal of Sociology*, vol. 29 (1978) also contains a useful section on the development of race relations in Birmingham. The theory of housing classes is thoroughly explored from the point of view of urban social theory in Peter Saunders, *Social Theory and the Urban Question* (Hutchinson, 1981), and assessed against the background of the literature on race in Michael Banton, *Racial and Ethnic Competition* (Cambridge University Press, 1983). Patrick Dunleavy's appraisal of 'urban managerialism' is taken from his *Urban Political Analysis* (Macmillan, 1980). John Rex's *Key Problems of Sociological Theory* was first published in 1961. Theoretical developments in the quarter of a century since are clearly and concisely reviewed in Ian Craib, *Modern Social Theory* (Wheatsheaf, 1984).

8   The rise and fall of the mods

MacGibbon & Kee first published *Folk Devils and Moral Panics* in 1972. The more popular paperback edition was issued by Paladin during the following year. A second edition, published by Martin Robertson in 1980 (and again by Basil Blackwell in 1987), contained a lengthy new introduction ('Symbols of Trouble') reviewing the literature on British youth subcultures that had appeared during the intervening years. Cohen's review includes a controversial (though in my view quite damning) assessment of the work of the Centre for Contemporary Cultural Studies. I have drawn extensively on this, and on Ken Plummer's excellent defence of the labelling perspective, for the latter parts of my own argument. Plummer's article, 'Misunderstanding Labelling Perspectives', appears in David Downes and Paul Rock (eds), *Deviant Interpretations* (Martin Robertson, 1979). Among the earlier studies drawn upon by Cohen I mention David M. Downes, *The Delinquent Solution: A Study in Subcultural Theory* (Routledge & Kegan Paul, 1966); Howard S. Becker, *Outsiders: Studies in the Sociology of Deviance* (Free Press, 1963); Edwin M. Lemert, *Human Deviance, Social Problems and Social Control* (Prentice-Hall, 1967); and Leslie T. Wilkins, *Social Deviance: Social Policy, Action and Research* (Tavistock, 1964). A good example of the work of the Centre for Contemporary Cultural Studies is Stuart Hall and Tony Jefferson (eds), *Resistance through Rituals* (Hutchinson, 1976). This collection contains an article on Mods and Rockers which can usefully be contrasted with Cohen's book. The arguments of the critical criminologists are fully spelled out by Ian Taylor, Paul Walton and Jock Young, in *The New Criminology* (Routledge & Kegan Paul, 1973). Personally, however, I much prefer Young's essay on 'New Directions in Sub-cultural Theory', which offers a less doctrinaire assessment of the complementary strengths of the original American subcultural and labelling theories, and can be found in John Rex (ed.), *Approaches to Sociology* (Routledge & Kegan Paul, 1974). Alvin Gouldner's critique of labelling, 'The Sociologist as Partisan: Sociology and the Welfare State', is included in his essays *For Sociology* (Penguin, 1975). This is largely an *ad hominem* attack on Becker himself, and is particularly scathing about his celebrated and often reprinted defence of labelling theory entitled 'Whose Side are We On?', first published in *Social Problems*, vol. 14 (1967). I must confess, however, to never having understood the alleged significance of the much discussed 'Becker–Gouldner Controversy'. The original article seems to me to be a remarkably slight contribution to the literature about the role of values in social science. Gouldner's reply is notable mainly for its excessive wordiness. A good overview of almost all the American and British literature that is relevant as background to Cohen's study is given in Mike Brake, *The Sociology of Youth Cultures and Youth Subcultures* (Routledge & Kegan Paul, 1980). Paul Wiles's introduction to volume 2 of his edited text about *The Sociology of Crime and Delinquency in Britain* (Martin Robertson, 1976) gives a useful history of the emergence of the new criminologies of the late 1960s and early 1970s. The subsequent articles in this book give some indication of the diverse theoretical standpoints that were embraced by, and developed out of, the National Deviancy Conference. Alternatively, see Paul Rock (ed.), *A History of British Criminology* (Oxford University Press, 1988), or Stanley Cohen's own 'Footprints in the Sand: a Further Report on Criminology and the Sociology of Deviance in Britain', in Mike Fitzgerald *et al*, (eds), *Crime and Society* (Routledge & Kegan Paul, 1981).

9   Sociologists and scientologists

The Road to Total Freedom; A Sociological Analysis of Scientology was published by Heinemann in 1976. Roy Wallis recounts the history of his strained relationship with the Church of Scientology in an article about 'The Moral Career of a Research Project', in Colin Bell and Howard Newby (eds), *Doing Sociological Research* (Allen & Unwin, 1977), to which is appended 'A Scientologist's Comment', by David Gaiman, offering the Church's view of the ethics of Wallis's research. This research is set into the general context of the new religious movements in Wallis's *The Elementary Forms of the New Religious Life* (Routledge & Kegan Paul, 1984). The debate about the importance of networks in recruiting converts to social movements can be followed in D. A. Snow, L. A. Zurcher and S. Ekland-Olson, 'Networks of Faith: Interpersonal Bonds and Recruitment to Cults and Sects', published in the *American Journal of Sociology*, vol. 85 (1980); Roy Wallis and Steve Bruce, 'Network and Clockwork', *Sociology*, vol. 16 (1982); and D. A. Snow *et al.*, 'Further Thoughts on Social Networks and Movement Recruitment', *Sociology*, vol. 17 (1983). James A. Beckford's objections to Wallis's approach will be found in *Cult Controversies* (Tavistock, 1985), but can easily be anticipated in his earlier article 'Accounting for Conversion', *British Journal of Sociology*, vol. 29 (1978). C. Wright Mills's classic statement about the sociology of motivation, 'Situated Actions and Vocabularies of Motive', is reprinted in his *Power, Politics and People* (Oxford University Press, 1974). For an overview of the subsequent literature see Laurie Taylor, 'Vocabularies, Rhetorics and Grammar: Problems in the Sociology of Motivation', in David Downes and Paul Rock (eds), *Deviant Interpretations* (Martin Robertson, 1979). Both Mills and Beckford are taken to task by Wallis and Bruce in 'Accounting for Action: Defending the Commonsense Heresy', *Sociology*, vol. 17 (1983), and 'Rescuing Motives', *British Journal of Sociology*, vol. 34 (1983). The latter article prompted a reply by two ethnomethodologists, W. W. Sharrock and D. R. Watson, entitled 'What's the Point of "Rescuing Motives"?', and rejoinder by Bruce and Wallis, '"Rescuing Motives" Rescued', in the *British Journal of Sociology*, vols 35 and 36 (1984 and 1985) respectively. Those who are not easily frightened can gain some idea of the huge literature now available on new religious movements from T. Robbins's lengthy bibliographical essay, 'Cults, Converts and Charisma', *Current Sociology*, vol. 36 (1988). The faint-hearted are recommended to try Alison Lurie's much published and hugely enjoyable *Imaginery Friends*, a novel about two sociologists conducting research into an exotic religious cult, itself based loosely on an earlier sociological study by Leon Festinger *et al.*, *When Prophecy Fails* (Harper & Row, 1956).

10   On the social origins of clinical depression

Social Origins of Depression was published by Tavistock Publications in 1978. As is indicated in the chapter, the book was preceded by a series of journal articles reporting various aspects of the project, the most complete of which is George W. Brown, Maire N. Bhrolchain and Tirril Harris, 'Social Class and Psychiatric Disturbance Among Women in an Urban Population', *Sociology*, vol. 9 (1975). Much of the subsequent debate about the Camberwell project took place in the pages of the journal *Psychological Medicine*, and is not readily accessible to sociologists (see, for example, the exchange between Tennant and Bebbington and Brown and Harris in volume 8, 1978). However, some of the principal protagonists have also published critical pieces elsewhere, including Paul Bebbington, whose article on 'Causal Models and Logical Inference in Epidemiological Psychiatry' was published in the *British Journal of Psychiatry*, vol. 136 (1980). The article by David McKee and Runar Vilhjalmsson, 'Life Stress, Vulnerability, and Depression: A Methodological Critique of Brown et al.', was published in *Sociology*, vol. 20 (1986), with a reply by Brown in the same issue. The exchange between Keith Hope and the Camberwell team can also be found in that journal, vols 10 and 11 (1976 and 1977). By far the best contribution to the controversy about 'interaction' effects in the aetiology of depression is the paper by Paul D. Cleary and Ronald C. Kessler, 'The Estimation and Interpretation of Modifier Effects', in the *Journal of Health and Social Behaviour*, vol. 23 (1982). A number of critics claim that Brown and his co-workers have failed (as yet at least) to explain the relationships between wider social processes, including for example 'the structure of power and production', and the causes of depression located in women's immediate social circumstances. See, for example, Uta Gerhardt, 'Coping and Social Action: Theoretical Reconstruction of the Life-Event Approach', *Sociology of Health and Illness*, vol. 1 (1979), and G. H. Williams, 'Causality, Morality and Radicalism: A Sociological Examination of the Work of George Brown and his Colleagues', *Sociology*, vol. 16 (1982). For a useful overview of the sociological and related literature about mental illness as a whole see Agnes Miles, *The Mentally Ill in Contemporary Society* (Basil Blackwell, 1987).

11   Families and social networks – a conclusion

Elizabeth Bott's *Family and Social Network: Roles, Norms, and External Relationships in Ordinary Urban Families* was first published by Tavistock Publications in 1957. A second edition, incorporating a sustantial Preface by Max Gluckman and an even lengthier set of 'Reconsiderations' by the author herself, was issued by the Free Press in 1971. The nub of the argument about conjugal roles and network connectedness can be found in Bott's essay on 'Urban Families: Conjugal Roles and Social Networks', in *Human Relations*, vol. 8 (1956). The secondary literature on these topics is positively voluminous. Fortunately, the principal contributions are reviewed in Gluckman's 'Preface' and Bott's 'Reconsiderations', both of which strike a proper balance between documenting the empirical amendments to Botts's arguments and conceding the essential soundness of her analysis. Stephen Edgell's *Middle-Class Couples* (Allen & Unwin, 1980), and Graham Allan's *Family Life* (Basil Blackwell, 1985) both offer good discussions of the more recent literature and issues surrounding Bott's study. The best general text on the family and kinship is C. C. Harris's excellent *The Family and Industrial Society* (Allen & Unwin, 1983).

Index